FLYING WITH DRAGONS

FLYING WITH DRAGONS

Notes, Practices, and Anecdotes from the Xiu Lian Purification Journey

STEPHEN R COLWELL

Contents

FOREWORD

Our spiritual journey is the most important journey we will ever make.

For most of us, our spiritual journey has spanned many lifetimes in many universes. Our soul is the traveler on this journey, incarnating in different points in space and time. Sometimes male, sometimes female. Sometimes as a human being, sometimes as another form of conscious entity. All the time as a child of God.

Heaven determines when and where our souls get reborn. To what extent our future lifetimes will be filled with love and happiness, or challenges with health, finances, and relationships is the result of our past karma.

The purpose of life is to serve. Our souls know that to serve other children of God unconditionally is the only way to clear negative karma from our current and past lives, advance on our soul journey, and ultimately return to the Source from which we have received the breath of life.

I began writing *Flying With Dragons* four years ago, primarily as a collection of anecdotal experiences from the time of my teenage years until my retirement forty years later. I had no aspirations for publishing the work for the general public, being of the opinion that my personal story would be of limited interest to others outside of my immediate family and closest friends. If I harbored any secret hope, it was that my children, grandchildren, and descendants might read the journal in the distant future, and gain some insight on how "Papa C" lived his spiritual life.

However, in September, 2015, I received encouragement in the form of a direct "task" from my spiritual Father, Dr. and Master Zhi Gang Sha. I was given four months to complete the project, and publish *Flying With Dragons* for the potential benefit of spiritual seekers everywhere awakening to their soul journey. If the stories and practices within are helpful to even one person looking to move forward on their journey, then I have fulfilled my task.

The spiritual journey for each person is unique. My journey is not yours. The lessons I have learned and have yet to learn in this life are different than your lessons. I have no agenda and harbor no fierce desire that you should follow the same path I am walking. If I have any expectation at all, it's a hope that when your own souls whispers to you to awaken, seek out answers to who you are, and why you're here, you'll be inspired to venture out onto your own path, and ultimately reunite with Heaven, the Divine, the Tao, and the Source.

May you enjoy the journey and find love, peace, and harmony along the way.

Master Stephen Colwell
Boulder, Colorado
June, 2016

"Consider that you are certainly placed between heaven and hell, and that both the one and the other lie open to receive you according to the choices you make."

—Saint Frances de Sales (1567–1622)

RAINBOW BRIDGE

We chase misprinted lies.
We face the path of time.
And yet I fight, and yet I fight
This battle all alone.
No one to cry to, No place to call home.

—Alice in Chains, *Nutshell*

"Where do I go?" I mumble, more to myself than to the Canadian Customs and Immigration official rudely squeezing my arm. His hands wrapped in oversized military-issue black leather gloves. Holding me fast with the authority of a police officer concerned his charge might attempt to wrestle free of his grasp and escape into the jet-black shadows of the night.

"You've got *assets,* Mr. Colwell. Get a hotel in Buffalo tonight while you figure things out," the officer addresses me. The tone of his voice tinged with hostility. It's 10 o'clock in the evening on December 30, 2010. I'm being led to my vehicle outside the Rainbow Bridge Border Station in Niagara Falls, Ontario. Frigid Canadian winter air whips across the parking lot.

Five hours earlier, while crossing the border from New York into Ontario, I was directed into the Canadian Immigration office to answer questions about my legal status in Canada. I'm in the parking lot now with the Immigration Officer because I've excessively irritated the magistrate who heard my case, summarily rendered a judgment against me, and ordered my immediate deportation back to the United States.

⚜ ⚜ ⚜

The unfortunate affair occurred while I was driving home from Boston after spending the Christmas holidays there with my family. Identified as a "person of interest" when examination of my passport triggered some type of red flag warning at the Niagara Falls checkpoint, I was directed to park my black Chevy pickup truck at the Customs and Immigration Office and proceed inside for "additional processing." After politely answering a series of routine questions and assuming I would soon be able to resume my journey back to my home in downtown Toronto, I instead found myself sitting uneasily in a hastily convened Immigration Inquiry hearing.

A beefy government official wearing a drab khaki uniform sat beside me looking extremely bored. His primary charge was to ensure I didn't attempt an ill-advised dash for the exit during the proceedings. A female clerk, looking older than time itself, took up residence in a straight-backed metal chair, recording the trial transcript onto the hard drive of an out-of-date PC. The magistrate in charge of the proceedings, a Canadian bureaucrat maybe twenty years younger than me, presided as my judge and jury. He'd nestled his frame into a comfortable-looking leather chair behind a wooden desk. His Honor eyed me with suspicion while shuffling piles of manila folders overstuffed with papers that apparently included my personal data pulled from official Canadian government records. Data he presumed that, once fully examined, would surely expose me as an illegal alien and pave the way to my conviction and justly deserved punishment.

The magistrate probed me with questions for over an hour, his grilling becoming Kafkaesque in its intensity and futility. The interrogation focused on the details of my private life in Toronto for the last three years, my two rejected attempts to become a Permanent Resident, and my inability or unwillingness to find gainful employment in Canada. An examination of my financial resources aroused the judge's curiosity and suspicion since my cash was spread across multiple US and Canadian banks.

From my admittedly biased perspective as the accused, the magistrate conducted his interrogation in an excessive and overly zealous manner. The bureaucrat appeared unreasonably driven to uncover patterns of behavior in me that he could link to international criminal activity worthy of further investigation and prosecution, eventual incarceration for a felon like me, and a notable and well-deserved promotion for himself.

His Honor exuded a rather pompous bearing, barely able to contain the airs of jurisdiction, influence, and control that filled his frame like helium being pumped into a balloon whenever he felt he might be zeroing in on flaws or contradictions in my story. He was running out of angles to pursue. His final attack—a last gasp effort—was directed at my truck.

"Is that your vehicle, Mr. Colwell?" the magistrate inquired, his squinting eyes gazing fixedly out the window towards the dimly lit parking lot.

"Yes, your Honor," I answered, nodding my head.

"And tell me Mr. Colwell…just how did you manage to acquire Ontario plates for that vehicle?" he asked while leaning towards me threateningly. Anxious to pursue this line of questioning he seemed sure would trip me up and expose me as a criminal worthy of harsh treatment.

"I went to the Service Ontario office in Toronto with my insurance documents…they registered the truck after I showed them all my paperwork." I offered in a helpful manner.

"And are you telling me that no one at Service Ontario asked if you were a citizen of Canada?" the magistrate inquired, sounding a bit surprised that proper and prudent protocol may have been overlooked at the Ontario agency that had processed my application. Knowing glances exchanged by the judge with the court clerk and the Immigration officer shifting nervously in polished black boots.

"No, your Honor. I did show them my Canadian driver's license." I volunteered. In retrospect, it may have been a bad move on my part to submit that bit of testimony into the official record.

"You have a Canadian driver's license?" the magistrate asked, tilting his head forward and appearing very surprised. Scanning me up and down over the tops of his reading glasses.

"Yes, your Honor. Would you like to see it?" I generously offered. Okay, another bad move on my part.

"I *would* like to see it, yes." the magistrate replied drily. I confess I suffered a bit of wishful thinking at that point. Foolishly hopeful that this whole misunderstanding might get cleared up if the judge just accepted the fact that the friendly folks at Service Ontario had validated me as worthy of an Ontario driver's license years ago. "And when you got this license Mr. Colwell ... I assume prior to registering your vehicle ... did anyone at Service Ontario ask you *then* if you were a citizen of Canada?"

"Not that I recall, your Honor ... I believe they asked for my condo address in Toronto and for some proof of residency ... I think they wanted to know if I'd lived in Toronto for at least three months ... your Honor, have I broken any laws?"

The magistrate paused, taking a deep breath. "Technically, Mr. Colwell ... no." he replied, whispering the words apologetically. Suddenly becoming weary of the entire affair. Concluding that I was no longer of interest to him. Disappointed that any prospects for recognition or career advancement that might be enhanced by further questioning of me would be futile. Arriving at the denouement that my actions were less than criminal.

"But you can't stay in Canada." he continued. "I'm barring you for a period of 12 months because you've lived in our country for three years without acquiring a proper visa. You can return if you like no earlier than this date in December 2011. Re-entry prior to that to be considered only if a close relative is dying. Do you have any close relatives in Canada who are dying, Mr. Colwell?"

"No, your honor." I answered, feeling strangely disappointed at knowing no terminally ill Canadian Colwells. My head felt like it was filling with some type of syrupy liquid, a source of dizziness upsetting my equilibrium and seeping throughout my entire being. *Barred for one year? What does that mean? I can't go back to my condo? Where am I supposed to live?*

"The clerk will prepare the paperwork. Wait here. The officer will escort you to your vehicle and ensure you cross back to the American side of the border when you leave." The magistrate stood up, leaving the room without looking back, and leaving me no opportunity to question the implications of his judgment or appeal to his humanity.

⚜ ⚜ ⚜

And now, thirty minutes after the verdict against me, I'm sitting in my truck on a sub-zero degree mid-winter evening, waiting for the heater to kick in. The Immigration Officer has removed his gloves and fumbles with a chunky padlock hanging like some rap singer's oversized bling on a silver chain decorating the gate separating Canada and the United States. The sign on the fence warns the passage is for use by "Official Vehicles Only". Apparently, Canadian Immigration is happy to make an exception for me. My oversized truck tires rudely and angrily spit up gravel in the general direction of Ontario as I forcefully accelerate away from the Canadian half of Rainbow Bridge onto the lanes leading back to New York State. I'm homeless and alone. My only possessions are a small suitcase with toiletries and four days worth of dirty clothes.

The next five weeks I spend most of my time on my sister's couch in Nahant, Massachusetts doing nothing but feeling sorry for myself in the cold New England winter. I suffer the trauma of having had my life blown apart in self-pitying silence, complaining mostly to Max, my sister's Wheaten Terrier, who joins me for solitary walks along the beach, my only form of exercise. I have no place to live permanently in the US and I'm barred from returning to Canada, where all of my belongings are interred in my off-limits and inaccessible Toronto condo. My shortage of clothes compels me to do laundry every few days; it's my only source of activity. Computer programmers—like I used to be—call this repetitive process an "infinite loop," a coding blunder to be avoided at all costs as the endless cycle wastes time and resources going nowhere, just like me.

BLUE DIAMOND, RED ROCK

What is it that calls us?
Why must we pray screaming?
                    — Patti Smith, *Dancing Barefoot*

Mother Guan Yin, Goddess of Compassion

I'm reasonably bitter and, to my mind, justifiably depressed after my unexpected and unceremonious exodus from Canada, a country in which I'd resided happily for over three years. A country to which I'd retired to chase a girl I never caught. A country where I was introduced to *Dr. and Master Zhi Gang Sha*, the world-renowned healer and spiritual Dragon whose teachings would become the driving transformational force in my life.

Daily meditation, forgiveness, and gratitude practices, as well as the chanting of sacred mantras, are part of what mystics call the *Xiu Lian Purification Journey*. Xiu Lian is an ancient Taoist term defining the totality of one's spiritual journey.

Xiu Lian is difficult for me now, the time between my meditation sessions becoming longer and longer. Some days I skip my practice altogether. My physical body is not grounded, and my spiritual mind has fractured. I know the Divine is testing me, but while this awareness helps at a subconscious level, my conscious self struggles with the implications for practical existence.

Winter storms relentlessly pound the Northeast coast of New England in one of the most severe winters on record. Temperatures hover in single digits for weeks on end; many nights dipping below 0°F. *I need to leave this place*, I think to myself. I'm digging my pit of despair deeper each day and I don't think I can last until the warmth of spring arrives in an unforeseeably distant future.

My younger brother Joe owns a condo, currently unoccupied, in Las Vegas. He takes pity on me and offers me the residence and use of the Cadillac he keeps there for as much time as it takes me to figure out my life's next steps. And although I'll miss Max, I jump at the chance to sleep in a real bed instead of on the couch. My heart tells me a change of climate and location will be a good thing right now if I intend to resume my purification practice. But my soul has doubts. *Las Vegas? That's where you're going to do your Xiu Lian? Are you kidding me?*

Despite those misgivings, I soon find myself in Sin City. Not many seekers on the spiritual path would choose this spot willingly as a preferred destination in which to meditate and practice their *sadhana*, the Hindu form of Xiu Lian, which includes purification disciplines such as meditation, asceticism, worshipping God, and living correctly. Yet, for better or worse, Las Vegas is exactly where I find myself in February of 2011. Feeling like a total loser. Barred from my preferred country of residence. Unable to access my possessions. Having nothing specific to look forward to. Being a bit bored and desperately lonely, I try to convince myself that maybe Las Vegas with all its hedonistic attractions will be the perfect place for me to spend my winter of exile. After all, Las Vegas is full of losers just like me.

How did it all come to this? Have I done something wrong and am now being punished by God? Are the guardians of my karma playing with me, leading me to this time and place to play out some miniscule role in the infinite drama of the cosmos? Can I find spiritual redemption on the Las Vegas strip wandering amongst the perpetually neon-lit casinos, the caffeine and vodka-fueled sleepless gamblers, the vacant-eyed street girls, and the barely legal kids here to party? Will Maria, the girl who works the bar down the street and who's taken a romantic interest in me, become my savior and lead me by the hand into a new chapter of love, light, and physical bliss?

Questions like these haunt me nightly and I realize I haven't really progressed much at all since leaving New England. I've simply swapped my sister's couch there for my brother's spare bedroom here. I'm spending too much time in questionable pursuits of physical pleasures and the once vibrant flames of my soul's spiritual journey have burnt down to just a few coals glowing in a heap of embers, turning slowly but inexorably into a lifeless pile of gray ash.

It's time to stop feeling sorry for myself. Time to get up off the couch, get out of the condo, go for a run, or at least a long walk. Time to turn 180-degrees away from the enticing distractions of nighttime Las Vegas. Time to explore places the vampires and karmic demons haunting the Strip can't be bothered to visit.

Red Rock National Conservation Area is just the place to start. Arguably the most beautiful nature preserve in Nevada, this park turns out to be only a short drive from the condo. There's a road that winds through Red Rock canyon, bending up and down moderately steep slopes and wrapping around 3000 foot-high sandstone cliffs stained a startling crimson due to the oxidation of iron in the rock that's occurred over the course of eons of geologic activity. Serious bikers train on this 13-mile route through the canyon, exerting their legs to push hard up the hills before reveling in the desert breeze brushing their faces while coasting downhill. Day campers and hikers scatter over dozens of trails around the park. Local rock climbing enthusiasts choose from an endless supply of verticals here on which to practice their dizzying sport.

My first of many visits to Red Rock Canyon finds me driving my brother Joe's Caddy leisurely up Blue Diamond Road away from the city. Scarlet-hued mountains loom ahead of me, jutting out starkly in the crisp desert air. There's a minimum of industrial pollution here to blur the sharpness of the peaks thrust up into the cold, dry, winter sky.

The one curve in the road takes me past the hamlet of Blue Diamond, where I stop for gas. Blue Diamond is a miner's village of about one hundred run-down homes, dilapidated shacks, and ramshackle trailers. The town looks like the abandoned set of an old Western movie that might have starred John Wayne. The modern day inhabitants seemingly lucky to have electricity and a single general store selling groceries and cold beer.

Blue Diamond Road straightens for the final run to the canyon of about twelve miles, the two-lane blacktop mildly ascending and descending through a series of gentle hills. I pass Spring Mountain Ranch to my left. I later learn the state park was once owned by the Las Vegas recluse and multi-millionaire Howard Hughes who purchased it from Vera Krupp, a well-known German film actress of the 1930s. Vera was famous for fleeing Nazi Germany before Adolph Hitler gained supreme power, and for her ownership of the

Krupp Diamond, an insanely huge 33-carat stone she sold to the actor Richard Burton who in turn gave it to Elizabeth Taylor shortly after starring with her in the 1963 epic film Cleopatra. I was just a kid when the movie came out but I remember my grandmother, mother, and aunt—we all lived together in an extended family of 11—being deliciously appalled at the scandalous tabloid affair between Hollywood's two biggest—and adulterous—celebrities.

About six miles from the park entrance, on either side of Blue Diamond, a few Joshua trees spring up in the desert. These lonely, eerie sentinels stretch their gnarly limbs towards heaven. As I get closer to Red Rock, more Joshuas group together into a desert forest, dozens of trees clustered on either side of the road. Joshuas don't grow very tall, and images of Middle Earth's Ents futilely searching for their lost wives spring to my mind. Beyond the last stand of Joshuas lies the entrance to the park. I stop at the visitor center to pick up a map and decide to tackle the Sandstone Quarry Trail which will lead me to Turtlehead Peak, a journey there and back again of almost six miles to a summit 2000 feet higher in altitude than where I'm starting. The guide map characterizes the trail as "strenuous" and the trail condition as "bushwhacking". *Huh? What does that mean? Am I going to need a machete to chop my way up brush-filled slopes?* I'm not sure I can handle it as most of my exercise the last few months has consisted of barefoot treks in my underwear from whoever's couch I've been occupying to the refrigerator for more beer and leftover pizza.

At the entrance to the trailhead, Bureau of Land Management signs display images of some of the wild creatures that inhabit the park. I'm drawn to the warning about bobcats and mountain lions prowling the upper elevations. Wandering off the marked trails is discouraged even though an encounter with a predator like a puma or a venomous snake is unlikely.

With the morning sun nearing its zenith and the desert heat rising, I fortify myself with a can of *Red Bull* pulled from my knapsack. The trek begins alongside a dry riverbed strewn with tan and gray stones worn smooth over the millennia. Clear skies reveal the occasional red-tailed hawk or golden eagle circling lazily above the briars alongside the river. They're waiting for rabbits and other delights to expose themselves and become eligible dinner offerings.

After the first mile or so of leisurely walking over more or less level terrain, the trail pitches sharply upward. Huffing and puffing on the ascent, I wind my way amongst elephant-sized boulders precariously perched aside steep-sloped drop-offs. Except for the sound of my own labored breathing, the world here is silent; not even the rustle of a desert breeze teases the ears. I now understand what was meant when the sign advertised the climb as "strenuous". Poisonous toxins seep from my pores with each painful step. My out-of-shape body undergoes a forced withdrawal from the intoxicants and stimulants consumed while playing games at my favorite downtown casinos. It's a healing kind of pain though. I find my spirit getting rejuvenated as my soul urges me to keep struggling towards the summit. But if there's a specific spiritual purpose for me making this climb, I haven't a clue what it might be.

The upward trek becomes a meditation. Having no one else to converse with, my mind generates random thoughts to distract me from my goal. *Why not turn back now? Isn't this enough for one day? You're not in shape yet for any kind of mountain climbing! Just what are you trying to prove anyway? What could possibly be calling you to the top of this mountain?*

I find myself spontaneously repeating the *Om Mani Padme Hum* mantra, which I haven't used in years. This Tibetan mantra is associated with *Guan Yin*, the Bodhisattva of Compassion for both Buddhists and Taoists. Its meaning is untranslatable to any specific English phrase and this fact is comforting to me since all I have to do is repeat each syllable and trust that beneficial effects will occur to ease my route up the rocky slope. Just why the *Om Mani Padme Hum* mantra shows up in my consciousness today, I'm not sure. But its arrival doesn't really bother me, since long ago

I gave up questioning the *why* associated with the occurrence or timing of spiritual processes. Mind-induced analytical dissection of soul-driven events is to be avoided at all costs according to *St. John of the Cross*, a legendary Christian mystic and Dragon.

About two-thirds of the way up Turtlehead Peak, I have to stop and catch my breath. The trail, branded at lower levels with stone cairns and flat-rocked resting places, has disappeared entirely, or if the path is marked, it's beyond my skill to find it. I harbor no sense of panic since the summit is looming before me and can't be missed. I merely have to trust my instincts and pick a route up and around the boulders. However, I do get stuck in a few spots and am forced to use my hands to pull my body vertically through several difficult stretches. But once I reach the ridge top that leads to Turtlehead Peak, the rest of the climb becomes a cakewalk. *Om Mani Padme Hum*... the mantra repeats itself over and over and I sink into a kind of walking meditation that Zen Buddhists call *kinhin*. Temple acolytes find kinhin walking a welcome break for the body after hours of motionless sitting in full lotus position contemplating koans delivered from their Rishi masters.

My body starts to shake from small muscle spasms. With each step up the slope, minor tremors explode in me—not from overexertion—but because the mantra's healing energy is transforming blockages in me, releasing stress, fear, anger, and my still-bottled up resentment at being deported from Canada. The center of my chest is pounding, and while my spiritual Third Eye is by no means fully open, I can see as well as feel vibrant red energy blasts pulsing and radiating outwards from my heart chakra with each labored breath. My steps hasten as if I have only a limited amount of time to reach the summit of Turtlehead Peak before some sort of disaster strikes. At last I arrive at the domed pinnacle overlooking adjacent, smaller mountains separated by grooved valleys winding far below me.

I slip off my backpack and lean it against the large boulder designating the top of Turtlehead. Las Vegas flickers in the distance, a tiny oasis in the form of a mirage floating over a limitless expanse of desert.

I sit down. Resting my back against the warm sandstone, the release comes slowly. I begin to sob between continuing recitations of the mantra. *Om Mani Padme Hum ... Om Mani Padme Hum ... Om Mani Padme Hum.* Gulping for air, I finally let it out. An angry scream directed at God, the world, everyone I know, and all the spiritual guides and Dragons in the heavens above me. The outcry doesn't last long. My wail is a mixture of many conjoined forces: a plea for help, a response to the throes of mental and physical agony, and surprisingly, *gratitude* for the experience of the last two months. I'm actually *happy* to be undergoing this mess of a spiritual test. I look around quickly to be sure I'm alone, worried I'll be found out and embarrassed. But as far as I can tell, I'm the only person on Turtlehead Peak right now and my solitude is not in jeopardy. My breathing slowly calms. My heartbeat relaxes. I pull a peanut butter and jelly sandwich from my knapsack and find it to be most certainly the best sandwich I've ever made.

Some sort of page has turned in my Xiu Lian practice ... some test has been passed. I know I'll be all right and I wonder—was I called to the summit by the Dragon Guan Yin to receive this healing blessing from the Mother of Compassion? *Om Mani Padme Hum ... Om Mani Padme Hum ... Om Mani Padme Hum.* I continue to chant. I consider the spiritual presence of Mother Guan Yin who has chosen to visit me today, and I wonder: *How many other Dragons have I flown with? How many other blessings have I received, whether consciously aware of them or not, on this spiritual path, this Xiu Lian Purification Journey I've been traveling since I was a teenager? And what lies ahead for me now?*

Buddhist Prayer of Forgiveness

Without exception, all of my spiritual fathers and mothers stress the importance of *Daily Forgiveness Practice*, a great way to self-clear karma. Master Sha teaches:

"Forgiveness brings inner joy and inner peace."

We can practice in two ways. First, we ask for forgiveness from those we've harmed. Secondly, we offer unconditional forgiveness to those who have harmed us.

Below is a traditional Buddhist Forgiveness Prayer that also accommodates forgiving ourselves, a necessary and beneficial practice for those of us who have not only harmed others, but our own selves as well.

You can chant this forgiveness practice at any time, silently or aloud, while cooking food, driving your car, or quietly meditating. If you're like me, some days you'll find yourself crying when connecting with the souls of those you've hurt. Let your tears of compassion flow!

Buddhist Forgiveness Prayer
*If I have harmed anyone in any way either knowingly or unknowingly
through my own confusions, I ask for their forgiveness.
If anyone has harmed me in any way either knowingly or unknowingly
Through their own confusions, I forgive them.
And if there is a situation I am not yet ready to forgive,
I forgive myself for that.
For all the ways that I harm myself, negate, doubt, belittle myself,
judge or be unkind to myself through my own confusions,
I forgive myself.*

HEJIRA

"Make yourself familiar with the angels,
and behold them frequently in spirit,
for without being seen,
they are present with you."

—St. Francis de Sales

Medicine Buddha Thangka
Hand-made for me in Nepal by Buddhist Monks in 2012
Consecrated with 200 hours of continuous chanting

Encouraged by my successful trek up Turtlehead Peak, and with my soul buoyed by my unexpected blessing from Mother Guan Yin, I determine not to lose the momentum that germinated in Red Rock Canyon and returned me to the Xiu Lian path, depositing me there like the long lost Prodigal Son in the Bible returning home after a long absence.

My body is painfully sore after the arduous climb up and down the mountain. Still, the next morning I join a 24-hour gym that's newly opened down the street from the condo, knowing I need to establish a regimen of physical training to keep me energized and moving forward.

I begin a 90-minute daily routine on the Nautilus gear and the treadmill, jumping right into the program rather than working up to speed with a more gradual, saner approach. Following the morning workouts, I return to the condo for a 45-minute meditation session before lunch. I feel like I'm slowly getting back on track. I'm healthier now and more focused on resuming my Xiu Lian Purification Journey.

Exploration Peak Park is a half-mile down the street from the condo. The family-friendly park is encircled by a mile-long oval walking trail surrounding green-grassed playing fields used primarily by little kids playing soccer and baseball. I begin taking late afternoon daily walks around the park and am intrigued by a winding dirt track leading to the top of Exploration Peak overlooking Las Vegas to the north. After my first week at the gym, I decide I'm fit enough to try to run up to the summit.

Exploration Peak quickly humbles me.

My first, second, and third attempts at racing up the dirt track are disastrous. The back of my legs cramp and I'm only able to jog about halfway to the summit. I'm forced to accept this predicament as a sure indication that I'm still not anywhere near the shape needed to run outdoors in the Las Vegas desert sun at midday. Jogging around the oval track around the park's perimeter might be a better option. Besides, there are lots of girls that use the path to walk their dogs and that will occasionally pause for conversation if their canines approve me after sniffing around my legs.

While living in Toronto after becoming a student of Master Sha in the spring of 2010, I developed a spiritual connection with the *Medicine Buddha* after learning how to chant *Soul Language*. Master Sha explains all about Soul Language in his book *Soul Wisdom: Practical Soul Treasures to Transform Your Life*[1].

The soul of the Medicine Buddha started expressing itself through my Soul Language in a joyous, healing manner. I also received multiple visions from a prior lifetime in which I lived in a Himalayan mountain monastery with a bunch of Tibetan monks. Heaven has showed me many images from that lifetime in which I sit in brightly colored robes on a balcony overlooking a mountain valley, pounding a drum while chanting in a deep voice that vibrates from the area of my abdomen. Master Sha refers to this part of the body as a foundational energy center known as the *Lower Dan Tian*. "Dan" means light ball. "Tian" means field. I am not a reincarnation of the powerful Medicine Buddha. But when practicing Master Sha's soul healing techniques, I do call upon the soul of this Dragon often to assist in the healing of others and myself.

Buddhist practitioners believe in the principle of cause and effect known as *karma*. Illness, sickness, and diseases that show up in our lives are the result of past negative actions on our part such as impure thoughts, impure speech, and impure deeds. When the karma from these negative actions manifests in the form of minor physical illnesses, Buddhists believe these sicknesses can resolve themselves naturally without the need to take medicines. If our mistakes are more serious, but we have received some amount of virtue—good karma—from past positive actions, we can use

---

1 Soul Wisdom: Practical Soul Treasures to Transform Your Life, New York/Toronto: Atria Books/ Heaven's Library, 2009.

modern healing techniques, including medicines, to recover. Buddhism also teaches if our karma is extremely heavy from serious past mistakes, then *no* amount of medicine and traditional healing modalities can cure us and we have to find other ways to pay off our karmic debt.

Master Sha is more optimistic and teaches that we can remove much of our bad karma by doing Forgiveness Practice and serving others unconditionally to make them happier and healthier. Using Soul Power, one of Master Sha's *Four-Power Techniques® for Self-Healing*, we can invoke the souls in need of healing ("inner" souls) as well as souls such as the Medicine Buddha ("outer" souls) to assist us spiritually to self-clear our serious or life-threatening bad karma.

After connecting with the soul of the Medicine Buddha when first chanting my Soul Language in Toronto a year earlier, I was curious to learn more about this high-level Dragon expressing himself through me during Master Sha's practices. I found a copy of *The Sutra of the Medicine Buddha,* which contains the principles guiding the Medicine Buddha's service to humanity, and studied the meaning and intent behind each of the Medicine Buddha's 12 vows.

When I begin my first lap through Expedition Park, I invoke the soul of the Medicine Buddha using the Sanskrit form of his name as first spoken by the Shakyamuni Buddha:

"Namo Bhagavat Bhaisajyaguruvaiduryaprabha-rajayatathagataya arhate samyaksambuddhaya tadyatha Om bhaisajye bhaisajye bhaisajye-bhaisajya-samudgate svaha."

On the very first day of my practice, and much to my surprise, a manifestation of the Medicine Buddha, deep blue in color, arrives above Exploration Peak! His body is huge, almost as big as the hill over which he sits poised in the lotus position. With his back turned to the Strip of Las Vegas—no surprise there—the

Medicine Buddha's gaze is focused instead on the visitors to the park. He is offering blessings to the souls below him, all the souls beyond the park, and all souls in all universes. All the while smiling serenely. This Third Eye image is very tangible to me, to the point where I would not be surprised if any of the other people in the park can also see the Buddha hovering above them in the clear desert sky.

Buddhist teachings say that if one chants the name of any high-level Buddha as death approaches, they will be avoid being reborn in the lower realms and receive the blessings of that Buddha in their next incarnation.

I recite the "12 Aspirations of The Medicine Buddha" as best as I can remember them after calling his name. Truth be told, I don't always get it right. I'm not rigid as to the specific order of the 12 vows, and I haven't memorized the exact wording of the aspirations or learned the original Sanskrit. Though I've been meditating for over 30 years, I still consider myself somewhat of a novice at spiritual practice and justify my laziness by assuring myself that it's my heart's intention that counts with the Divine, not my ability to be perfect in the mechanics of practice, be it the recitation of mantras or the ability to sit for extended periods of time in perfect posture with a straight spine.

Each day in Exploration Park I am graced with the presence of the Medicine Buddha after chanting the mantra and the 12 aspirations. Although I've been taught not to have any expectations regarding the continued appearance of this Buddha or any other spiritual Master during my practices, I can't help but eagerly look forward to this Dragon's daily blessing. I feel extremely grateful to be offering service to the people and animals in the park by facilitating his visits and presence through my chanting. As Master Sha would say: "We are extremely blessed!"

While continuing to gain in strength spiritually, mentally, and physically over the next two months, I receive an email from Lynda Chaplin, one of Master Sha's advanced students and teachers from

Toronto. Lynda is coming to Las Vegas on business. She's heard unsettling rumors about my deportation, my flight, and exile from Canada. She suggests we meet on a free day at the end of her business conference and is not interested in spending any time on the Las Vegas strip. I pick her up and take her to Red Rock Canyon instead. The canyon is a perfect place for a leisurely drive with a few stops to enjoy the views, have lunch, and exchange war stories about our respective Xiu Lian purification experiences. I don't remember the specific advice Lynda gave me, but she must have said something that affected my heart deeply because, after dropping her off for her return flight to Toronto, my soul whispers to me: *It's time to go.*

Leaving Las Vegas will not be difficult. There is a lot of dark energy hovering around this adult's playground and I'm a little fearful an extended stay here may derail the Xiu Lian progress I've managed to attain since my deportation from Canada.

Hejira is the act of physically escaping from any hostile environment. In the Muslim tradition, hejira refers to the flight of the *Prophet Muhammad* from Mecca to Medina in the year 622, the beginning of the Muslim calendar. Ready to undertake my own hejira from Sin City, all I have to do now is find a place to live that feels right. I decide to give Colorado a try.

My brother needs someone to drive his Cadillac back to Denver, where he lives, for the summer—he won't drive the Caddy in snowy winter climates and so keeps it at the Vegas condo. I offer my service to help him out but also to check out the Rocky Mountains near Boulder, the site of Master Sha's first Divine Temple in the US. Boulder is also home to the Shambala Meditation Center and Naropa University founded by the Buddhist Guru *Chögyam Trungpa Rinpoche*. Boulder is filled with many other Asian tradition temples and ashrams.

I leave Las Vegas around 4 a.m. on a Tuesday morning hoping to reach Boulder by late afternoon if the State Police don't catch me racing past one of their hidden speed traps. The drive through

Nevada, Utah, and Colorado is one of the most scenic drives in America across US Highways 15 and 70, and winds through Zion, Bryce Canyon, and Moab National Parks. As far as I can tell, there is no one living in Utah, no cell phone service there, and no radio stations to listen to. I'm totally alone on my road trip with only Mother Nature for company and am looking forward to the solitude, which will permit me time to chant Master Sha mantras and sing Soul Songs for hours at a time.

Pre-dawn orange light glows above the mountains in the East, signaling a warm day before me. Land and sky blend together as dawn breaks. Heaven and earth fuse into a coalesced fabric of unity and oneness. The view through my windshield reminds me of a Vincent Van Gogh painting like my favorite, *The Church at Auvers,* where the artist's brushwork melds all the objects on the canvas into a single homogeneous fabric. Vincent was said to be madly and romantically insane. The renowned artist never received artistic or monetary reward for his precious paintings while alive. Years earlier, when counseling patients in the Massachusetts State Mental Health system, I would learn why society often locks up individuals like Vincent for no reason other than that they see the world differently than the rest of us. I chuckle aloud thinking back to my college years when pot-smoking, LSD-tripping students pinned cheap prints of Van Gogh paintings like *Starry Night* to their dormitory walls. Van Gogh was so popular amongst hippies back then because, at the height of a psychedelic drug high, all space and time unite, all duality disappears and—at least for a short time—the canvas of the universe becomes a unified landscape.

My personal hejira, an 11-hour exodus from Las Vegas, is happening at just the right moment in my Xiu Lian Purification Journey. And with no distractions on the drive to Colorado, I have time to recount the key elements of my spiritual journey from my teenage years up to now, a trek that's taken me from my New England roots to my new home in the slowly approaching Rocky Mountains.

12 Aspirations of the Medicine Buddha

In the future, when I attain perfect awakening and become a Buddha:

May all sentient beings be replete with the bodily appearance of luminosity and clarity of the Buddhas by hearing and recollecting my name.

May all sentient beings see luminosity and clarity by hearing and recollecting my name.

May all sentient beings come to have wealth and no being be deprived of anything by hearing and recollecting my name.

May all sentient beings that are on a negative path take the positive path of virtue, kindness, and selfless compassion by hearing and recollecting my name.

May all sentient beings be virtuous and keep their vinaya discipline. May those who have broken their discipline immediately see their own faults, and cultivate renunciation and purification until attainment of full enlightenment by hearing and recollecting my name.

May all sentient beings that are diseased or disabled be replete and immediately cured of sickness and disease by hearing and recollecting my name.

May all sentient beings that suffer the burdens and anxiety of poverty and loneliness attain abundance, wealth, joy, and peace by hearing and recollecting my name.

May all sentient beings that take a negative birth, who are despised for their presence and wish to be free, be free and never again take a negative rebirth by hearing and recollecting my name.

May all sentient beings that have wrong views give rise to correct views until attainment of enlightenment by hearing and recollecting my name.

May all sentient beings who are oppressed, beaten, terrorized by fear of a ruler, and those whose body, speech, and mind are plagued by torture and suffering and therefore endure great humiliation, grief, despair, and persecution be liberated by hearing and recollecting my name.

May all sentient beings who suffer from hunger be satisfied and taste the flavor of Buddha Dharma and ultimately attain enlightenment by hearing and recollecting my name.

May all sentient beings be free from the sufferings of extreme heat, cold, and exposure. Furthermore, may all beings that are suffering from such a condition be provided with fine clothes and other excellent, proper, material offerings by hearing and recollecting my name.

Source: www.rimayrinpoche.com

The Rising Young Executive

"But something is happening here,
And you don't know what it is,
Do you, Mister Jones?"
—Bob Dylan, *Ballad of a Thin Man*

Timothy Leary and Richard Alpert (Ram Dass)
Harvard University Professors fired for
experimenting with LSD in the 1960s.

"Here he comes." I announce to my best friend Steven. Two teenagers sitting on a stone wall. Kicking out our restless legs. Watching late afternoon traffic pass by on Main Street.

"Who?" Steven asks, turning to look in the direction I'm pointing.

"*The Rising Young Executive.*" It's kind of a mean nickname we've given this guy who walks home from the bus stop every weekday touting a brown briefcase we're sure is stuffed with important business documents he intends to review after dinner. His evening meal prepared by an unseen wife who's cooped up in their house all day long on the adjacent side street. The Rising Young Executive always wears an uncomfortable looking oversized brown or blue suit—he seems to own only two—brown wingtip shoes, and a few non-descript ties that he never takes off or loosens regardless of the temperature. We don't know where he works or what type of business he's in, but assume he's pursuing a career somewhere in the big city. His commute each day is a loop of walking to the bus stop, taking the bus to the Orange Line subway station to downtown Boston, then reversing the process to get back to his suburban home after work.

The Rising Young Executive engages in a daily battle fighting the crowds heading in and out of a maze of skyscraper office buildings before at last reaching a cubicle most likely shared with another junior corporate employee with similar aspirations much like himself. We've taken notice of The Rising Young Executive because he walks extremely and unnecessarily *fast* as if perpetually on a mission for the benefit of the senior management team he's trying to impress in hopes of gaining a future promotion.

Steven and I are way too young to understand any of the intricacies of corporate life and capitalistic moneymaking occupations, but the moniker with which we've anointed our neighborhood executive seems appropriate enough to us. On the weekday afternoons we encounter the man, he appears focused, but stressed.

In control, but unhappy. Ambitious, but struggling. And although we are only 14, Steven and I are quite sure we don't *ever* want to grow up to be anything like The Rising Young Executive. It feels to us like we are privy to some secret of life that he's not. We know he notices us because he occasionally flashes a frown of distaste and frustration our way when he passes. He never says hello. Clearly, to his mind we are lazy teenagers who aren't studying as we should and this lack of initiative on our part will most assuredly catch up with us when we are of age to enter the working world and need to look for a career job to support our families and ourselves.

It's the spring of 1967. Steven and I are finishing 8th grade in the accelerated studies division and pursuing our usual after-school activities of hanging around waiting for dinner after waging ferocious ping-pong battles in Steven's garage. We live in Melrose, a suburban commuter town just north of Boston. At around 5 p.m. on any weekday evening, my Mom and live-in grandmother are getting supper ready for my Dad, me and my brother, my three sisters, my aunt, and two girl cousins who live with us. Any additional guests or neighborhood kids who happen to be in the vicinity and are hungry are always welcome. My friend Steven is a frequent guest for dinner. One more chair squeezed around the table and one more mouth to feed won't make a noticeable difference in the amount of available food with the possible exception of the Duncan Hines chocolate cake my Mom prepares once or twice a week. Steven is a big fan of Duncan Hines chocolate cake and seems to have a pretty accurate sixth sense about what nights Mom's likely to bake the frosted dessert.

Driving my brother's Cadillac from Las Vegas to Colorado, I have plenty of time to reflect back on those days and those family meals with incredible fondness because, since my deportation from Canada, most of my current dinners consist of leftovers brought back from local restaurants or unhealthy frozen food meals micro-waved into submission and eaten alone.

1967 is a year of social upheaval in the US:

- *Elvis, once the King of pop music, has been exiled to Las Vegas. Driven to sudden insignificance in the music world by the invasion of British rock bands like my favorite, The Rolling Stones.*
- *The Cold War against Communism rages. Vietnam is the current battleground to which 18-year old kids are shipped by President Lyndon Baines Johnson to do battle with determined Viet Cong forces who will never be defeated.*
- *High school and college kids from the same neighborhoods—many from the same families—take up socio-political stances against each other, not unlike extended families that lived in the North and the South during America's Civil War. The "hippies" sport long hair, smoke pot, and preach Peace and Love. The "jocks" have buzz-cut "wiffles." drink beer, and look for someone to punch out in a friendly fight on any given Friday night.*
- *The Beatles release Sergeant Pepper's Lonely Hearts Club Band, which includes* Within You, Without You, *a mystical musical collaboration by George Harrison and Ravi Shankar after the rock group visits India and learns about meditation from Maharishi Mahesh Yogi.*
- *NASA gets the US closer and closer to landing on the moon with the Apollo Space Program that will culminate successfully in two years time fulfilling President Kennedy's dream announced at the start of the decade.*
- *Martin Luther King champions civil rights for Blacks. Things get ugly in America's Deep South, and King is assassinated a year later.*
- *Young women celebrate demands for freedom and equality by burning their bras—to the delight of the boys. They shout for their voices to be heard in government halls and the boardrooms of America—to the dismay of aging, white, power brokers.*
- *Debt becomes fashionable. Families "keep up with the Joneses" by acquiring credit cards and sending formerly stay-at-home Moms out*

to work as cheap labor for a second income so the family can buy "one of them color televisions."

And in Boston,

- *The Red Sox generate record levels of excitement for local sports fans—hippies and jocks alike—becoming the first team ever to go from last place to first in one year, winning the American League pennant, but, alas, losing to the St. Louis Cardinals in an excruciatingly painful seventh game of the World Series.*

It's a time in America's history when one is forced to take sides, a Swiss-neutral stance on any of the social issues of the day just not acceptable. White Judeo-Christian America is getting scared. Young people are exploring alternatives to the 9–5 corporate lifestyles their fathers and grandfathers pursued with unbridled passion and which "made America great!" College kids are shirking degrees in Business Management to go off and live on a farm or, God forbid, join an ashram in the Himalayas with a guru preaching reincarnation of the soul. Use of psychedelics to expand consciousness is happening on college campuses all across America. Martini-sipping parents don't understand their kids. Dope-smoking kids shun their parents. Eastern philosophies and lifestyles are gaining footholds in the once uninterested West. Yoga, meditation, Qi Gong and Tai Chi exercise groups take root around college campuses, their message of alternative lifestyles sprouting like seeds in fertile earth watered with the curiosity of those who will become the New Age seekers of the 1970s. Buddhism, Taoism, Hinduism and other non-Christian religions start to interest the younger generation who question the ideologies propounded by priests and pastors at Mom and Dad's Sunday services. Change is coming and most everyone over the age of 30 is of the opinion that "No good will come of it!...And by the way, just *what exactly is wrong* with what we've been doing in America anyway?"

And that includes our friend The Rising Young Executive, who isn't at all comfortable trying to stay afloat in the shifting social landscape. He feels he's doing everything right but, like Mr. Jones in Bob Dylan's ballad, he's also acutely aware that *something else* is happening around him, he's not a part of it, and he doesn't even know what "it" is.

Social culture and the issues of the day come to a head in my house on Main Street on May 3, 1967. My parents learn of a debate to be televised that evening on PBS that they inform us kids will require our "mandatory attendance." *Timothy Leary,* a professor who's been thrown out of Harvard University along with *Richard Alpert*—who later became *Ram Dass*—for experimenting with LSD and psilocybin, will debate the merits of hallucinogens, only recently mandated as illegal, with *Jerome Lettvin,* an MIT professor who believes such drugs are dangerous and justifiably outlawed.

I'm the second oldest of the kids in the house, and at 14, I have no idea what drugs are or why the adults are insistent we watch these two professors argue with each other. However, there's a noticeable level of excitement in the air as we scramble to the living room for the 7 p.m. show. Like a gala Hollywood movie premiere, every seat gets filled. Dad claims his recliner, reserved exclusively for the breadwinner of the family. Mom, Grandma, Auntie Sis and the girls squeeze into the two sofas, and my brother and I are relegated to cushions and pillows on the floor directly in front of a large-at-the-time black and white console TV.

Tim Leary comes out like nothing I've ever seen before. He has long wavy hair, unkempt and uncombed, and wears a white loose-fitting cover-all shirt—probably an Indian lungi—that clearly wasn't sold in any store that I had access to. Tim is barefoot. Sits down cross-legged on a floor cushion. Lights a candle.

"Well, would you look at that…he's got no shoes!" one of the women mutters disdainfully from the sofa behind me.

"And will you look at that hair…on a grown man!" says another, her disapproval of radical Tim's entire presence quite evident. Professor Lettvin, a last-minute replacement for another MIT professor originally scheduled for the debate, wears a white shirt and tie and speaks from behind a desk and a stand-up microphone. Professor Lettvin projects a far more professorial and appropriate demeanor for such a serious event than "that oddball Leary."

What fascinates me is that when Timothy Leary speaks, advocating a "Turn On, Tune In, Drop Out" philosophy that became the mantra of hippies everywhere in the 1960s, he simultaneously projects a display of patterns, lights, and music on a gigantic movie screen behind the stage in what was a pre-cursor to all the MTV music videos and rock show stage effects that spawned in the years to come. To me, the effect is entrancing, peaceful, loving, and well... *pretty*. My Dad is fairly quiet during the debate—not unusual for him—but the adult women continue to be noticeably unimpressed and at times become even violently upset.

Comments spontaneously spew forth from Mom, Auntie, and Grandma, new variations on these admonishments cycled round every few minutes, all for the children's benefit. "Just what does he think he's doing showing those crazy pictures?" or "I'm getting a headache just looking at this!" or "If that's what taking drugs does to you, I don't want any part of it!"

I believe now that the adults in my family truly believed that these hallucinogens that made you see things, and distorted— Tim would say expanded—consciousness were dangerous and that Timothy Leary was a nut. But their well-intentioned declarations had just the opposite effect on me. What I witnessed was a nice man, clearly intelligent, talking about using LSD to promote religious communion with the Divine, to actually *talk* to God, and to experience expanded dimensions of reality—albeit only while the drug's effects lasted. Yes, I was only in junior high school, but LSD was something I decided then and there I wanted to try, and I silently resolved to get some in the future even though I knew no one who had any or would know how to get it.

Of course, I couldn't voice anything about my intent with the antagonistic and openly hostile crowd in the room, so I just kept my silence for the duration of the debate that ended abruptly for us when Jerome Lettvin shouted "Bullshit!" at Tim for likening LSD flashbacks to mystical experiences. I believe this was the first time that expletive—followed shortly thereafter by a "Goddamn"—was blurted out "live" on public television—no HBO back in the 1960s! Well, the adults had seen enough. They were as outraged at Tim Leary as was Jerome Lettvin. Common sense and Christian decency dictated the end of the fun before who knew what would be said next and The Great Debate was turned off.

I'm sure if The Rising Young Executive had come out for a walk after dinner that evening in May, 1967 and somehow found himself invited into my parent's living room to watch the debate with our family, he would have experienced a level of comfort with the adults, being of similar opinion and holding a value system much like theirs. His beliefs, under siege daily in those tempestuous years, may have been shored up for a time by Professor Lettvin's common sense warnings not to attempt consciousness expansion via LSD, magic mushrooms, or any other hallucinogenic drugs. But I also believe his comfort would be short-lived, and his uneasiness would soon return because the karma of the times was beginning to rumble like a long dormant volcano soon-to-explode. We all had to take a stance for our beliefs, weather the antagonism of those against us, and learn to survive in those turbulent times. Timothy Leary and Richard Alpert were two of the earliest spiritual Dragons I would fly with in the 1960s and '70s. A few years later, inspired by Tim Leary and his televised debate, I would get the chance to take my first psychedelic trip using LSD, an experience that acted as a spiritual catalyst for my soon-to-get-active Xiu Lian Purification Journey.

Daily Gratitude Practice

It is important to express *Gratitude* each day to all of our spiritual fathers and mothers in Heaven for all they have done and continue to do to help us on our Xiu Lian Purification Journey. We can also express gratitude to any souls on Mother Earth or in Heaven such as family, friends, loved ones—and even pets!—whose helpful actions we are thankful for.

You can personalize this Gratitude Practice and use it anytime, anywhere. Expressing gratitude from your heart can be much deeper than just saying "Thank you" after a kindness, or saying grace before meals. Make every day in your life a "Thanksgiving"!

Daily Gratitude Practice

Dear Divine, Dear Tao,
Dear All Heaven's Committees, All Heaven's
Generals, All Heaven's Soldiers,
All Souls in all Heavens serving all souls in all universes,
Dear Souls of all my spiritual Fathers and Mothers:
I love you, honor you, and appreciate you.
I bow down to you countless times in thanks for my
life, my health, my trials and tribulations.
I bow down to you countless times in thanks for
Your love, guidance, teachings, protection, and support,
Dear all of my Divine and Tao treasures, downloads, blessings, and orders,
I cannot bow to you enough.
Please continue to heal, teach, love, guide, protect, and support me.
Hao. Hao. Hao.
Thank You. Thank You. Thank You.

ATTACK OF THE GIANT GREEN FROGS

One pill makes you larger.
And one pill makes you small.
And the ones that mother gives you
Don't do anything at all.
Go ask Alice When she's ten feet tall.

—Jefferson Airplane, *White Rabbit*

Stephen Colwell
1053 Main Street
Mysteriously quiet on the
outside . . . inside lies a solid
mind . . . a faithful Rolling
Stones fan . . . Big Four . . .
golfing at Mt. Hood . . . en-
chanted journeys to Colton
Forest.
Golf; Cross Country 1;
J.C.L.; LOG.

Melrose High School Class Yearbook – 1971

My first LSD experience happens in July 1969, two years after I'd watched the Timothy Leary-Jerome Lettvin Great Debate about using psychedelic drugs to facilitate consciousness expansion. LSD, mescaline, and psilocybin "magic" mushrooms are all illegal, and all in vogue now amongst the rock-music-loving, rebellious, long-haired hippies of my generation. Jimi Hendrix is dead, but his music lives on, and a new British group, Led Zeppelin, releases a debut album that changes the rock music scene forever. American boys are still being killed daily in Vietnam; we watch the horror every evening on the nightly news. If the war continues for two more years, I'll have to enlist for the draft or flee to Canada. Technology advances occur at the speed of light and the US will land a man on the moon for the first time on the 20th of the month.

My friend David and I venture downtown to Caruso's, a local pizza joint with a dimly-lit parking lot that gets taken over by bad-ass motorcycle gang members on Friday and Saturday nights. David's older brother Andy buys drugs from the gang and pushes them to high school kids. He's "working" tonight and David says that, although Andy will let us tag along with him to the parking lot, we have to let him do his thing alone since he's a known entity to the gang members and we are not.

The three of us head down the street decked out in bell-bottomed Levi's, swaggering with the false bravado of zit-faced teenagers trying to look hip. My nervousness is barely held in check, fueled by the excitement of our anti-social behavior and impending criminal activity. I'm feeling very cool hanging out with David and his brother because "bad" girls like them and we expect to run into a few of them at a party later tonight once we score the acid.

We linger clandestinely in the doorway of a barbershop across the street from the motorcycle gang. Wait warily for the deal to go down. Anxiously scan the perimeter, paranoid that narcs with guns drawn might be lying in wait for us behind the nearby manicured hedges outside law-abiding citizens' homes. *My parents would kill me if they knew I was here.* Andy tells us to stay put and not talk to anyone. Ventures into the midst of the motorcycle gang smoking pot openly under dead, dark street lamps. Returns a few minutes later to make a clandestine handoff to his brother before quickly walking away. David hands me the tiniest orange pill I've ever seen. Tells me to pop it in my mouth *now*. I blindly follow his command after he swallows his own LSD tab. I'm expecting immediate results but David laughs at me and says it will take about 20 minutes for the acid to kick in. He says I'll know my trip has started when things start to look different to me—though he doesn't explain what that means—and that I may start to hallucinate and see stuff that isn't really happening. He assures me that if I start to freak out, he'll be there to help and won't let me do anything stupid. I feel comfortable with David and decide he's exceptionally wise for his age.

We head downtown to see who's out and what our friends are up to as if tonight is just another typical Friday in our small hometown. But of course it's not a normal Friday and tonight we are not-so-typical teenagers. Tonight we are about to expand our consciousness and experience multiple dimensions of the universe firsthand.

We sit on a stone wall in front of Melrose City Hall, watching the night people perform their socially choreographed weekend rituals up and down Main Street. Girls in mini-skirts and colored tights advertise premature sexual sophistication. Packs of skinny, sneakered boys pick up the females' scent and follow them around hoping to get noticed. Cliques of Barbie-doll cheerleaders drive by in Daddy's borrowed car. Honk the horn on their way to exclusive parties with older boys living beyond the borders of high school. The less pretty and less popular girls stare with envy. Varsity wrestlers wearing skin-tight T-shirts with cut-off sleeves show off ripped abs; the jocks are mean paragons of hostility, anger, and resentment. 17-year old novice drunks stagger about dangerously, dizzy eyes unfocused, trying mightily to avoid sidewalk collisions with disapproving adults who can smell two-dollar-a-bottle Boone's Farm Apple Wine on their breath. Authority-inspired cops patrol in pairs, desperate for a violent crime to be committed. Then the moving picture show before David and I starts to *slow... down*, just like David told me it would.

Like a wide-angle camera panning away from a close-up shot in a movie, my visual perspective withdraws and I feel "myself" looking down on Main Street from a vantage point in the sky high above the city's rooftops. The world is becoming a swirling stew of people, cars, buildings, sounds, and colors, and I'm no longer part of the mix. "I" have left. I'm somehow outside of my body gazing down at the person sitting on the wall far below me. This experience will repeat itself many times in the years ahead when I go deep into meditation. But tonight is the first time I'm aware that it's possible for my soul to separate from my physical body. I'm too young spiritually to understand what's going on and my guide David has no insight or interest in the "why" of what's happening. David is content to just laugh and go with the flow.

Soon, the noises of downtown diminish in volume, replaced by another sound, a not unpleasant humming that vibrates my sternum. It's the *OM* sound, the "primal sound" of the universe, though I don't recognize the mantra at this stage of my Xiu Lian Purification Journey, a journey only just beginning in this lifetime. I'm relaxed now, just riding along—David tells me I've now started tripping—and "watching" my mind wake up and sense more than it ever has before. This strange ride is happening just like David told me it would.

I comprehend what he means when I see the traffic light suspended over the intersection of Main and Upham Streets. The green has switched to yellow and it takes what feels like a million lifetimes for the yellow to switch to red. I *know* I could have safely crossed the street during the yellow light, gone back and forth a hundred times without hurrying, and been perfectly safe.

Or if I was caught in the crossfire of a downtown gunfight, I'm sure I could see any stray bullets coming my way and dodge them without effort like that sun-glassed dude in *The Matrix* movie that came out 30 years later.

Of course, these types of experiences contribute in large part to why psychedelics are illegal. When used outside of a controlled session being guided by someone who is *not* tripping, LSD users might decide to try something that violates the laws of classical physics and have to pay the price. Our high school Health Class teachers are enamored of telling and re-telling the story of the boy who—while tripping—told his friends he could fly and jumped off a rooftop only to splatter his brains on the ground below. I'm fortunate to have David along as my guide. He's experienced enough with LSD to handle his own trip, but also keep an eye out for me.

The effects of the psychedelic maximize over the next few hours and the fabric of space and time begins to warp, literally. Walls of the buildings around me start to melt. I'm entranced by the atoms that define solid matter vibrating and oscillating visibly before me. My ability to delineate between material objects is blurring. The molecules that comprise people, cars, and the shops on Main Street all blend together. My senses get cross-wired. My eyes can view sounds, sounds are heard in color, and colors each have their own unique texture.

This show is amazing and hilarious! David and I laugh incessantly at the ever-new stream of kaleidoscopic images flowing before us. For me, it's as if the nature of reality is being revealed in its true form for the first time. And this glimpse of visual creation, beyond the rainbow light spectrum my normal consciousness is constrained to, begins to feel somehow like ... *God*.

The Van Gogh-like nighttime landscape becomes a new reality for me. What existed before now is recognized by my soul as just an illusion. I will learn about "life as illusion" in a few years when I study Buddhist texts in college. But for now my soul simply rejoices at getting to directly experience this normally hidden view of what lies behind the doors of perception.

Difficult to explain after the fact and in simple words, but for the duration of the night there are two versions of me. *Straight Steve* is the high-school student out with dissident friends, lounging on a ratty basement sofa at someone's party we've managed to find. Laughing continuously at whatever anyone says. Earning teenage "status" in high school for months to come when the other party-goers figure out David and I are tripping—but not dying—and not going insane like we were warned would happen by overly-zealous authority figures.

Psychedelic Steve is a soul watching the show from outside my physical body. For most of the night, the soul's perspective comes from the sky above me, urging me to *go outside* instead of trapping myself indoors at the party.

Some Southwest American Indian tribes use peyote and psilocybin legally as part of their religious rituals that are always performed outdoors. When tripping, it seems to me you need to go outside literally to facilitate going out of your body spiritually. And when I do, I understand why I was getting the message. Because outside, I can look up and *touch* an infinite number of stars, galaxies, and universes. I *love* them and for the first time I realize the unity of all things that I am an integral and equal part of. No duality exists, and like a Zen Buddhist hit on the head by his Master to facilitate enlightenment, or a new-born baby whacked on the bum to start crying and get his lungs working, *Psychedelic Steve* has been whacked by God and "awakened" to a higher—though short-lived—state of consciousness.

The Dragon Timothy Leary precipitated all of this soul arousal within me a few years earlier. My awakening foreshadowed by that television debate that hooked to something in my own soul that was yearning to open up spiritually. This LSD trip is the catalyst that has started to unfold the previously closed flower of my soul and reveal its eternal and true nature to me.

Curious friends will ask me later what my trip was like and I can only offer a half-assed metaphorical explanation borrowed from someone else: *"tripping is like watching color television for the first time."* If all you've ever seen is black and white TV, you can watch the shows and understand the plot, but the stories are enhanced and more expansive when viewed in color. Just like *The Wizard of Oz* movie starting in black and white and then changing to Technicolor when Dorothy enters Oz and says to Toto: "Now I know we're not in Kansas."

Over the course of the evening, the effects of the acid inevitably start to wear off. David wants to abandon me around midnight after finding an older girl with a car. She's pretty and wants to go and make out with him. I tell him I can't go home and don't know what to do. He leads me to the kitchen and tells me to call my parents to say I'm staying at his house. My grandmother is the one who answers the phone as my parents are out at a Friday night dance at the local Elks Club with my Dad's golfing buddies and their wives. She tells me she'll leave a note for Mom and Dad. If she suspects something is amiss, she doesn't say anything to me. I sense David will stay with me if I ask him despite wanting to experience for himself the charms of the girl he's hooked up with, but I tell him I'm fine. He leaves quickly before I change my mind.

Normal Steve decides a long walk back up Main Street towards home is the best course of action. I haven't formed any kind of definite plan about what to do as I get near my house. All I know is *Psychedelic Steve* wants to stay out under the stars. The effects of the acid are fading after five or six hours. But the trip is not quite over. There turns out to be one more hurdle, a "crossing of the Rubicon" of sorts before I can begin my return journey back to the "straight" world.

The *Attack of the Giant Green Frogs* takes place as I'm walking past Ell Pond. Subconsciously facilitated by my hyper-attuned hearing, I'm aware of the maleficent croaking of an army of green amphibians squatting on the banks of the water. After passing the pond, I "sense" something ominous behind me. I turn and, sure enough, there are a dozen or so slimy, gargantuan pond frogs jumping out of the moonlit lake up onto Main Street. Ferociously sinister. Each monster as large as an elephant. Evil eyes filled with hate. Hopping closer and closer to me. Their croaking hostile and grim, portending my imminent destruction. *Where did they come from? Why didn't anyone know these monsters were living in Ell Pond? Are they going to kill me? Why do they hate me?* Panic sets in and I quicken my pace. At around 2 a.m., there's no traffic on Main Street, so I cleverly determine that running along the white line in the middle of the road is the safest course of action. *Don't look back! They're getting closer! Keep to the middle of the road! Maybe the cops will come by, see the frogs chasing me, and shoot them all dead!* I stumble. Fall to the street. Rip my jeans on my left knee. Observe the blood from the wound but don't feel any pain. Roll over and prepare to face my pursuers. I'm ready to accept next week's Melrose Free Press newspaper headline announcing my unlucky fate to friends and family:

> *"Stephen Colwell: Eaten to death by evil frogs at the age of 16 in the middle of Main Street only blocks from the safety of his house."*

I turn to face my imminent demise. But, miraculously, the frogs are gone. Nowhere to be seen. And *Straight Steve* soon realizes *Psychedelic Steve* has had his first hallucination. My first encounter with paranoid delusions, as the drug counselors would describe it. And I'm lying in the middle of Main Street at 2 a.m. with a bloody knee and laughing out loud at my predicament for a good long while. I then realize I'm in a *real* predicament if a car comes by and doesn't see me in time to swerve and that this undesirable situation is most definitely *not* a hallucination. Picking myself up, I still have to make my way up Main Street towards my house. I end up spending the rest of the night lying on soft moss under a tree in a wooded area two blocks away. The comedown from the acid is gentle, and I float in bliss, surrendering to the magic of the Middle Earth-like forest around me, a safe environment for the remainder of my LSD experience. When it's light enough, I sneak in through my kitchen door around 7 a.m. No one is up and I creep silently to my bedroom before anyone realizes I'm home.

When I wake up about 2 p.m., I'm feeling pretty much back to normal physically. But spiritually, I've undergone a major transformation. My way of thinking about God's universe is forever changed. The glimpse of forever I experienced showed me a place I want to return to, and this *Return to Forever* becomes my heart's desire.

To paraphrase Ram Dass: *The problem with psychedelics is that the high doesn't last.* No matter how much LSD or other psychedelic drugs you take, the effects are temporary. They just fade away and you can't stay in that elevated state of consciousness permanently. The difficulty Ram Dass and many other acid trippers of the day found with psychedelics was that although they liked the aspects of expanded consciousness and God-realization they felt during their highs, what they really wanted was to stay in that "enlightened" space all the time *without* using drugs. What they wanted was to cross over once and for all into an eternally higher realm of existence. And there didn't seem to be any way to do that with psychedelics. Swallowing greater and greater dosages of LSD or eating lots more psilocybin mushrooms couldn't *permanently* change their consciousness.

Ram Dass's own Xiu Lian journey eventually led him to India where he found his guru and began following a path towards spiritual enlightenment via meditation under the direction of his loving Master. Tim Leary's path was not a journey to the East and he gradually faded from the culturally significant role he played in society in the 1960s and '70s. LSD usage also declined amongst the younger generation. Smoking pot and hashish seemed to be safer and certainly less risky psychologically amongst kids looking for a milder high and not a face-to-face conversation with Jesus. Those seeking the spiritual path like Ram Dass found a more natural approach to physically and emotionally balanced living by eating whole foods, practicing yoga, and attending meditation retreats with a host of Eastern Masters and teachers who found Western culture overdue to receive the primeval teachings.

I would dabble in LSD usage for a few more years, acting as an occasional guide, "turning on" friends and lovers interested in trying out psychedelics. But, like Ram Dass and so many other seekers of my generation found out, psychedelics were not the tools that could facilitate a permanent *Return to Forever.* My spiritual path would soon point me to India and Tibet. Ancient Eastern teachings and practices began to whisper to my soul to come and find them.

Self–Heal Using Master Sha's Four-Power Techniques

We face all kinds of sicknesses and challenges in life because of the mistakes we've made in our past that created negative karma. Master Sha teaches that everyone and everything has a soul and that if we heal the soul first, then healing of the mind and body will follow. By focusing on the soul and the underlying karmic root cause of our illnesses, we can self-clear our negative karma and heal physical, mental, emotional, relationship, and financial challenges.

Master Sha's *Four-Power Techniques* are tools that are, generally speaking, used in combination with each other to heal, prevent sickness, rejuvenate, prolong life, and transform every aspect of life, including relationships and finances. The *Four-Power Techniques* are so simple!

1. **Body Power:**

   Special hand and body positions. Place your hands on the area of the body in need of healing.

   "Where you place your hands is where you receive healing and rejuvenation."

2. **Soul Power:**

   "Say Hello" to "inner" and "outer" souls. Connect with the souls of the area needing healing (inner souls). Then invoke outer souls such as the Divine, your spiritual fathers and mothers, and other spiritual beings to assist.

   "Apply 'Say Hello' Healing and Blessing to invoke the Divine, Tao, Heaven, Mother Earth, and countless planets, stars, galaxies, and universes, as well as all kinds of spiritual mothers and fathers on Mother Earth and in all layers of Heaven, to request their help for your healing, rejuvenation, and transformation of relationships and finances."

3. **Mind Power:**

   Use creative visualization to receive healing and rejuvenation.

"Where you put your mind, using creative visualization, is where you receive the benefits for healing, rejuvenation, and transformation of relationships and finances."

4. **Sound Power:**

Use of sacred sounds and mantras to receive healing and rejuvenation.

"What you chant is what you become."

Here's an example of using the Four-Power Techniques to heal a physical condition of the body—"knee pain":

1. **Body Power:**
   - Sit up straight, feet on the floor, spine straight.
   - Put the tip of your tongue to the roof of your mouth (without touching).
   - Put one hand on your knee and on hand on your lower abdomen.
   - Relax and close your eyes.

2. **Soul Power:**
   "Dear soul, mind, and body of my knee,
   I love you, honor you, and appreciate you.
   You have the power to heal yourself.
   Do a good job!
   Thank you. Thank you. Thank you.
   Dear soul, mind, and body of Jesus, Mother Mary, and the Medicine Buddha,
   I love you, honor you, and appreciate you.
   Could you please give me a healing for my knee as appropriate?
   I am honored to receive this healing."

3. **Mind Power:**
   - Visualize golden healing light flowing to your knee from 360-degrees all around you.

4. **Sound Power:**
   - Chant "Light" repeatedly for 5–10 minutes at a time, 3–5 times a day. You can chant aloud or silently.

After the practice, say:

> *"Hao. Hao. Hao.*
> *Thank you. Thank you. Thank you."*

Hao means "perfect, get well." in Mandarin Chinese.

Students of Master Sha use the Four-Power Techniques in virtually all soul healing practices. This method of self-healing is so simple. Give it a try for any health challenges you are facing and you may receive amazing results! The guidance for chronic or life-threatening conditions is to practice for two hours or more per day. You can practice for a 10–15 minutes at a time throughout the day and add up all your practice time to equal two hours.

Migraines to Maharishi

"You must learn to take life less seriously and to laugh."
—Maharishi Mahesh Yogi

Maharishi Mahesh Yogi (1918–2008)
Founder of Transcendental Meditation Movement

The pain of the migraine is unbearable. Sears my brain on both the left and right sides of my skull. Pressure points like hot coals burn the flesh of my forehead from the inside. Gorged blood vessels squeeze my optic nerves like a python constricting its prey. Hundreds of explosions of white light dazzle my field of vision like miniature strobe lights. My balance lost to waves of dizziness. Sounds become torture. Sweating becomes profuse. Fear builds on itself. Once started, there is no way to shut down a migraine headache. A climax of ceaseless vomiting reached until there is nothing left to spit up. Crying aloud because of the agony. *Kill me to make this pain go away!*

My first migraine attacks me in Mr. Haggerty's mathematics class. It's mid-afternoon and all of a sudden I can't focus on the blackboard due to the onset of light flashes. Opening and closing my eyes, I wait in vain for my vision to adjust, but things just get worse. Then, Mr. Haggerty's raspy voice becomes distant, as if he is speaking to the class from a hilltop far away. I manage to raise my hand and ask to be excused to go to the washroom. Permission reluctantly granted, I rush to the toilet and throw up lunch. After vomiting, my blurred vision clears but is immediately replaced by a new symptom, a pulsing, throbbing headache. I'm not thinking straight. I should ask to see the school nurse and go home, but instead I return to my seat and rest my head on the desk with my eyes closed. Nancy, the girl sitting next to me, whispers in sympathy. Asks if I'm ok. "No … headache" is all I can muster.

A few hours later, I'm home in my room. Shades pulled down. Door closed. A wet facecloth lying across my forehead. No light, no sound. I learn over the next few years that the only recourse to resolving a migraine that's already begun is to find a dark, quiet room and try to sleep until the agony passes.

No one in my family, least of all me, understands what I'm suffering from. When I'm in school, the attacks come more frequently, and I know I can expect to get hit at least once a week. My Mom finally figures out something's not right when I get sent home from class for the second time in a week. She schedules a visit to the doctor down the street. All he does is tell me to try to relax. His counsel is that if everything is all right at home, then the headaches are most likely caused by stress about school. I take some consolation in his assessment. At least he's not sending me to the hospital for tests because he thinks I've got a growing brain tumor or something.

I begin to recognize patterns to the problem. The headaches usually arrive 24–48 hours before some significant event is about to occur. Sometimes it's a test at school I'm worried I haven't studied enough for. Other times, the pain is brought on in anticipation of an upcoming holiday or school vacation. Once I start dating girls in my junior year … well, suffice to say, girls can be the cause of lots of migraines.

I am pretty much resigned to these headaches as a permanent part of my life. None of my friends suffer from this curse so there isn't any opportunity for empathy from any of them. In the springtime of my senior year, a few months before graduation, the migraines peak in frequency. I get attacked for stretches of three or four days in a row and often have to call in sick to school as well as my after-class kitchen staff job at the local hospital so I can suffer in silence in my darkened bedroom. I'm sure my anxiety and excitement about graduating from Melrose High and attending the University of Massachusetts in the fall are significant contributing factors to my accelerating number of migraines. But at 18 years old, I don't think negatively about much of anything and I certainly don't analyze possible psychological causes for my problems. I've also never heard of karma, so the fact that my past actions in this life or a prior life might be contributing causes to my frequent attacks are beyond my ken.

When I'm not suffering, life is good. I've got a steady girlfriend with whom I've been intimate for two years. I'm going away to live in a co-ed dorm and study what I want, not what I have to. I own a 1967 Chevrolet Impala that I can fill with gas for under $10, and

I have the best summer job ever working for the City of Melrose Parks Department. I go to work in cut-off jeans and sneakers. No shirt is required so I get tanned while mowing grass 8 hours a day. As far as I can remember, the migraines pretty much cease in the summer of 1971 and don't resume in intensity until my first semester at college.

At the University of Massachusetts, I'm overwhelmed at the *freedom* I experience my freshman year away from home. I'm living in a coed dorm with a bunch of female students who float around at night wearing casual but enticing bedtime attire, lounge in hallways smoking joints and telling stories, and share the bathrooms and showers with the boys without shame. We behave more like a large group of brothers and sisters than a mix of hormone-driven potential sex partners—although there is plenty of that type of activity happening as well. If I want to skip a lecture, there are no repercussions. I can always borrow the notes from someone else in the class and return the favor at a later date. I join the dorm's volleyball and softball teams, find a female partner for the mixed doubles badminton league, and generally fit into the dorm's culture as a normal college freshman.

The migraines return in force around the time of mid-term examinations. I know the tests are coming up in mid-October and although I'm outwardly confident of success in all my classes, subconsciously I must be stressing out. My roommate Lou, a junior, is seldom around. He's scheduled all his classes for Tuesdays, Wednesdays, and Thursdays and drives home to Connecticut every Thursday night to stay with his girlfriend until Monday. That leaves the dorm room my own private haven each weekend in which to entertain the occasional female guest I like who lives on the floor below me. It's also a room that becomes my sanctuary. A place to retreat from the music, sights, sounds, and smells of academic life when the migraines hit me.

After a particularly vicious migraine attack, I spend nearly two days in bed before deciding it's time for a visit to the campus medical center. Something is clearly wrong with me. I need some sort of help. When in the throes of a serious migraine, I'm thinking drastic thoughts including the idea of ending it all. I let myself grow slightly paranoid about my condition, envisioning a diagnosis that I'm surely the unlucky victim of a nameless, incurable disease the doctors have never seen and won't be able to treat.

The nurse on staff ushers me in to see the doctor at the walk-in care center in the middle of campus after a wait of only about ten minutes. He clinically asks about when my headaches started, how long they typically last, and confirms for me that I suffer from migraines just like a lot of students. He assures me the headaches will eventually go away and apologizes that, for now, there is no medical treatment to prevent migraines. He prescribes Seconal to help me sleep once the headaches start.

Seconal is a barbiturate or "downer" as it's known on the street. Seconal is a sedative that relaxes your body and induces sleep. Seconal is addictive if used to excess by persons who become dependent on taking the drug each and every day to avoid and relieve stress. The first few times I take Seconal, I experience something like a drunken state of euphoria. I stagger around for a bit before crashing dreamlessly into sleep for endless hours. Seconal works dangerously well at relieving the pain of a migraine headache. I have an open prescription for the narcotic at the campus pharmacy, and load up on an overly ample supply of "Mother's Little Helpers". I keep a bottle in my knapsack when I go to class, ready to pop a pill at the first pinprick spark of light signaling the onset of a new migraine. Friends soon find out about my stash and ask if they can buy some from me since I have a seemingly endless and renewable supply of "reds."

So I have a temporary fix for my headaches that works, and I can sell extra pills for $5 a pop to my dorm coeds who want the drug intoxication without drinking tons of alcohol. So what's wrong with this picture?

Well, just about everything.

The fact that I'm selling spare pills to my friends so they can get high means I'm putting myself at risk for criminal prosecution and getting thrown out of UMass if I get caught. The fact that the pills work to put me to sleep once the migraine has started is nice, but doesn't address the underlying issue of why I get the headaches in the first place. I can feel myself slowly edging nearer to the cliff of dependency—I won't say addiction—and I know from firsthand experience that's not good.

Auntie Sis got hooked on painkillers after she suffered complications having her second child. She was forced to stay in the hospital for a few months and was fed sedatives every day. Back then in the late 1950s, the addictive dangers of daily painkillers either weren't understood or weren't paid much attention by the medical community. It literally took her years to get herself straightened out at great personal and emotional cost to her family and mine. So I'm a bit wary about going down that road and pay attention to my usage so that taking the painkillers doesn't become a habit.

Help comes unexpectedly from my friends Katy and Fred when they tell me they are going to a lecture to learn about Transcendental Meditation (TM) and suggest I join them. I don't know much about meditation but I do know it's an Eastern practice that Ram Dass talks about extensively in his seminal book: *Be Here Now*. Katy had let me borrow her first edition copy and I read the whole thing in one pass sitting on a bench beside the campus pond. I was unable to put the book down and decided to skip my afternoon classes so I could finish it. Katy and I discuss *Be Here Now* frequently, debating just what it is exactly that Ram Dass is trying to teach us. And although I find the front half of the book fascinating regarding Richard Alpert's history using LSD, the back half of the book is nearly incomprehensible to me. Ram Dass's pages are drawn in pictures and non-linear text describing mystical perspectives of reality similar to, but at the same time, well beyond where an acid trip will take you.

And now it's time to make a decision that will have far-reaching ramifications for my Xiu Lian Purification Journey: *Yes, I'll go to the lecture* or *No, I'm not ready for meditation.* I'm thinking: *Okay, I've done acid a number of times, but nowhere near as much as Tim Leary and Ram Dass. And Ram Dass seems to be saying that the ancient path of meditation is a "better" road to take. That meditation can take anyone beyond the boundaries of their minds/egos to realms of reality that our souls are all trying to get to anyway. But I don't understand anything about what meditation is or how it works.*

"Don't worry." Katy tells me, "We'll find all that out at the TM lecture."

"Okay, I'm in." I tell her. "I'm curious. I'll go."

Katy smiles. And looking back with the benefit of historical hindsight, I think my soul was so ready and so magnetically drawn to the idea of meditation, that the choice I made was inevitable.

The following Thursday evening, Katy, Fred, and I find ourselves seated in an overly crowded lecture hall. A few grad students wearing jackets and ties are here to explain Transcendental Meditation (TM) as taught by this long-haired Indian Master and Dragon, *Maharishi Mahesh Yogi.* Maharishi is getting popular now in the US, in large part because the Beatles went to India to meet him and learn TM. From a soul marketing perspective, the time is right for the Maharishi. Western souls, overly ripe for Eastern knowledge and practices, flood to TM lectures all over America.

It's the premise of meditation that appeals to me. As I learn at the lecture, all I have to do to meditate is sit, close my eyes, be quiet, and empty my mind of all thoughts as they arise. Okay, this is almost exactly what I do when trying to get rid of a migraine headache. So why not give it a try? There is also something called a *mantra* involved, a word or phrase that will be picked especially for me. My mantra is to be kept secret and not revealed casually to others. By repeating my mantra whenever pesky thoughts arise during meditation, I'll return immediately to the intended state of relaxation and maybe even bliss. The long-term beneficial effects of meditating include becoming relaxed and calm for extended periods of time. They tell me meditation will also be good for my emotional and physical health by lowering blood pressure, generating more energy, and facilitating a saner mental approach to dealing with life's problems.

At the lecture, Katy, Fred and I are sold on Maharishi's concepts. I'm thinking—and Katy's encouraging me—that maybe, just maybe, TM will help me with my migraines and I can stop taking Seconal. And that's all I'm looking to get out of Maharishi's practice. If there's any goal of meditation for me, it's to suffer fewer migraines. I'm not tying the appeal of TM to anything spiritual. In fact, there's little or no inference made at the introductory lecture that there is *anything* spiritual or religious about TM.

A week or so after attending the introductory lecture, Katy, Fred, and I receive our mantras and become full-fledged meditators and students of Maharishi Mahesh Yogi. I practice twice a day for twenty minutes per session, usually alone in my dorm room, but occasionally joining Katy to practice together. I not only find that I like to meditate but that some days, I *really* like to meditate. Once I become consistent and established with my daily routine, my soul gets *excited* as meditation time nears. Not only do I get to mentally disengage from the noises around me like the TVs, phones, and hallway conversations impossible to avoid in college dormitories, but I find that the state of meditation or "going inside" actually causes the world to disappear, as the Indian Guru *Osho* teaches. There is an emptiness that I occasionally get a glimpse of, and it is into this emptiness that all meditators and I are trying to go. Meditation is a non-drug induced way of *Returning to Forever*!

Most "beginner" meditation practitioners face the same challenges. We are novice travelers on the Xiu Lian Purification Journey. We become aware there is an "I," that is, an ego, that is reluctant to see us "go to emptiness" via meditation and we become roadblocked. The "I" or ego has to dissolve in order for us to become "empty vessels" as St. John of the Cross teaches. Many meditation practices address this problem by the use of mantras. Mantras are sacred words like "OM" or sacred phrases given to students by their teacher. When we realize our minds/egos are having thoughts of any type—it doesn't actually matter *what* we are thinking about—we are taught to repeat our mantra and let those distracting thoughts magically melt away.

In the early stages of meditation, when we are just beginning our journey, our minds don't get overly concerned about our dabbling on the spiritual path. The ego considers us to be like little kids at the beach sticking our toes gingerly into the ocean to see how cold it is, to see what it feels like, but certainly not ready to dive in. Our egos are quite sure we are just entertaining meditation as a passing fancy, and that we'll move towards pursuits and new hobbies soon enough. But when we continue to practice, the ego can't entirely ignore our efforts. And when meditation becomes a highly anticipated regular and routine part of our daily lives, the ego stirs and decides to take action against us. Why?

Osho, the Indian mystic, Guru, and spiritual Dragon who lived from 1931–1990 warns students that the ego becomes aware of its impending death as we progress in our practice and get nearer and nearer to enlightenment. And if we meditate long enough and devoutly enough, we *will* reach enlightenment, even if it takes us thousands of lifetimes. Our ego doesn't want to die and so it vigorously defends its turf and fights back against the soul and the direction the soul is leading us: *You don't have to meditate now, have another cup of coffee first. You really should respond to that email from your sister before you begin practice, it's important to get back to her. Go put a load of laundry in the washer before you start, that way it will be done when you finish meditating. If you go to the grocery store now, there won't be much traffic, so you'll save time and have even more time to meditate later.* Later. Later. Later. Your mind will always find seemingly rational reasons why we should wait until *later* to meditate.

When we encounter ego-driven resistance to meditation practice, our souls just smile back at us in love. Secure in the knowledge that all we have to do is find a way to make it physically to the place we sit, quietly begin our practice, and within minutes we will be transported to emptiness and move beyond time and space. And when we get there, we laugh at ourselves for the hollow excuses we entertained for putting off, for delaying, meditation. What were we thinking?

The full benefits of meditation are not received immediately. Meditation is not a "fast food" shortcut to enlightenment. It can take most of us years before we see significant transforming changes in our lives, our relationships, our health, and our finances. It's my own experience, and that of many other students like me, that the positive changes do come— eventually. But many new meditators can receive near-term benefits and I am one of them.

When I start TM as a teenager, I'm a stressed-out, barbiturate-abusing, bit of a mess. Not a total wreck, but someone who's facing daily struggles without a roadmap to freedom. And for me, TM calms me down. My migraine headaches begin to diminish in both frequency and intensity. After a few months, I flush the Seconals down the toilet and tell my disappointed dorm roomies I can't get the pills anymore.

I decide to take a Logic class offered by the UMass philosophy department and find I can actually handle the mathematical concepts that would have totally intimidated me before TM. Learning the structure of Formal Logic will serve me well in the future when my post-collegiate studies in Computer Science at Wentworth Institute of Technology in Boston land me a lengthy and lucrative career in Information Technology. Logic class also introduces me to the Taoist concept of yin and yang—1's and 0's in computer lingo.

My TM practice at the University of Massachusetts helps me get through many challenges and struggles. I relax and learn to laugh again. Meditation becomes the impetus to sign up for Eastern philosophy classes and take yoga. My Xiu Lian Purification Journey is well underway now and I just have to remain consistent in my practice, display infinite patience, and let the process unfold for as many days, weeks, months, years and lifetimes as are karmically necessary. For me, that first step is meditating on a regular basis.

Of course the Xiu Lian path is not always straight. We often encounter setbacks and make irrational decisions on impulse when aspects of our life don't go exactly the way we think they should. Like the saying goes "Life is what happens while you're making other plans."

The Girl With Infinity Eyes

Adilah and I are taking a Kundalini Yoga class together at the University of Massachusetts during the spring of my freshman year in 1972. Kundalini yoga has recently been brought to the West by the spiritual Dragon Yogi Bhajan, a Sikh who immigrated to Canada from Punjab, India in the early 1970's. Kundalini Yoga is becoming extremely popular amongst the hippie culture in North America.

Adilah's long brown hair flows like a waterfall running straight down her back. The coed is attractively skinny in a time when Twiggy, the world famous androgynous model from the UK, rules the runways. And like the iconic fashion model, Adilah sports not an ounce of fat on her lithe frame. Adilah is Malaysian—her name means "honesty"—and she's shy. I don't believe she knows anyone in our class held on Monday, Wednesday, and Friday mornings at 8 a.m. I'm entranced by her beauty on the first day I see her, and look for ways to maneuver myself beside or behind her in each session, hoping we might connect. If she does notice my stealth schoolboy pursuit of physical proximity, she never says a word. I finally work up the courage to introduce myself and she seems okay with me, granting me silent permission to sit beside her from that point forward, but that is the extent of our relationship.

We practice the *Breath of Fire*, a supremely powerful foundational energy exercise in which the abdomen is moved in and out while breathing rapidly and intensely through the nostrils under the guidance of an experienced teacher. Breath of Fire releases toxins and poisons from our bodies while at the same time strengthening our *Qi*, the spiritual energy that maintains life and health written about a few thousand years ago by the Yellow Emperor (the legendary first ancestor of the Chinese nation.) The philosophers of ancient times regarded the source of the cosmos as "essential qi," and that everything in the world was produced by essential qi.[2] If

---

2 The Medical Classic of the Yellow Emperor, Beijing China: Foreign Languages Press, 2001.

practiced for lengthy periods of time in correct posture and form, Breath of Fire raises Kundalini energy like a serpent uncoiling up through the seven chakras or soul houses of the body.

Beware!

This energy movement can happen spontaneously and explosively, which is why you *must* practice Breath of Fire with a qualified teacher. Of all the yoga or foundational energy practices I've ever done, Breath of Fire Kundalini is by far the most intense.

Do not try this at home alone!

Today, the instructor asks us to perform a new practice created by Yogi Bhajan after our Breath of Fire practice. We will attempt to connect deeply with the soul of another student. He motions for us to pair up, sit cross-legged facing each other, and prepare to stare into each other's eyes without blinking for as long as we can. The practice will last a minimum of five minutes.

Adilah and I glance meekly at each other. Exchange weak smiles. Neither of us sure we want to attempt the practice together, but also quite sure we don't want to try this with anyone else. We are warned that anything can happen during the practice, and that some people may have a negative experience if they are not ready for what they "see". *Okay, so I really want to do this practice with Adilah, but I really don't want to freak out on her or have her freak out on me.*

We inch our bodies closer to each other. The heat from the earlier Breath of Fire practice lingers, coloring our cheeks rosy red. Both nervous, we avoid eye contact until the gong is rung signaling the beginning of what will become a secret journey into each other's inner world.

Adilah's brown eyes, perfect circles the same color as her hair, lock onto mine. Our breaths synchronize. Heavy and a little too fast at first. Laden with trepidation and anxiety. Adilah looks afraid. As if I'm the first person she's ever invited to enter this deep space inside of her. Her fear shows. I'm sure I look the same way to her, trying hard not to speculate on what Adilah might be seeing inside of me. As far as I recall, we did blink a few times in violation of our instructions, assuaging our mutual fears by mercifully gaining a few microseconds of privacy before resuming the practice.

Our breathing slows after a few minutes, and the nervous tension in our bellies slowly subsides. And it's at this point that an amazing experience occurs for me. Adilah's eyes alter in their depth, morphing into brown tunnels infinite in length. I follow her energy down the vortex behind her pupils like Alice falling down the rabbit hole towards Wonderland. It's like I'm riding a rollercoaster into another dimension of space and time. I receive no images. No Third Eye visions. But what I do sense is an incredibly expansive void of "nothingness". Adilah has become a portal, her eyes a gateway to a universe beyond both of us. It's my first non-drug induced experience of *No Time, No Space* and I am forever grateful to Adilah for sharing such an intimate moment with me.

We close this special practice by group singing the traditional Irish Sun Blessing:

"May the long time sun shine upon you,
All love surround you,
And the pure light within you
Guide your way on,
Guide your way on."

ROAD TRIP

"What is it you have learned? What are you able to do?"
"I can think. I can wait. I can fast."
　　　　　　　—Hermann Hesse, *Siddhartha*

Castalia Seminar Poster from Harvard Square, 1972

"**D**ad, I'm quitting college." I try to sneak the words past my father, who's driving us to Mt. Hood Golf Course on a Saturday morning in May, 1972. I've come home for the weekend to study before spring semester final exams begin. I'll have soon completed my freshman year at the University of Massachusetts in Amherst, a year of satisfying basic requirements for my major in Psychology with a minor in Philosophy. Two subjects my Dad, who's paying for my education, is less than thrilled about. He's quite sure that my post-graduate employment prospects would be better served by obtaining a Bachelor's Degree in Accounting or another business skill set that could lead to gainful employment in a promising corporate career when I graduate.

I've become an avid meditator in the TM tradition of Maharishi Mahesh Yogi. But that spiritual practice hasn't constrained a typical male college social life of unbridled partying three or four nights a week, coed dorm living with a trove of female lovelies, unchecked recreational drug use, and a serious relationship with a girl that generates so much passion, ecstasy, and ultimately misery in me that when I learn she's coming back for the fall semester of sophomore year, I decide I am not.

My Dad reacts calmly. Keeps his eyes on the road ahead. "Why do you want to *quit*?"

"I don't like it... I just want to do something else." I reply, unable to tell him what's really going on.

"Like what? Get a job?"

"No... I want to go to Switzerland... to a seminar about the author Hermann Hesse and the psychologist Carl Jung they're having this summer. It's being run by a bunch of professors from Harvard and MIT. It costs $1375 but I'm thinking that's less than tuition will be next fall so I'm wondering if I can borrow the money and pay you back later... I'll get a job when I come home."

This is the best I can do in terms of constructing a formal request for Dad's cash. I'm trying to make it sound like I want to go to the Alps for educational purposes, not to get away from a painful relationship by traipsing around Europe for the summer on my father's nickel.

Dad doesn't put up too much of an argument. I'm kind of surprised. Maybe he's impressed by the pedigree of the Ivy League professors that will be teaching the classes. And he does lend me the money, which I use to enroll in "Castalia," the name of the summer retreat to be held at The American School in Montagnola, Switzerland.

Castalia, a fictional city described in Hermann Hesse's novel *The Glass Bead Game,* is a glorified university setting. Funded by working taxpayers, it's a private community where the intellectually elite members of society go to study liberal arts, engage in debates on various existential topics regarding the human condition, and otherwise ponder their navels. Hesse won the Nobel Prize for Literature three years after publication of *The Glass Bead Game* in 1943 and became a kind of literary cult hero in the 1960s and '70s largely because of his more readable works such as *Siddhartha, Steppenwolf,* and *The Journey to the East.* It's too bad most of his fame and literary influence—and certainly most of his financial success from book sales—all happened after his death, to the benefit of his heirs.

I'm a big fan of Hesse's books, and *Siddhartha* is still one of my favorite novels of all time. In 1972, I'm only 19 and have never been out of the country, so when Dad says *"Yes"* I can go and *"Yes"* he'll foot the bill, I get pretty excited at having manifested a summer overseas and an escape from a maddening teenage love.

The Castalia seminar is set in Montagnola where Hesse did much of his writing, undoubtedly inspired by the panoramic views of the southern Alps overlooking Lake Lugano on the Swiss-Italian border, a few hundred kilometers north of Florence. Our residence is the Villa De Nobili, a 17th-century mansion situated on a plateau high above the city overlooking the expansive lake below.

Just the kind of Castalian atmosphere where *Huston Smith,* the head of MIT's philosophy department and my assigned mentor, will feel right at home alongside his Ivy-league professorial comrades also looking to enjoy a relaxing summer hiatus and engage in lively philosophical dialogue in the rarified atmosphere of the Swiss/Italian Alps.

I find Huston Smith to be an animated, amiable, friendly teacher who takes a personal interest in each of his students. It's relatively easy for me to recognize when someone I'm dealing with is far more intelligent than I, like Professor Smith. I listen respectfully when he speaks and try to gain some of the knowledge and perspective he imparts to sink into my own less developed intellect. Huston Smith has that rare ability to sense the level of receptiveness and capacity to understand in those he's addressing, be it a casual conversation or a more formal teaching setting. He's a professor able to adapt his delivery to his target audience. The "deer in the headlights" syndrome seldom, if ever, manifests in his students at Castalia when this MIT Department Head teaches.

Professor Smith shuns our assigned classroom and holds most of his daily sessions outdoors around a fountain in the courtyard of Villa De Nobili. The classes are relaxed, informal, and stimulating. We students, maybe 25 or so in Smith's group, are a mix of a few teenagers like myself, a lot of university graduate students, maybe a dozen teachers in their 30s and 40s, a couple of aspiring writers, and a handful of well-to-do intellectual hippies, one of whom I manage to offend from the very beginning of the summer session by displaying a lack of adoration for his persona.

The gentleman shall remain nameless, his true identity hidden. Let's just call him "Anton" for now. Anton is a rather scruffy character. Sports an unkempt beard made up of squirrely gray and black hairs. Hard to tell his age. Maybe late forties, maybe older. Glares at me with Charles Manson-style "crazy eyes." Wears clothes a homeless person would find barely suitable. And smells funny, not from a lack of personal hygiene, but as if his body cells create and exude their own unpleasant odor like a wet cat curled up on a living room couch.

In 1969, three years prior to the Castalia seminar, The Rolling Stones released their *Beggars Banquet* album. The first track on side one of the vinyl is *Sympathy For The Devil*. One verse of Mick Jagger's lyrics refers to Grigori Rasputin, the Russian mystic healer who served the last czar, Nicholas II. Czar Nicholas and the entire royal family were killed after the Czar was forced to abdicate his throne during the Communist Revolution in 1918. Rasputin's true colors are still debated amongst Russians and the mystical healing community, but he's characterized in the Rolling Stones song as a manipulative charlatan responsible for much evil manifested via his powerful connection to Nicholas's wife Alexandra, their daughter Anastasia, and their son Alexei.

Well, since Anton is a fellow student at the Castalia seminar, I find I can't avoid being around him. And I find that he somehow reminds me of Rasputin! My soul warns me Anton's a character to be shunned at all costs, a villain that will suck my soul dry if I give him the slightest opening. I have little or no experience dealing with these types of characters at this point in my life—I'm only 19—so there's some legitimate level of vulnerability to my getting manipulated.

My friend Daniel, another student at Castalia, invites me to meet with Anton and a group of students after dinner one night. I agree to go along, having nothing else to do, and not especially concerned about being around Anton in a group setting. We sit in a circle around a fire pit piled high with wood and spewing out an unnatural amount of heat for a summer evening. Anton is speaking—holding court as it were—to a rapt group of fellow students. Daniel and I are waved into the circle and squeeze in amongst the others.

Tonight's topic is "Using Sex as a Means to Achieve Enlightenment." I'm a little taken aback when Anton asks us all to have sex with each other later that evening to validate his teaching points. If I'm hearing him right, he's scheduling an orgy and looking to gather willing participants from those of us seated around the fire circle. Two female graduate students squirm around a bit. Giggle nervously. Agree to go with Anton and three other male students. I find my teenage mind wrestling with the idea of stimulating group sex with these older girls I don't even know, but something holds me back. This whole scene just doesn't feel right, and I'm pretty sure Anton is the source of my reticence. I wrestle with this predicament/opportunity before me. Because when teenage sexual hormones rage—like mine at that moment—the male ego usually sends caution to the wind. An invitation to have sex in Switzerland lies enticingly before me, but it doesn't feel "healthy." Anton stares at me in manner that suggests he knows exactly what my dilemma is.

Flames of the fire blaze high against the nighttime backdrop of the Swiss Alps. I stand up and back away from the searing heat. Anton bores into me with those crazy eyes. It feels like he's trying to hypnotize me, and my soul senses he's trying to steal something from some part of my core being. Anton feels wrong, negative, and *evil,* all at the same time. His gaze stays fixed on me and he won't let go, making me feel a bit like a fish that's been hooked and is being reeled close to the boat where it will be snagged by a net, pulled out of the ocean, and die gasping for water on the floor of a fishing trawler.

Anton asks me a question. I don't respond. His lips are moving but I can't hear his words. It's as if a guardian angel has suddenly dropped an impenetrable bubble of protection around me that's saving me from falling under the spell of Anton's mesmerizing voice.

I laugh. Anton frowns. He can't touch me. Can't get through my defenses to reach my soul, my inner being. I don't understand whose spiritual armor protected me while I balanced on the knife-edge of Anton's unclean devilish magnetism, but I do know I'm now safe from him. I'm not joining his clique of worshippers so eager to follow his every command even if it means I can get laid by cute Castalian grad students.

I hover on the outskirts of the fire circle for a bit longer before returning to my bunk in the men's dorm. Daniel returns late in the evening after participating in Anton's sex orgy. I feign being asleep so we don't have to talk. A barrier forms between Daniel and me over the next few days, not totally disrupting our friendship, but making conversation awkward. And soon after, Daniel confronts me about the night at the fire pit.

"Steve ... you've upset Anton."

"What do you mean ... upset Anton?"

"He doesn't understand why you don't come back to his meetings ... why you don't want to become part of his ... sessions. Everyone in Castalia wants to join his group, but he only invites certain *chosen* ones."

"He's a weirdo, Daniel! There's something ... creepy about him. Don't you feel that?"

"No ... no, I don't. I think he's got some interesting ideas about people's sexual hang-ups that could help them if they work with him ..."

"Work with him by doing what? Fucking everyone and telling them it's sex therapy or something?"

Daniel starts to respond, but pauses, thinking how to change the direction of the discussion. "Why don't come you back to the fire circle just for tonight ... give him another chance."

"Another chance for what? To get me to join the orgies you guys have with each other every night?"

"He just wants you to keep an open mind ..."

I interrupt Daniel. "Just what did he say about me, exactly?"

"He said you've confused him. You're the only one he's invited who's rejected coming to the fire circle. He doesn't know why and he just wants you to give it another try."

I don't offer a reply and Daniel stares at me forlornly, like a puppy dog that knows he's misbehaved. After the discussion with Daniel, I feel like I've won some type of victory over Anton. That I've defeated a dark force attempting to gain unnatural control over my beliefs, my actions, and my soul. To this day, I feel I must have had what Master Sha calls my *Heaven's Team* watching over me back then. Silent protectors that wouldn't let Anton's dark energy infect me. Maybe I had some good karma working for me. Maybe I just displayed common sense. But from that time forward, I would start trusting my intuition more fully when dealing with people with questionable motives, or if I found myself in spiritually uncomfortable situations that didn't feel right.

We gain valuable experience when we have encounters with dark forces. And as we learn to trust our intuition more and more, we can avoid at least some of the myriad perils and pitfalls that lie in wait to test us on our Xiu Lian Purification Journey.

When you recognize you're the beneficiary of angelic assistance—of your Heaven's Team guarding you—don't forget to offer thanks to the light beings that protect you! They've offered you incredible service. Expressing your gratitude is a powerful indicator of your appreciation. I didn't appreciate or acknowledge the help I'd gotten from my own Heaven's Team at the Castalia seminar—I was too much of a novice on the Xiu Lian path back then—but I recognize it now and give thanks to all my spiritual fathers and mothers for protecting me during that critical moment of spiritual testing.

⚜   ⚜   ⚜

Towards the end of July at Castalia, a buzz of gossip circulates amongst the students. "Tim's coming. Tim's coming." Whispers in the dining hall and the dormitory hint at some clandestine happening, but I'm not in on the secret and have no idea that "Tim" is Timothy Leary, the ex-Harvard professor, advocate of LSD for consciousness expansion, whose debate with MIT's Jerome Lettvin I'd watched a few years earlier prior to my first LSD trip.

I've already told you about my initial experience with taking acid. Well, here was a chance to hang out with the high priest of

LSD himself! President Richard Nixon once described Timothy Leary as *"the most dangerous man in America,"* verbalizing the fear of mainstream capitalists and politicians that if the current generation adopted Leary's mantra of "Turn On, Tune In, Drop Out" en masse, it would signal the imminent and assured demise of the United States of America and all that it stands for.

Leary was imprisoned for drug possession, but in an ironic twist of fate, he managed to get himself assigned to a low-security prison after filling out a psychological profile that quantified him as a "normal" personality and, more importantly, a non-flight risk. What the State of California officials didn't realize was the test Leary took to determine his placement in the California penal system was one he had designed himself while at Harvard, so how surprising is it that he was able to fill out a profile that resulted in his getting assigned to a low-security penal site?

After his transfer to the minimum-security prison, Leary easily escaped and made his way to Algeria, which does not have an extradition treaty with the United States. In 1971, he slipped quietly into Switzerland. The following summer, when he learned so many of his university colleagues from Harvard were teaching at the Castalia seminar, Tim decided to pay a visit to his buddies.

Suffice to say there were many endless evenings that summer in Castalia in which a small band of intellectual hippies from Harvard Square, Cambridge lay out under the Alpine stars drifting along in short-lived chemically-induced journeys carrying them off to realms far and away. I was not a part of that group, although it would have been easy enough to join in the psychedelic fun and games. At that point in my life, I wasn't against using LSD per se, but was already moving down the path of meditation and yoga as a preferred way of *Returning to Forever*. It would certainly make for a more exciting story to say I dropped acid with Timothy Leary during my summer in the Swiss Alps. But psychedelics had lost their appeal for me by then and my encounters with the acid-taking group in Castalia occurred on the sidelines only.

When I returned from Castalia at the end of summer, I wrote a long essay about Hermann Hesse's novel *The Journey to the East*, first published in 1932. Hesse's story involves a group of spiritual seekers on a quest to discover "Ultimate Truth" by traveling to India in hopes of meeting high-level beings guarding the secrets of ancient spiritual traditions. I mailed my paper to Huston Smith at MIT and asked the philosophy professor to "grade" my work as a favor. To my pleasant surprise, Professor Smith found my essay—now long lost and forgotten—worthy of a B+. I subsequently submitted the paper to the Dean of Philosophy at UMass who—astonishingly to me—gave me 8 credits for attending "summer school at Castalia in Switzerland."

Encouraged by my B+ grade and thinking maybe I had a calling to pursue a major in Philosophy instead of Psychology, I promptly re-enrolled in UMass for the spring semester of my sophomore year. I was able to reconcile my relationship and become friends with the girl who'd driven me mad enough to leave school in the first place, and ended up having an affair with her roommate instead.

My TM practice and scholarly interest in Eastern spiritual traditions grew more intense. And in the coming years, my Xiu Lian Purification Journey would lead me to continue my search for and ultimately find spiritual Dragons from India, Tibet, the Himalayan mountains, and China just like the characters in Hermann Hesse's *Journey to the East*.

Practice to Boost the Snow Mountain Energy Center

One of the 5 key foundational energy centers of the body goes by different names in different spiritual traditions:

1. *Snow Mountain* for Buddhists
2. *Kundalini* for yogis and Hindus
3. *Golden Urn* for Taoists
4. *Ming Men* or *Gate of Life* in Traditional Chinese Medicine

You can locate the middle of this fist-sized energy center by making a straight line from your navel to your back and going 2/3 of the way along this line. Then go down 2.5 cun (a cun is a Chinese measurement representing the width of your thumb joint).

The Snow Mountain is a pre-natal energy center that connects with energy of your ancestors. The four major meridians (Ren, Du, Dai, and Chong) referenced in acupuncture and Traditional Chinese Medicine originate at the Snow Mountain. Taoists consider the Snow Mountain a key center for longevity that nourishes the kidneys, brain, and Third Eye.

If you want to open your Third Eye, you need to have a strong foundation in the Snow Mountain. Using your Third Eye without a strong foundation will drain your energy quickly to the detriment of you physical health, so it's a good idea to build up this center daily. We can practice building the energy of our Snow Mountain by doing a practice using Master Sha's Four-Power Techniques:

Practice to Boost the Snow Mountain Energy Center

1. **Body Power:**
   Place your hands on your kidneys in your lower back.

2. **Soul Power:**

   Say Hello to your Snow Mountain Area for an energy
   boost:

   "Dear soul, mind, and body of my Snow Mountain Area,

   I love you honor you, and appreciate you.

   You have the power to boost my foundational energy."

   Say Hello to the outer souls you request to assist in the
   healing:

   "Dear Divine, Tao, all my spiritual fathers and mothers,

   I love you, honor you, and appreciate you.

   Please assist me in boosting the energy of my Snow Mountain Area.

   I am so honored and grateful.

   Thank you. Thank you. Thank you.

3. **Mind Power:**

   Visualize golden light entering and nourishing your Snow
   Mountain from 360- degrees around you. Some practitioners can "see" or visualize an actual snow-capped mountain
   in the area of the Snow Mountain and receiving light from
   all planets, stars, galaxies, and universes. Visualize the snow
   melting and turning to steam. The rising steam nourishes
   your body.

4. **Sound Power:**

   Chant "Light" repeatedly for 5–10 minutes. Repeat the
   practice 3–5 times/day.

Close the practice, say:

"Hao. Hao. Hao.
Thank you. Thank you. Thank you."

Because a developed Snow Mountain Area nourishes the Third Eye, if you are able to do this practice on a regular basis, don't be surprised if your Third Eye begins to open or—if it's already open—that the images the soul world sends you become more powerful, more detailed, and contain more depth and substance to aid you on your Xiu Lian Purification Journey.

PRELUDE TO TAO

The Tao that can be told is not the eternal Tao.
The name that can be named is not the eternal name.
—Lao Tzu, *Tao Te Ching*

In the spring of my sophomore year at UMass, I sign up for a Comparative Religions class. One of the required texts is *The Religions of Man,* authored by Huston Smith, the MIT philosophy professor who'd been my mentor at the Castalia seminar in Lugano, Switzerland the prior summer. Feeling spiritually uneasy, I'm searching for some sort of organized religion or sacred tradition I can connect with to fill a void in my being. I'm hoping maybe I'll find a religion that resonates with me by reading Professor Smith's book and taking the class. My soul senses that, somewhere out there, there's a path I can follow and connect with the Divine. I just need to exhibit some patience and find it.

My family was Catholic on both my father and mother's side. Growing up, I was a big fan of the stories of Christian saints, especially the martyrs with unshakeable hearts who had total trust in the Divine. These soldiers of Christ represented Jesus to the masses and were often able to manifest miracles just by calling the name of the Lord in their hour of need. My father often brought home books from the Catholic bookstore in downtown Boston. The books— stories of Christian saints written for children—were gifts for all my brothers and sisters, but I think I was the only one who actually read them.

The story of *Daniel* was particularly appealing to me. I loved how this Biblical hero got unjustly persecuted, sentenced to death, and then thrown into the lion's den by his accusers expecting him to suffer an excruciating death. Daniel called upon his God to protect him, then slept peacefully amongst the host of hungry predators in the cage, greatly upsetting King Darius of Persia who found him alive the next morning instead of torn to shreds by the killer beasts who had miraculously become Daniel's protectors.

Both my grandmothers recognized a spiritual aspect to my personality. When I was in grade school, without being overtly obvious, they gently guided and reinforced the direction of my spiritual path towards becoming a Catholic priest. This future livelihood might have been realized seamlessly for me were it not for my discovery of girls in high school. Any longing being nurtured in me to live exclusively for God got ruthlessly overridden by the insatiable hunger for the opposite sex that complicates the lives of the vast majority of teenage boys and girls all around the world. My grandmothers might have been slightly disappointed at my hormonally driven desire to turn away from the priesthood as a vocation, but their sentiments were never expressed openly in a way that made me feel guilty.

The Catholic Church's mandates about having no sex before wedlock—and absolutely no sex for pleasure—were a bit too constraining for me, and so, like many of my friends, I stopped going to Mass on Sundays and gradually eased myself away from what I considered an oppressive set of rules and regulations that, while appropriate for acolytes living in a seminary and training to become priests, were not at all practical for laypersons residing in 20th century America.

⚜   ⚜   ⚜

My exodus from Catholicism created a void in my being. Colloquially speaking, a great big hole formed in my heart, a gaping pit that's still with me in my sophomore year at UMass.

My soul is anxious, and nudges me to seek a way to fill the spiritual vacuum. Excited about taking the Comparative Religions class I've signed up for, I'm hoping to make an objective assessment of the smorgasbord of organized religious options out there. Kind of like going into a pizza parlor, scanning the menu for all the possible toppings, then ordering the one you like.

When I purchase my copy of *The Religions of Man*, I'm intrigued by the short chapters describing the history, tenets, and beliefs of each of the world's major spiritual traditions. If you ever need to quickly figure out the difference between Sunni and Shiite Muslims, Catholics and Protestants, Hasidic Jews and Modern Orthodox Jews, then this is the reference guide for you.

I'm so anxious to take the class that I begin to read *The Religions of Man* before the semester officially begins. The descriptions and key elements of each religion are interesting but my soul doesn't connect with any particular tradition until I reach the chapter on Taoism.

The chapter is relatively short compared to the others in *The Religions of Man* because Huston Smith just doesn't have that much to say about this spiritual path that originated in China about 600 years before the birth of Christ.

Taoist teachings are derived from Lao Tzu, a government bureaucrat employed as Keeper of the Archives for the royal court of the Zhou Dynasty. When he was approximately 60 years old, Lao Tzu got fed up with society and its impure ways. He faced a choice. Either stay at his job in the big city in service to the Emperor and hang out with his fellow bureaucrats on Friday and Saturday nights, or walk away from it all and head to the mountains to meditate and practice "The Way," the path to longevity, enlightenment, and immortality. Lao Tzu made his choice to head for the hills, to "go to the mountain" and meditate in solitude for the remainder of his life. This was to be his way of *Returning to Forever*, of going back to the Tao, the Source of all things.

Lao Tzu found himself a water buffalo on which to ride away, leaving society, family, and friends behind forever. His route led him to Hangu Pass, south of the Yellow River in Henan Province. Hangu, a militarily strategic checkpoint, was not open to the general public, but Lao Tzu figured that as a government official, he wouldn't be questioned as to just who he was or why he was leaving. The guardian of the pass on duty that day was a perceptive individual named Yinxi.

When Lao Tzu arrived at the Hangu Pass gate on his water buffalo, Yinxi sensed the government bureaucrat was a highly advanced spiritual being. Yinzi begged Lao Tzu not to leave, not to abandon humanity desperately in need of spiritual wisdom. Lao Tzu must have felt some compassion for the guard's pleas because he turned aside for three days and wrote the *Tao Te Jing*.

The *Tao Te Jing* is a 96-chapter commentary, which reads like pure poetry. As Huston Smith writes, "the *Tao Te Jing* can be read in half an hour or over a whole lifetime."

Master Sha teaches that seekers on the spiritual path realize "Aha!" moments at the appropriate time, based on our readiness to receive deeper insights and guidance from Heaven to help purify and advance us on our Xiu Lian Purification Journey.

For me, the "Aha" moment occurs when I read the first two lines of the *Tao De Jing*:

> *"The Tao that can be told is not the eternal Tao,*
> *The name that can be named is not the eternal name."*

That is, if you are talking about the Tao, anything you can say in words can never adequately describe the Tao. The Tao is beyond time and space, beyond our comprehension. The Tao is "bigger than biggest, smaller than smallest," as Master Sha teaches.

This is all I need to know. This is my "Aha" moment. No amount of theological study, of struggling with Buddhist sutras, the *Bible,* or other spiritual texts can elaborate or improve upon this simple statement.

However, the problem I face is that, other than referencing any of the 96 short verses in the *Tao Te Ching*, there's nothing in classical Taoism to study. Nothing to practice. No rules to follow. There's no fear of punishment from a wrathful deity anthropomorphized to human likeness and watching our every move, waiting for us to make a mistake. The goal of life is simply to realize Tao. To connect with Tao. To return to Tao. That's all.

I rush out and buy the full text of the *Tao Te Jing*. I commit to memorizing the 96 verses. I don't make it all the way to the end. Years later, once I become a student of Master Sha, I'll memorize 75-line and 220-line new Tao texts from Master Sha's books *Tao I: The Way of All Life* and *Tao II: The Way of Healing, Rejuvenation,*

Longevity, and Immortality.[3] Like a Koi fish swimming to the surface of a pond and sticking its mouth out looking for food, I'm hungry for more Taoist sustenance, but am unable to find anything else to study or practice in my university world. My Comparative Religions professor spends only one lecture on Taoism, which he combines with Confucianism and the I Ching.

Confucianism is practical wisdom for living properly in a world comprised of thousands of nations and cultures. Taoism is spiritual wisdom that goes beyond the yin yang world. Professor Smith recounts the legend of *Confucius* hearing about Lao Tzu—they lived in the same time period—and deciding to visit the Taoist Master in his mountain retreat. After returning from the encounter, Confucius wrote:

> *"I know a bird can fly; I know a fish can swim; I know animals can run. Creatures that run can be caught in nets; those that swim can be caught in wicker traps; those that fly can be hit by arrows. But the Dragon is beyond my knowledge; it ascends into heaven on the clouds and the wind. Today, I have seen Lao Tzu, and he is like the Dragon!"*

My friend and TM partner Katy and I attend a campus exhibition displaying works by UMass's art students. My eyes catch sight of a woodblock print on parchment. It's a representation of a bald-headed Lao Tzu riding on his water buffalo. Tucked under his arm is a rolled-up scroll of the *Tao Te Jing*. I purchase the woodblock print, frame it nicely, and put it on my wall. It's my favorite piece of artwork—simple—just like the *Tao Te Jing*. I hang the framed woodblock print next to the front door of all the apartments, homes, and condos I reside in for the next 38 years. That way, I get to say hello to and acknowledge Lao Tzu whenever I'm leaving my residence or returning home.

Although I'm comfortable that the Tao is the answer to all my questions, the pot of gold at the end of the rainbow of all the

---

3   New York/Toronto: Atria Books/Heaven's Library, 2010.

different spiritual traditions I'll explore in my life, there's no outward or overt actions I can take to become a practicing Taoist. I would like to join a Tao Church. Attend a Tao Study class. Hang out with Taoist students and teachers. Read more books about Taoism. But there's nowhere to go. There's no one to talk to. 1972 is the pre-Internet, pre-Google era. There's no easy way to research Tao. My longing to fly with Taoist Dragons will have to wait many years until I meet Master Sha. As *Lao Tzu* states in the *Tao Te Ching*:

"The journey of one thousand miles begins with one step."

I've taken the first baby step on the path to reach Tao.

Five Elements of Traditional Chinese Medicine

Traditional Chinese Medicine (TCM) traces its roots back over 5000 years to the time of the historical figure known as the Yellow Emperor. TCM is used today in the Orient to treat illnesses using modalities such as acupuncture and natural herbs.

A major difference between TCM and modern Western medicine is that TCM acknowledges and focuses on the movement of *Qi* (energy) throughout the body. Qi circulates through channels called *meridians* that connect our bodies, systems, and organs. If it's helpful, you can think of the meridians connecting all parts of our bodies like the system of Interstate highways that connect all parts of the United States.

A basic premise of TCM is that when Qi is blocked, illness occurs. When Qi flows, one is healthy. Western medicine doesn't acknowledge the existence of Qi from a scientific perspective although some Chinese healing modalities such as acupuncture that have become well accepted in the Western world focus on removing blockages in our bodies that are preventing the free flow of Qi.

A few years ago, I was suffering from pain in my left shoulder and decided to visit a local Chinese acupuncturist at the recommendation of friends from Master Sha's Love Peace Harmony Center in Boulder, Colorado. Dr. Pao checked my pulse, looked briefly at my tongue, and told me to lie down. He then inserted a few acupuncture needles at various points along my upper leg and lower back. I was a little uncomfortable with Dr. Pao's approach since the pain was throbbing in my shoulder and not my leg. I was thinking maybe I hadn't explained my problem appropriately to the elderly healer who didn't speak English very well. But over the course of 24 hours after the treatment, the shoulder pain went from severe to almost non-existent. At my follow-up visit, Dr. Pao's assistant explained that the Doctor had placed the acupuncture needles in parts of my lower body because that was where the Qi blockages were in meridians running to my shoulder. She explained that the reason I felt so much better was because the Qi blockages had been removed and the energy and blood started to flow freely again to my shoulder area.

Master Sha teaches us that the root cause of Qi blockages is karmic and that when those blockages are cleared by a soul healer, or ourselves, we can experience the same type of healing results that I got from my eighty-year-old Chinese acupuncturist.

In TCM, there is a lot of focus on healing and maintaining the major organs in the body. These five major (yin) organs and five associated (yang) organs each have specific characteristics such as: body tissues, body fluids, senses, and even negative emotions:

Five Elements of Traditional Chinese Medicine

Element	Yin Organ	Yang Organ	Body Tissue	Body Fluid	Sense	Emotion
Wood	Liver	Gall Bladder	Tendons/Nails	Tears	Eyes/Sight	Anger
Fire	Heart	Small Intestine	Blood Vessels	Sweat	Tongue/Taste	Depression/Anxiety
Earth	Spleen	Stomach	Muscles	Saliva	Mouth/Lips/Speech	Worry
Metal	Lungs	Large Intestine	Skin	Mucus	Nose/Smell	Grief/Sadness
Water	Kidneys	Urinary Bladder	Bones/Joints	Urine	Ear/Hearing	Fear

For example, a person suffering from intense bouts of anger might get a liver treatment for that emotional condition from a TCM Doctor or acupuncturist since the liver is associated with the negative emotion of anger. Everything can be categorized by the Five Elements. Master Sha offers many practices to transform the Five Elements and teaches us that when we balance and heal our own internal Five Elements, we are also balancing and healing Mother Earth and countless planets, stars, and galaxies!

AN UNEXPECTED BLESSING

"Enlightenment is ego's ultimate disappointment"
        —Venerable Chögyam Trungpa Rinpoche

Venerable Chögyam Trungpa Rinpoche (1939–1987)

The silver Greyhound groans painfully, hinting the bus may be on its last legs. Limps into White River Junction, Vermont. I've ridden up from Boston on a muggy Sunday afternoon in August, 1973. Slinging my backpack over my shoulder as I step into the terminal, I'm a bit lost and make my way to the ticket counter to get help with directions. There's a woman sitting behind a Plexiglas panel cut with a crescent moon-shaped opening through which she exchanges tickets for cash. Her hair is the same color as the bus. She doesn't look the least bit friendly when she sees me approaching. I'm scanned up and down with a noticeable air of disapproval and informed that my destination, the village of Barnet, is "50 miles away... and no buses go that far north, honey."

I guess my long hair and unkempt looks stereotype me as one of those college hippie types that—far too often for her liking—invade the virgin forests of Vermont to smoke marijuana and have sinful sex with un-Christian girls who don't wear bras. Well, truth be told, she's not too far off the mark in her assessment. I'd be ok doing those sorts of things if given the chance, but in reality I'm on my way to a Buddhist meditation retreat and not some dope-fueled orgy in the woods. The disapproving ticket-seller reluctantly points the way to Route 91, the highway I'll have to hitchhike in order to reach Barnet and Karmê Chöling, the meditation center and retreat founded by the *Venerable Chögyam Trungpa Rinpoche* three years earlier.

I've never been to a Buddhist retreat before, and, in actuality, I'm not exactly sure just what it is that Buddhists *do* at retreats. The brochure I'd taken from an outdoor bulletin board in Harvard Square, Cambridge proclaimed I and the other aspiring Buddhists would be spending the coming days and nights in quiet repose, learning and practicing sitting meditation, and eating vegetarian meals silently together. We would be graced by the presence of a "real Tibetan Lama" to guide us through it all in what was sure to be "a rare and unique" opportunity taking place in a Tibetan-style monastery hidden in Vermont's Green Mountains.

My junior year at UMass is still a few weeks away and I've made enough money from my summer job to cover the fall semester's tuition. And if I can just catch a ride up Highway 91 in the next hour or so, I'll arrive at Karmê Chöling before dark and see just what it is I've gotten myself into.

The "real Tibetan Lama" alluded to in the retreat brochure is the Venerable Chögyam Trungpa Rinpoche. He was born in Tibet, but fled the country along with the Dalai Lama in 1959 when the Communist Chinese invaded. The Rinpoche lived in India and then England for the next six years before eventually settling in the United States where he established the Vajradhatu organization to promote the tenets and practices of Vajrayana Buddhism. He set up the Shambala Center and Naropa University in Boulder, Colorado, as well as Karmê Chöling, my intended destination, in Vermont.

This renowned spiritual leader has an impressive pedigree to support his efforts of promoting Buddhism in the West at a time when Eastern religions and all types of yoga and meditation practices are just beginning to reveal themselves to people like me, spiritual seekers undergoing the genesis of soul awakening. It seems to me *now* that most of us *then* didn't know what a spiritual path was, let alone realize we were traveling on it, and we certainly didn't have any clear idea about just what it was we were seeking. But our souls gently tugged us along, a group of like-minded individuals, bound together by the frayed strands of some type of cosmic rope. And like a troupe of blind beggars, we found ourselves stumbling along a road that would lead us onwards and upwards in search of spiritual enlightenment.

With the possible exception of only myself, the students that have found their way to Karmê Chöling are eagerly awaiting the teachings and blessings from the Rinpoche. Chögyam Trungpa is also a tülku, a reincarnated master born in 1939 who would hang around in this incarnation until 1987. His lineage is from the Kagyu sect of Vajrayana Tibetan Buddhism and his current incarnation is the 11th in that documented series of reincarnated Tibetan Lamas. Chögyam Trungpa Rinpoche is also a tertön, a finder and caretaker of ancient Vajrayana texts and teachings, many of which he's translated into English as part of his mission to educate Westerners who are curious and find their souls drawn to the story of the Buddha. A Xiu Lian Dragon indeed!

Having caught a ride with a truck driver on his way to Montreal, I arrive in Barnet at dusk that Sunday and am welcomed at Karmê Chöling just in time for dinner—the last non-silent meal of the retreat. But I can't help feeling a bit out of place here in the monastery. I'm just not sure I belong with this group of enthusiastic practitioners who all:

- *Have a deep understanding of Tibetan Buddhism, which I do not.*
- *Tell fascinating stories about their spiritual journeys at dinner, which I cannot.*
- *Have years of experience meditating in the Kagyu Buddhist tradition, which I do not.*
- *Display an intense longing and expectation for the arrival of Rinpoche, which I wish I had, but do not.*

These Buddhist monastics are not mean-spirited or conceited in any way; it's just that I'm not part of their club. I'm here alone—none of my Boston friends were interested in coming along with me—and I've no guide to help me navigate through and understand the protocol of living in a Buddhist monastery. So, besides being required to be silent from this point forward during our meals, eaten while sitting on the floor of the temple, I'm pretty much silent anyway except when allowed to question the kitchen manager about my assigned duties of chopping veggies and sweeping the floor. I sleep in a corner on the male's side of the bunkhouse with just enough floor space between me and my nearest neighbors to discourage even a forbidden late night whispered conversation.

On Tuesday morning, the excitement at Karmê Chöling reaches an apex. *Rinpoche is coming today!* The students are behaving like adolescent children running around on Christmas morning, on the verge of literally bursting apart with excitement and joy. I'm infected with their enthusiasm also, despite having no prior exposure to the Tibetan Master.

When I finish my cleaning chores in the kitchen after breakfast, I wander outside on this beautiful, clear summer morning. Fill my lungs with the pristine mountain air of Vermont. Wander down the side of a grassy slope away from the monastery's buildings. Alone again—of course—and thinking about a golf tournament I've signed up for once the retreat is over on the weekend before I head back to school. In what seems long after the fact to be an auspicious event, I find a fallen tree branch that is roughly the length of one of my golf clubs. The branch even has a knot on its end that resembles the shape and size of my driver. Picking up the stick, I start swinging it like a golf club while standing on the precipice of a graded slope below which lies the winding road leading off the highway and up to the retreat property. My practice swings are soothing, helping to relieve some of the uneasiness I feel about being out of place here, about feeling cornered by this group of people I have so little in common with. But my anxiety is not so great that I'm thinking of leaving—after all, Karmê Chöling is a beautiful, peaceful, and relaxing place to be—but I'm still not exactly sure why I came here. So I continue to swing my club, to balance my rhythm, and visualize golf balls, perfectly struck, arcing gracefully to imagined greens far below the promontory on which I'm standing.

I'm kind of out of it, just focusing on my swing plane, when a black Lincoln Town Car starts to snake up the road below me, ascending the gently sloping grade in near silence at a pace neither hurried nor unnecessarily slow. I'm studying the vehicle, which seems grossly over the top here. All the other cars parked haphazardly around the place could be right out of a Jack Kerouac novel:

beat-up Volkswagen Beetles, aging Ford Fairlanes, and bald-tired hippie vans with fading, scratched pastel exteriors; vehicles that in no way could ever pass a safety inspection test.

The limousine pulls up beside me. Slows to a stop. The rear power window on the passenger-side lowers. An Oriental face is revealed and stares at me without moving, without blinking. The Tibetan man is middle-aged with Asian-black hair and black-rimmed glasses. Our eyes lock. We don't speak. There is no need, the Asian man is communicating to my soul directly in the language of love. *But who is this man and how can he love me? How can I love him back when I've never even seen him before?*

I feel myself being cleansed, as if the power of his love is pulling me through some sort of spiritual car wash whose brushes and scrubbers are removing debris and detritus from my soul and recharging my life's battery. Then, the window is raised and the car moves on up the road. I have no idea how long the blessing from Rinpoche has lasted. I'm so spiritually ignorant, I don't even recognize it's an actual blessing that has been given to me! All I sense is that the world has changed. The scenic vista before me looks sharper, brighter. The ridges on the distant hills have become more—defined. It's like I'm now looking through once-dirty glass that's just been sprayed with Windex and wiped squeaky-clean with newspaper.

Turning around, I look up to see the entire congregation lining both sides of the road. Most people are bowing; many hold offerings of fruit and fresh-cut flowers for the Guru. At least half the group is crying tears of joy at Chögyam Trungpa Rinpoche's arrival. Some of the girls appear on the verge of fainting. By the time I walk back up to the monastery courtyard, Rinpoche is out of the car, smiling broadly, and walking up the steps to his Temple. His authority here is confirmed when, an hour or so later, we are summoned to the hall by a ceremonial gong rung three times. We take our places sitting lotus style on tiny cushions arranged in neat rows on the hardwood floor. When the Rinpoche enters and takes his seat on the dais in the front of the room, the energy shifts noticeably like nothing I've ever felt before. This man, this Master, just feels right.

True Masters are spiritual Dragons whose energy and vibration spin at a significantly higher frequency than the rest of us. When you sit in a room with an enlightened being, your own lower frequency attempts to adjust, to calibrate with the soul of the teacher for the duration of the time you'll spend together. This calibration period affects different people in different ways. Some feel lighter than air and have difficulty keeping their bodies physically grounded while their souls ascend to attune with the Master's vibration. I've witnessed new students react with spasms bordering on epileptic fits, the Master's energy too strong for them to handle upon a first encounter with such a high-level holy being. For me, there is initially a sense of ecstasy that's much stronger than the mere excitement, the buzz, of being in the room with such a Master. And when the session is over, I am always totally exhausted, happy, and drained. Without fail, I have to sleep immediately, and the sleep is always deep and dreamless while my soul repositions itself to a higher plane, never reaching the same level as what I experienced in the room while with the teacher, but higher than the frequency and vibration I had before being in the Guru's presence.

One of the tests I've used when I find myself around teachers who claim to have "spiritual insight and powers." is to let my intuition feel the vibration of those individuals. If I'm not experiencing the teacher's energy as high frequency, high vibration, and *totally loving,* I become suspicious of that teacher's intent. *Is the teacher a charlatan after my money? Is he or she trying to manipulate my soul to advance their own agenda? Does he or she have any real wisdom to impart to me or am I going to be asked to drink the poisoned Kool-Aid of some weird-ass cult?* Your intuition will *always* let you know when the teacher is right for you. Just bring your attention, your focus, and your mind away from your analytical brain and down to your heart and ask your soul how the teacher "feels."

You may have to accept some level of uncomfortableness when you first meet a true Master who is here to serve you by helping you work out bad karma, remove blockages, and advance on your Xiu Lian Purification Journey. This is a natural reaction that most spiritual seekers experience at some point in their multi-lifetime journey. But if your intuition warns you that the energy around the teacher is negative, that the vibration of the teacher is disruptive, *you have to leave the room right away.* If the teacher or other students are upset at your departure, they are only confirming your decision to go as a true Master never forces your attendance or makes demands on you if you are not ready.

All of Chögyam Trungpa Rinpoche's students stay for his teachings and blessings given over the days of the retreat. We have no doubt that Rinpoche is enlightened, that he is a vehicle like a rocket ship we've boarded, ready to transport us to realms beyond Mother Earth. His energy is intense and his love is boundless.

I endure the pain of sitting on my heels for hours at a time in the Temple practicing meditation with the Master and begin to learn how to use the pain to my advantage. To realize the source of the agony is my mind and that if I turn off my mind to focus on the mantra I've been given, the pain disappears. Or rather, it's not the pain that disappears, it's me. And for the first time in my life during these rich, golden August days in the mountains of Vermont, I catch fleeting glimpses of the goal of meditation. I begin to gain clarity around the purpose of my soul's spiritual journey and its intent to one day go back to the Divine, to meld with Tao, to return to the Source. My soul is awakening like a rose slowly unfolding in the light of the morning sun, but I'm not fully able to grasp the meaning of it all or decide what I should do next. It's like I'm a baby duckling about to be born; I've cracked the eggshell surrounding me from within—maybe that was what the Rinpoche helped me to do with his silent blessing—but there's still lots of work ahead before I break completely free of my blockages and am able to clear my karma. And it will take years of Xiu Lian practice for me to appreciate the significance, the compassion, and the loving generosity of my roadside blessing from the Rinpoche.

After meditating with Chögyam Trungpa at Karmê Chöling, for the first time in my life I develop a strong yearning to become a monk, adopt an ascetic lifestyle, and go live quietly in a monastery. I seriously entertain the idea of leaving the world of normal society just like Lao Tzu chose to do, but upon deeper reflection, I know I'm just not ready. If I quit college a second time and tell my family I'm going to move to the mountains of Vermont to meditate with a Tibetan Master, they'll accept my decision but be shaking their heads in dismay behind my back. They'll be wondering how long my enthusiasm for meditation will last before I tire of the spiritual life and return home with head down like a sorry puppy with its tail between its legs.

We learn ancient Buddhist wisdom and receive countless blessings from Rinpoche during my stay at Karmê Chöling. Returning to university for my junior year, I eagerly study the tenets of Tibetan Buddhism and the Four Noble Truths in an Oriental Religions class but find that Buddhism confuses me intellectually. And like lots of Westerners who grew up in the Christian tradition, I'm a bit overwhelmed by the sheer volume of deities that float in the different layers of heaven, the angelic Dragons all serving humanity in unique ways. My meditation practice becomes a mix of TM with my assigned mantra and practice in the style taught me at Karmê Chöling with Rinpoche. I am blessed by the soul of Rinpoche who is ever present with me. When I sit in the condition, it's like I am back in the Temple with the Master, resting on my heels, connected with his eternal eyes, dancing with his gentle vibrating love.

But, despite how wonderful it all feels, I don't return to Karmê Chöling the following summer. I don't become a student of the Rinpoche. And I don't know why.

A few years later, I will meet my Guru; I suspect that my time spent with the Rinpoche and his Buddhist students was planned in Heaven to prepare me for what lay ahead in my Xiu Lian Purification Journey. But as the Buddhist's teach us, it's best not to speculate on how or why the wheel of dharma turns as it does...

Food Offering Practices

This guidance was posted on the wall in the kitchen at Karmê Chöling in Vermont. It's a nice reminder of how one should approach the preparation of food in the kitchen and how everything we do can be a practice on our Xiu Lian Purification Journey.

Slogans for Kitchen Practice

~~~

Always clean up after yourself.
Do not take what is not offered.
Do not harm others with your speech.
Not too fast, not too slow.
Do not waste.
No one is finished until all are finished.
This food is prepared as an offering to the Three Jewels.
The sangha are your guests.

Master Sha offers two practices around meals:

Jin Dan Jin Gu

Chant this mantra *before* each meal to prepare your entire digestive system for eating food. *Jin Dan Jin Gu* prepares every organ and every cell in your digestive system for the intake of food.

Jin Dan Hua Gu

Chant this mantra *after* each meal to help your entire digestive system digest and absorb food well. *Jin Dan Hua Gu* boosts the functioning of every organ and every cell in your digestive system.

TRANCE WALKING

"I clearly reached a condition in which the weight of the body is no more felt and in which the feet seem to be endowed with an instinct of their own, avoiding invisible obstacles and finding footholds, which only a clairvoyant consciousness could have detected in the speed of such a movement and in the darkness of the night."
—Lama Govinda, *The Way of the White Clouds*

Lama Anagarika Govinda (1898–1985)

Three of my friends and I inadvertently become *lung-gom-pas*—Tibetan trance walkers—while scrambling about on the jagged slopes of Mt. Washington in New Hampshire on Columbus Day weekend in 1973. The sun has just set and what little daylight remains is fading fast. My buddies and me have foolishly decided to forego the marked trails in favor of an unmapped route across open and exposed terrain.

We are now paying the price for that ill-advised decision.

Only halfway down the mountain, we face the unattractive prospect of having to finish our descent in deepening, dangerous darkness. We left our flashlights behind at camp with our tent and sleeping bags, never anticipating a descent at twilight. We are fast becoming anxious and desperate. Acting reckless. Forced to jump amongst outcrops of large granite boulders to avoid getting mired in patches of thorny briars scratching out a tenuous existence on the darkening slopes of Mt Washington. The group is scared, but since we're 20-year-old males, no one admits to our fear out loud. Our attention is focused solely on returning to base camp as quickly as possible without twisting an ankle, breaking a leg, or worse, under an evening sky starting to speckle with stars.

We had scaled the summit earlier that morning, choosing the Ammonoosuc Ravine trail for our ascent, 4.4 miles in length and one of the steeper climbs up the highest peak in North America east of the Mississippi River. Our initial intent for the return route was to follow alongside the Cog Railway over which a rack and pinion locomotive built in the 1800s transports tourists up and down the mountain.

The evening before, sitting around our campfire sometime around midnight, undoubtedly high and having consumed an excessive amount of beer, I recounted a story from six years earlier when I convinced my friends it would be fun to race the Cog Railway train down Mount Washington.

❧ ❧ ❧

My first full summer away from home landed me in the White Mountains. I was 14 years old and a friend and I enrolled at a "caddy" camp affiliated with the Mt. Washington Hotel in the town of Bretton Woods. The white-walled hotel with a brilliant red roof is famous for hosting a global conference of the leading industrial nations at the end of World War II. A new economic system was needed for the civilized world to live by after the war, and the deal—known as the "Bretton Woods System"—got crafted in the shadow of Mt. Washington.

The caddies lived in an old-fashioned wood-framed bunkhouse. There were about 40 kids from all over New England, all competing to make $10–20 bucks a day lugging golf clubs around the Bretton Woods golf course for well-to-do tourists vacationing at the luxury hotel.

On our one-day-a-week off, a few of us liked to go and climb Mt. Washington. At 6,288 feet above sea level, the mountain is the tallest in the White Mountain range. There are approximately 20 major hiking trails up and down the massive uplift of granite. At the height of summer, Appalachian Trail trekkers and casual day hikers select their preferred trail and begin the ascent to the peak. Tuckerman's Ravine trail is the toughest trail to attempt. The deep clefts of the ravine harbor hidden pockets of winter snow and ice that slide off the mountain's higher elevations during the springtime warmth and don't fully melt until the steamy heat of mid-July. Climbers who make it to the summit find a weather observatory that's logged the highest winds ever recorded—over 200 miles per hour—a gift shop, and a restaurant that serves exquisite beef stew to boost exhausted hiker's energy after the 4–5 hour climb.

For the less physically fit and the elderly, there's an auto road that snakes all the way up the mountain. Not for the squeamish. Hairpin turns and precipitous drop-offs mandate speeds of

10 miles per hour or less. Make sure your brakes are in good working order before you attempt this "scenic drive"!

The preferred tourist route to the top for families with small children and those not wishing to suffer the anxiety of the auto road is the Cog Railway, a steam railroad built to the summit over 100 years ago. The railway boasts an average grade of 25%. The ride is approximately 3 miles in length. The train's engine tugs the single passenger car slowly up the mountain at about 3 miles per hour and "speeds" down at up to 5 miles per hour.

At age 14, me and the other caddies one day debated if we were fit enough and fast enough to race the Cog down the rocky slopes and beat the train to the bottom. On that hot summer day in July, we mustered up our spurting teenage testosterone-fueled energy and declared we were ready. After climbing to the summit, we boldly announced our intention to "beat the train" to the tourists leaning out the windows of the passenger cars and found unexpected and enthusiastic support for our cause. The excitement built to a fever pitch when the Cog blasted its horn for all on the mountaintop to hear. The great race was on!

The first leg of the descent found my friends and I jumping out to an early lead. We ran over a marked trail that parallels the tracks for the first half-mile. Once the trail diverged right towards Mount Jefferson and the other peaks in the Presidential Range, we were on our own and forced to scramble over the granite outcrops without the benefit of following a marked path. Negotiating the boulders beside the train tracks wasn't so bad in the light of the midday sun, and we looked to extend our lead over the slowly churning Cog engine chasing us from behind and huffing and puffing plumes of black smoke into the clear New England skies.

Then things got tricky.

There's a steep gorge called the "Great Gulf" the train must pass over. The Cog Railway engineers had to figure a way for the train to traverse the gulf when they originally designed the railway. The construction crew built what's called Jacob's Ladder, a stretch of tracks on wooden trestles 30 feet high that span the entire ravine. This part of the Cog route is beautiful if you're sitting inside the passenger car with your camera taking panoramic views of everything around you. But Jacob's Ladder presents a formidable obstacle if you are racing the train, since you are going to lose a lot of time navigating the steep slopes to get into and then out of the Great Gulf.

Exhibiting the reckless abandon of youth, we foolishly decided our best course of action was to avoid the ravine entirely by climbing up onto the tracks of Jacob's Ladder and running over the wooden railroad ties ahead of the train trying to catch us from behind. The only problem with this half-baked plan was that the Cog was steadily bearing down upon us and we weren't sure if we could cross the gorge and scramble off the trestles before the cowpusher on the front of the train swept us to our death on the rocks at the bottom of the Great Gulf!

Climbing up the beams supporting Jacob's Ladder, we soon discovered another problem. The railroad ties were spaced just far enough apart from each other that we had to gauge each step precisely to avoid stumbling and falling through the spaces between the wooden ties. The temptation to look back over our shoulders and see how quickly the Cog was approaching was intense, but I kept my mind focused on just reaching the end of Jacob's Ladder and didn't look down or back. My friends and I managed this part of the race safely and successfully, but our 10–15 minute lead on the train had shrunk to barely 5 minutes and we continued to have no trail to follow. No problem for a bunch of 14-year old boys! We prevailed in our task and when we reached the icy-cold creek at the bottom of the mountain that flows past the train station, the other caddies and I jumped out of our clothes and dove into the water. When the Cog passed over the creek, we were scowled at by the engineer and train porters, but wildly applauded by the passengers, and we basked joyfully in the thrill of our "victory" over the Cog.

✠   ✠   ✠

My fellow hikers are suitably impressed upon hearing my tale of "beating the train" down the mountain and we collectively agree to recreate the Great Train Race of my caddy camp days the following day.

After climbing to the summit without incident and arriving there around noontime, we hang around the summit of Mount Washington longer than prudence and common sense dictate. In hindsight, we should have chosen to race the Cog train that departs from the summit at 1 p.m. Instead, we inexplicably wait to race the last train leaving at 3 p.m.

We find ourselves paying the price for our inaction, our delay.

The loss of the sun as it sets behind the Presidential Range includes loss of light and heat. On this crisp October Indian Summer afternoon, the temperature drops quickly. We are fast approaching weather conditions that can be fatal if we are left exposed on the mountain for more than a few hours. Survival instincts kick in. We don't have to discuss our situation openly. Each hiker is well aware of our perilous predicament for which we have only ourselves to blame.

As we scramble to accelerate our journey, we suddenly and miraculously find ourselves seeming to "float" above the slopes of the mountain as we make our descent in deepening shadows. Our steps become unnaturally exaggerated in length and we bounce from boulder to boulder like light-footed elves guided by some higher power that's ensuring our safety. Our feet find footholds we can't see with our eyes in the dim light, and lightly brush the tops of the rocks as if we are weightless and walking on the moon.

When at last we arrive at the base of the mountain in the darkness of early evening, we are all stunned. No one can fathom what's happened. We can't understand how each one of us made it down without at least one of us getting a sprained ankle or other significant injury. There is no rational explanation for how we leapt safely from boulder to boulder with such limited vision, of how our feet found safe footholds and no one slipped and got seriously hurt.

Cooling our feet in the cold stream at the base of Mt. Washington, we awaken from the dream state in which we trance-walked down the rocky slope guided by an unseen force. We disconnect from whatever power protected and guided us on our perilous descent. There's an ecstatic gleam in everyone's eyes and we recognize something magical has happened but no one knows what to say or how to put our experience into words. On the ride back to Boston the following morning, our rational minds return to their seat of logic and control and quickly belittle and suppress any acknowledgement that something extraordinary happened the day before.

⚜   ⚜   ⚜

I won't come to understand the trance-state we entered until the next year when I read *Lama Anagarika Govinda's: The Way of the White Clouds*. Lama Govinda relates how Tibetan mystics are sometimes seen traveling great distances at great speeds in the Himalayan foothills. Witnesses recount how the mystics seem to glide above the terrain or bounce over rocks comprising mountainous Himalayan landscapes. Lama Govinda calls this unique talent *lung-gom-pa* walking. Lung-gom-pa walking is a special ability that serves a very practical purpose if one is spiritually advanced and in need of traversing difficult terrain in a hurry in order to offer service to those in need.

Theodore Illion published a book called *In Secret Tibet* in 1937. He recounts witnessing lung-gom-pa walkers firsthand:

"The lung-gom-pa's must rightly be described as one of the strangest phenomena in Tibet. They do not run, but move past like an elastic ball bouncing off the ground at regular intervals, their arms and

legs swinging like a pendulum. Although they move past at a speed of something like fifteen miles an hour, they are never out of breath. Their faces are curiously immobile. Their eyes remain wide open and they seem to exist in a strange state of trance."

I am not suggesting or implying in any way that my friends or I possess special powers of any type. But we did share a "magical" experience on Mount Washington that we weren't able to explain afterwards in rational, scientific terms. And it was only after reading *The Way of the White Clouds* that I started to wonder if maybe the Divine was giving me a glimpse of special spiritual abilities in the form of lung-gom-pa trance-walking that evening on Mt. Washington as a kind of "sneak preview" of the kind of mystical experiences that could lie ahead for me on the Xiu Lian Purification Journey.

It takes many thousands of lifetimes to develop these abilities on the Xiu Lian Purification Journey and these powers are not to be "displayed" to the public or nurtured by one's ego, but instead are available to be called upon when one is offering service to others. Miracle healers and high-level spiritual beings described in the texts of many of the world's religions are servants with such abilities. A good example might be Jesus who "fed the multitude of 4000" by manifesting unlimited amounts of food from seven loaves of bread and a few fish.

Baird T. Spalding's *Life and Teaching of the Masters of the Far East* recounts the experiences of a group of Western spiritual seekers traveling in India and the Himalayas in the early twentieth century who had first-hand encounters with many saints displaying extraordinary powers including the ability to heal physical injuries instantly.

Theodore Illion recounts that he twice observed a lung-gom-pa at close range:

"... judging by careful examination of his footprints, the weight of his body must have been diminished to some extent."

Here Illion is referring to the physical weight of the lung-gom-pa walker. From his observation, the "flying lama" appears, at least while in the trance-walking condition, to be physically lighter than when in the normal condition outside of a trance and this aspect of his "light body" is what enables the lung-gom-pa to "float" and "bounce" over difficult terrain.

Lama Govinda emphasizes the important point of developing and using spiritual powers for the right reasons:

"In the original system of Buddhist meditation, the attainment of magic power is a mere by-product and is looked upon rather as a danger than as a stimulus on the higher path, which aims at liberation and abhors the exhibition of occult forces. The peculiar conditions of Tibet, however, have sometimes made it necessary to make use of these powers to a certain degree, especially when nature placed insurmountable obstacles in the way of the adept or his desire to be of service to his fellow human-beings."

As Lama Govinda teaches, the purpose of having extraordinary abilities is not to impress our friends by walking through walls, traveling to distant places instantaneously, becoming invisible at will—to name just a few of the special abilities—but to develop spiritual capacities that allow us to humbly help others in need. And although stories of saints and high-level spiritual beings performing miraculous events and healings using extraordinary abilities are entertaining and inspiring, practitioners on the Xiu Lian path are discouraged from desiring or cultivating such powers.

As Lao Tzu says in the *Tao De Jing*:

"There is no greater sin than craving,
No greater curse than discontent,
No greater misfortune than wanting something for ourselves."

For the remainder of my college years, I don't get another chance to experience spiritual power or witness any more spiritual miracles. Continuing to be diligent in my daily TM practice, I'm inspired to read many books about the lives of lamas, gurus, and saints from India and Tibet. My soul yearns to travel to the Himalayas and find a guru, but lack of money and practical considerations force me to remain in the United States. If I have an Indian guru somewhere, he will have to come to me...

Weng Ar Hong Practice

Weng Ar Hong is a powerful healing mantra that originated in ancient China. Master Sha teaches that millions of people have received healings and blessings by calling upon the soul of the *Weng Ar Hong mantra*. The 3 syllables of this mantra have no specific meaning, but chanting each of them stimulates cellular vibration in different areas of the body to promote healing and rejuvenation.

In Traditional Chinese Medicine, the body is divided into 3 sections know as the Triple Burner, or 3 Jiao:

- *The Upper Jiao is the area above the diaphragm, and includes the heart and lungs.*
- *The Middle Jiao is the space between the diaphragm and navel, and includes the pancreas, stomach, and spleen.*
- *The Lower Jiao is the space in the body from the level of the navel down to the genital area. It includes the small and large intestines, urinary bladder, kidneys, reproductive organs, sexual organs, and liver.*

Use Master Sha's Four-Power Techniques to practice *Weng Ar Hong*:

1. **Body Power:**
   - Weng Ar Hung is most effective when standing up.
   - Hold your right hand, palm up, a few inches above the navel, close to, but not touching the body to promote energy flow and healing.
   - Hold your left hand, palm up, a few inches below the navel, close to, but not touching your body to promote energy flow and healing. (If you have hypertension, glaucoma, pain, inflammation, or a tumor or cancer in the brain, eyes, or head, turn your right hand over so that

the right palm faces down. The right hand is still held a few inches above the navel.[4])

2. **Soul Power:**

"Dear soul, mind, and body of Weng Ar Hong,
I love you, honor you, and appreciate you.
Please heal my 3 Jiao and all organs within them as appropriate.
I am so honored and grateful.
Thank you. Thank you. Thank you."

3. **Mind Power:**
   - Visualize colored light flowing in each area as you chant:
   - Visualize the color red in the Upper Jiao.
   - Visualize the color white in the Middle Jiao.
   - Visualize the color blue in the Lower Jiao.

4. **Sound Power:**
   - Take a deep breath and exhale very slowly for approximately one minute or as long as is comfortable for you. While exhaling:
   - When chanting Weng (pronounced "wung"), concentrate on the Upper Jiao.
   - When chanting Ar (pronounced "ar"), concentrate on the Middle Jiao.
   - When chanting Hong (pronounce "hohng"), concentrate on the Lower Jiao.
   - Chant each syllable for approximately 20 seconds. When you chant *Weng Ar Hong*, you vibrate the cells in the Upper, Middle, and Lower Jiao respectively.

---

4 *Soul Mind Body Medicine: A Complete Soul Healing System for Optimum Health and Vitality*, Novato, California: New World Library, 2006.

After the practice, say:

"Hao. Hao. Hao.
Thank you. Thank you. Thank you."

I love *Weng Ar Hong* practice in part because it's very easy to physically experience the vibration of the mantra in each part of your body. Students who are new to the concepts of Master Sha's soul healing and Traditional Chinese Medicine almost always relate to *Weng Ar Hong* from the first time they practice this ancient method of healing.

Master Sha also teaches that whenever we chant *Weng Ar Hong* (or any ancient mantra), all the souls that have ever chanted this mantra in the past join in with us and that this "group chanting" at the soul level helps to balance and heal Mother Earth, and all planets, stars, and galaxies!

GURU

"When a devotee prays intensely to God to know truth,
God sends him a true guru to guide him.
This Divine grace comes to the devotee when he demonstrates
his desire for liberation by sincere constancy in supplication to God."
—Paramahansa Yogananda

Paramahansa Yogananda (1893–1952)

So how do you know for sure that the teacher standing before you is the right one? How do you know the one representing himself to you as your eternal guide, mentor, friend, and loved one is here to serve *you*? That his or her purpose is to guide you back to the Divine, the Tao, and the Source?

Well, you will know in your heart, not in your mind. If you are a seeker waiting for your spiritual pilot, you may have encounters with many potential candidates that don't measure up, or fail the heart test outright.

Some teachers will appear quite promising to you. Nice eye candy that upon deeper examination have little substance and little to offer that you don't already know. Some may try to manipulate you. They'll say all the right things. Ask for your commitment to their way. Insist you practice using only their techniques and no others. Promise you enlightenment if you adhere strictly to their rules.

Other teachers seem intent on building a critical mass of disciples, the more people that follow them the better. These types of teachers won't have the time to guide you as an individual on your Xiu Lian journey.

False prophets also exist, easily identified by huge egos hiding behind smiling facades of spurious humility. Get suckered in with one of these guys and you're soon likely to find yourself feeling empty and drained, a result of your spiritual energy, your emotions, and all too often your finances, getting siphoned off to feed the "engine" of the teacher's movement.

I'll say it again: If your heart tells you the teacher doesn't feel right: trust your intuition. Listen to your heart—it's incapable of lying to you or tricking you like the ego—and look elsewhere!

This is not to say that you might not experience some level of anxiety when you first meet a true Master. If you've been plodding along slowly on your Xiu Lian Purification Journey for hundreds or thousands of lifetimes, and suddenly a true guru shows up in front of you, you can be sure things are going to start shifting in a hurry. Your body will probably start to undergo physical changes and you might actually feel sick for a time. Your emotions may start to go haywire. You'll find yourself subject to outbursts of crying for no apparent reason. You are likely to start feeling a bit disconnected from family, friends, and your spouse/partner. Your job and career may become meaningless, unfulfilling, and unimportant, an actual hindrance impeding your spiritual journey.

You may feel like you've lost touch with reality because when you finally meet your guru, your mind transcends its grasp of what reality is. And what was important yesterday can suddenly become trivial today. These mental conditions and experiences are "normal" occurrences on the Xiu Lian path and they are often quite beautiful, not from the viewpoint of our threatened egos, but from the perspective of our souls and those high-level souls watching us who understand what is happening and smile at us offering empathy, sympathy, encouragement, and love like parents watching their first-graders board the bus on the opening day of elementary school.

The mind rebels when an enlightened Master first appears before the student. The ego fights furiously to maintain its dominance over our life because it foresees the beginning of its ultimate demise, the death of its existence. Be assured our ego is not going to go down without a fight. And similar to the resistance the ego puts up when we first start to meditate seriously, the "battle of Kurekshetra," as the Hindus refer to it in the *Bhagavad Gita*, gets even more intense when we meet our Master. Arrows of doubt get hurled at our soul to challenge the validity of the guru:

"Who is this guy who's shown up out of the blue? He's not going to teach you anything special! This man has no spiritual powers! You're going to lose all your family and friends if you take up with this character! And he'll definitely take all your money, how are you going to explain that to your wife and kids? Are you really going to give up everything you've worked so hard for to go with this guy, to

join his cult? Have you lost your mind completely? Shouldn't you hedge your bet and check this guy out a bit more before you fully commit to the path he's asking you to follow?"

In the early 1980's, I read Paramahansa Yogananda's *Autobiography of a Yogi* for the second time. I had first tackled the story of this Hindu spiritual Dragon's life in college and found it interesting, but not life transforming. The first reading didn't galvanize me to deviate from my daily TM practice. Nor did I seek to become a student of Yogananda's Self-Realization Fellowship, the organization he founded in the US in 1920 when his Guru, *Swami Sri Yukteswar,* informed Yogananda that his divine task was to spread the message of love and light beyond India to anxious souls waiting in the West. The autobiography ended up on a shelf in my living room along with a bunch of other spiritual texts I'd picked up at University. Those books got boxed and carried from apartment to apartment over the course of eight years. Eventually, I would meet my future wife, settle into our first house, and display the books on shelves in my home office. They were a pleasant reminder to me of my carefree days on campus before "real life" happened and I found I needed a career and money to survive in the modern world after getting married.

Resting quietly in the background, maybe becoming impatient at my lack of spiritual progress in the years since I'd graduated college, my soul woke up at some point and guided me to pick up *Autobiography of a Yogi* and read it again. And this second reading proved much more inspirational than the first. I must have been spiritually ripe—maybe on the verge of becoming rotten! —But I was certainly in a state of readiness to absorb more of Yogananda's teachings. As a result of the second reading, I restarted my daily TM meditation practice that had stalled since my commitment to an IT job installing computer systems all over the world— exciting and financially rewarding, but not very spiritual—while simultaneously trying to raise a family of three boys that my wife and I had over a period of four years.

I would set my alarm for 5 a.m. each weekday morning, take my shower, then return to our bed to sit cross-legged, my back supported by fluffy pillows propped up against the wooden headboard. My daily TM meditation sessions lasted 30 minutes after which I'd rush downstairs and head off to work in downtown Boston. Sadly, I was morphing into a 1980s clone of the 1960s "Rising Young Executive" corporate guy I'd so hoped to avoid becoming.

My daily meditation routine propagated itself for several years and I clung to it tenaciously even when struggling with many rough spots in my work and my marriage. After seven years of struggle, my wife and I ended up getting a divorce. Being the man, I was the one expected to move out of the house to a basement apartment overstocked with boxes of my stuff, including all of my spiritual books. I'd escaped a functionally dead marriage at huge financial and emotional cost, and found myself living a lonely lifestyle very much akin to what I'd gone through after graduating college. And it was here, in my bachelor apartment, alone, spiritually treading water and horribly depressed, that the Guru revealed himself to me.

⚜   ⚜   ⚜

It's a rainy Saturday morning in springtime, but I don't remember the exact date. Because of the weather, I'm not golfing today and have slept in. Around mid-morning, after coffee and Cheerios, I pull out my blue meditation cushion and sit down in my underwear facing south to begin my practice. About ten minutes into it, I've slowed my breathing and am drifting along in *No Time, No Space* while silently chanting my TM mantra. Standard stuff for me—nothing unusual going on. Then I sense a presence in the room. I open my eyes to see what's going on. The Guru is here, standing right in front of me!

How can I explain this in words? I know his name: Paramahansa Yogananda. The Guru smiles at me. Yogananda is cloaked all in white, not the orange robe he's traditionally pictured wearing, the symbol of his Indian Swami monastic order. We are in sacred space, my dreary apartment magically transformed by the Guru's presence. The room now a veiled bubble of utter peace and calm. The Guru and I are alone in a mystical moment and spiritual sphere created just for the two of us. Just for this meeting. A prelude to the impending union of our souls that will occur many years later when I become a Disciple. And it dawns on me as surely as the sun rises each morning that I've been waiting for this moment all of my life. All of my lives. He is here. He has come. Not in the physical form I might have expected, but instead, as a light being from some higher realm, his image appearing before me like an ethereal collection of transparent particles held together by an unseen mystical force. This Guru is eternal love! This Guru is shining white light!

Paramahansa Yogananda and I share the same birthday, January 5, but he was born in 1893 and transitioned in 1952, the year before I was born. His presence before me is as real as if he were here in person, maybe more so. This is no hallucination, no visualization manifested to become reality. There is not the least amount of doubt or concern on my part: *I've melded into an incredibly loving higher presence and feel like a baby being cradled in the arms of an angel*!

The Guru holds a slender white candle lit with a golden flame. He moves towards me and gently places the candle in my heart, his hand moving through my flesh as if I have no substance, as if I am made of the same transparent spiritual matter as he. The fire from this candle in my heart will burn eternally and my soul is certain it will never be extinguished even after I ultimately attain enlightenment by following the Guru's path wherever it leads me. My soul rejoices in this knowledge, this realization that I've found my spiritual Master, and that I will never be alone again! Without having asked the Divine specifically for Paramahansa Yogananda or any other spiritual teacher to come and help me, I've been found, found wanting, and healed. The bond between us is eternal, the Guru's love is forever, and I've been given a permanent priceless treasure in the form of the candle and flame now burning steadily in my heart.

My eyes blink and, just as quickly as he appeared before me, the Guru disappears leaving his energy and a fragrance of flowers lingering in the room. I'm overwhelmed with joy and cry profusely. I prostrate myself on the floor to give thanks to my Savior.

My meeting with the Guru was an introduction—more of a wake-up call really—with a spiritual Master who was inviting me and accepting me to partake of his teachings as a *student.* There is a huge difference between being accepted as a *student* of a Master and being accepted as a *Disciple.*

On the day of my meeting with my Guru, I am given the opportunity to become a *student* only. I agree in my heart to study and learn the teachings and practices of Paramahansa Yogananda in order to advance my spiritual journey.

I've found spiritual students of Eastern traditions like Buddhism, Hinduism, or Taoism to be a lot like Christian parishioners. They aren't priests, nuns, or pastors, fully devoted to serving God and humanity 24 hours a day, but instead make their best efforts to meditate and not create any really bad karma for themselves. They're like Christians who attend Sunday church services while trying to do good and avoid evil in their daily lives the rest of the week. These types of practitioners live primarily in the secular world. They have jobs, families, hobbies, and interests and are able to devote only a portion of their time to practicing their faith. *Disciples,* on the other hand, are like or may be actual monastics. *Disciples* voluntarily give up worldly ambitions for fame, money, power, and sexual relationships in order to focus on the Divine full time, all the time. *Disciples* often live in monasteries or cloistered communities in order to support each other on the spiritual path and avoid the temptations of samsaric life beyond the temple gates.

Once your soul guides you onto the Xiu Lian path, the meeting with your Guru occurs only when you are ready. Your Guru is always ready to receive you, even though you may not know it. You may see him but not recognize him. Have no worries, he'll recognize you. When that time comes, you'll really have no choice but to follow your spiritual guide. Your ego may still put up a spirited resistance, but your Guru's love will quiet that part of your being, nourish your soul, and encourage you to start or continue your journey home to God, the Tao, the Source.

If we are lucky enough to experience the human condition of falling in love, we catch a glimpse of what the guru/disciple relationship will be, but it is only a glimpse. When you feel love's chemistry with another person, you rush to share sentiments with your friends like "I'm in heaven when I'm with her," or "She touches my heart so deeply." You feel that deep connection forming between you and your lover's hearts, your souls. Everything in the universe changes and you become "one" with each other. The guru/disciple relationship is a thousand times, a million times more powerful than that glorious human experience! When you meet your guru, you find total, unconditional, never failing love that will carry you home *to God*! This love can never be equaled at the human level and is one reason why so many monastics on their Xiu Lian Purification Journey focus entirely and willingly on divine love and not the physical love of two people that can never approach the intensity of God's love given through the guru.

Paramahansa Yogananda teaches that anyone can ask God for a guru, a teacher to help them navigate the path of purification and enlightenment, at any time. The Divine will always answer, just maybe not in the time, place, or manner you expect. But he will answer. How can he not? God loves us forever, despite our faults, our sins, or our apathy towards him. And yet I've known so many people who seem so lost when it comes to asking for help answering questions like: *Why am I here? What am I supposed to do? Is there life after death? Do I really have a soul? What is my task?* They don't or can't bring themselves to ask God directly for help. So sad...

After my meeting with my Guru, I gently put aside the TM and Buddhist meditation practices of Maharishi Mahesh Yogi and Chögyam Trungpa Rinpoche and spend the next twenty years studying the Self-Realization meditation techniques of Paramahansa Yogananda with a frenzied zeal. My life gets miraculously transformed in so many ways. Daily Kriya Yoga practice and on-going study of Yogananda's teachings expanded upon at SRF Retreats and by reading his many books keep me emotionally stable and spiritually excited about going deeper and deeper on the path home to God.

But the Xiu Lian road is not smooth. There are countless distractions, temptations, and alluring detours that hinder our journey. My soul is elated at having met my Guru and wants to focus exclusively on one day becoming a Disciple of Paramahansa Yogananda. But my ego shouts: "Not so fast!"

I am *OM*, I am *OM*

Paramahansa Yogananda wrote many spiritual books, poems, and chants before his transition back to the soul world on March 7, 1952. Almost all of the poems and chants are heartfelt epistles to the Divine praising God in all of his myriad names, forms, and denominations.

OM—often written as AUM—is an ancient sacred Sanskrit sound and mantra originating from Yogananda's Hindu spiritual tradition. *OM* represents the primal sound and origin of the Universe. The Christian Bible in the book of Genesis makes reference to this primal sound as "the Word".

Hindu texts are derived from the *Vedas*, the oldest known scriptures in the world. The Vedic texts, most notably the Upanishads, which includes the Bhagavad Gita, were first written in Sanskrit after having been orally transmitted from high-level spiritual beings in the form of "sounds" thousands of years ago. These Sanskrit sounds carry sacred frequency and vibration and continue to be used in Hindu and Buddhist rituals and meditation practices today.

When you chant or sing Yogananda's *I am OM, I am OM,* open your heart and soul fully to the Divine and to the cosmos. Feel free to add a verse wherever you'd like calling upon the soul of any special saints you have a connection with. Let yourself meld with the primal sound of creation and all of your spiritual fathers and mothers!

I am *Om*, I am *Om*

I am *Om*, I am *Om*,
Om, *Om*, I am *Om*,
Omnipresent, I am *Om*,
All-blessed, I am *Om*,
Omniscient, I am *Om*!
Om, *Om*, come to me,
Come to me, O come to me;

O my Guru, come to me,
Come to me, O come to me;
O my Jesus, come to me,
Come to me, O come to me,
Swami Shankara, come to me,
Come to me, O come to me;
O my Allah, come to me,
Come to me, O come to me;
O my Moses, come to me,
Come to me, O come to me;
O my Nanak, come to me,
Come to me, O come to me;
O my Krishna, come to me,
Come to me, O come to me;
Om, Om, come to me,
Come to me, O come to me;
O my Father, come to me,
Come to me, O come to me;
I am *Om,* I am *Om,*
Om, Om, Om! Om Tat Sat, Om!

—*Paramahansa Yogananda*

Running With Scissors

"A lot of people enjoy being dead.
But they are not dead, really.
They are just backing away from life.
Reach out! Take a chance! Get hurt even!
But play as well as you can…
Otherwise… you've got nothing to talk about in the locker room."
—Maude, *Harold and Maude*

Harold and Maude Movie Poster - 1971

This chapter will be short.

If you want to hear tales of sin and adventure, you can read my semi-autobiographical novels: *The Ivory Monkeys* and *Kissing Carmen*. Suffice to say, for most of us, what's called "real life" often gets in the way of our Xiu Lian Purification Journey. Only a few spiritual seekers choose to commit to the path of becoming a monk, a priest, or a monastic able to spend 24 hours a day in continuous service to God. Many human beings remain blissfully ignorant of the Divine and never worry at all about their soul journey. Most of us believe there is a God and know in our hearts we should be paying more attention, but—someone has to spend time working to make money to pay the bills. Someone has to do the laundry. Someone has to go grocery shopping. Time for meditation and God-communion sometimes has to wait if the kids need to be picked up at the soccer field before 5 p.m.

Ascetics have it hard. They voluntarily give up a "personal life." The rules of engagement for monastic living pretty much discourage, if not outright exclude, sensory pleasures, the pursuit of money, or owning possessions.

Ascetics have it easy. They don't have to deal with the monumental tasks of managing a career, keeping a spouse happy, raising kids, or finding the money to pay the rent on time each month.

Non-ascetic spiritual seekers are always dealing with a question of balance. How much time should they allocate to God and how much time to family, friends, and careers?

When I was not practicing meditation, studying holy texts, or attending Self-Realization Fellowship retreats with other seekers on the spiritual path, I lived a secular lifestyle. And for approximately 33 years—post-college to retirement—the vast majority of my time was spent fighting in the corporate wars of global capitalism, raising a family, and playing a lot of golf. Truth be told, I was nowhere near ready to commit to the Xiu Lian journey on a full-time basis.

Spiritual progress for me happens slowly but surely while I'm meditating and doing Kriya Yoga practice in Paramahansa Yogananda's Self-Realization Fellowship in my 30s and 40s. You can't rush the spiritual journey. I "bake in the oven" for decades. A work in progress. Profound insights into one's soul journey reveal themselves only when you are ready, and for me, it's taking years and years of practice to yield only a few "Aha!" moments.

Setbacks occur when I'm distracted and find myself taking an occasional extended hiatus from meditation practice. School vacations with the kids to Disney World wandering the entertainment park day and night; repeated trips to Space Mountain and Haunted Mansion tiring everyone out quickly. Meditation passed up for naps on the couch when I'm tired. Traveling around the globe on flights that induce jet lag lasting days. Spending days, nights, and weekends configuring computer systems as part of a global network. Paying strict adherence to business social protocol requiring 10-hour workdays followed by drinks and dinner before crashing at the hotel. Getting up to do it all over again the next morning at 6 a.m. Feeding my competitive fires by playing in lots of golf tournaments on summer weekends once the kids are older. Going to Myrtle Beach, South Carolina once a year with the guys to golf, drink, feed dollar bills to strippers, and pass out in smelly clothes. All activities that some guys consider fun, but those types of activities come at a cost to making spiritual progress on the Xiu Lian Purification Journey.

Finding myself single again after years of marriage, I wonder what to do for companionship. Lost and gun shy, I go almost seven years with only a few dates that end disastrously. My friends call what happens to me next a mid-life crisis on a grand scale.

In my late forties, I meet Tracy, a 23-year-old singer in a rock band. We fall totally and hopelessly in love. Back then, although I was practicing Kriya Yoga meditation daily in Paramahansa Yogananda's Self-Realization Fellowship tradition, I wasn't totally committed to the spiritual path as a full-time vocation. That commitment would come a few years later when I decided to retire. When I met Tracy, I enjoyed an active social life in the bars and clubs of whatever city in the world I was traveling, and I certainly wasn't immune to pursuing the occasional temptations and pleasures of a hedonistic lifestyle when the sun went down.

Tracy lives a decadent lifestyle that comes with the territory of her profession. Over the next 7 years, she records 3 CDs with her band, films a handful of music videos, and gets published interviews in Hustler and Playboy magazines. The chemistry between my girlfriend and me is potent right from the beginning and I eagerly look forward to my monthly combined business trips and hotel trysts in Toronto. Long-distance relationships spent in luxury hotels can be both exotic and exciting. Tracy and I live that lifestyle to the fullest.

Why Tracy is hanging out with me is a mystery. We've got an impossibly strong soul connection that can't be undone as well as some heavy karma to be worked out between us in this life and maybe for a thousand more to come. I fall victim to the perils and pitfalls of hanging out with a rock star more than I would ever have thought possible. Try to juggle weekend trips to Toronto staying up all weekend partying with Tracy before turning 180-degrees back to corporate life in a suit and tie on Monday mornings.

Tracy provides me with inspiration. Inspiration for my first novel. Inspiration for moving from Boston to Toronto. Inspiration for living a lifestyle that will ultimately end in a "crash and burn" scenario if I'm not careful. Meditation practice suffers when you hang out with a pretty girl. My schizophrenic lifestyle leads to many ups and downs in my Xiu Lian practice. The spiritual flame in my heart doesn't expire completely, but it often burns low and is often in need of re-ignition after spending time with Tracy.

Male friends are jealous. Female friends are annoyed. Family members are concerned. When drunk and sitting around discussing our lives, I'm portrayed by some of my buddies as foolishly extreme. Reckless. Immature. Sure to suffer. Heading for a fall.

Running with scissors.

Other friends tell me I'm lucky. Fortunate. Blessed. Encourage me to ride the wave for as long as I can. They counsel me like Maude counsels Harold in the movie from 1971 that if I go down in flames, at least I was in the game, not passively watching from the sideline, afraid of the bad things that can happen in life.

Thirty-three years of secular life and ample doses of non-spiritual activities ultimately resolves itself. As my 55th birthday approaches, my soul re-awakens. Nudges me. Whispers that *now* is probably the time for a change in lifestyle. It's time to consider leaving the corporate world in which I spend my days, nights, and weekends prowling the world of sex, drugs, and rock 'n roll. I meet with the financial advisors at my firm and they inform me I can retire now if I live modestly. They project conservative earnings estimates on my investment accounts that should fund my retirement until the age of 92. Joke around the table that I should plan on dying at that age since my 401k money will likely be exhausted by then.

It's time to jumpstart my Xiu Lian Purification Journey again. Time to retire from the working world completely. Time to prepare to become a Disciple of my Guru. I kick off this stage of the journey with a retirement gift to myself in the form of a trip to Kyoto, Japan. I make the spiritual decision to become a *Forest-Dweller* and go live in the mountains like Lao Tzu.

Winter Coat

It's −10 degrees Celsius on a brutally windy February afternoon in Toronto. My girlfriend is out to a doctor's appointment and we're supposed to hook up later once she returns. She hates going to see the psychiatrist since the waiting room at the clinic is filled with degenerates and addicts just like her struggling mightily to get by day-to-day on Canadian government-supplied Methadone.

When I'm not with her, she gets hit on by guys and girls as soon as she enters the always-crowded waiting room that smells like a cross between a barnyard and a bar. Gets followed to the street by rundown girls wanting to bum a cigarette if they see she's gone downstairs for a smoke. The doctor schedules mandatory weekly appointments to test her urine for heroin. If she's stumbled in her sobriety, she'll have to walk five blocks in the cold to the pharmacy every morning to receive her daily methadone dose. If she's behaving, she'll be able to bring a week's supply home to keep in the refrigerator. If she slips badly, she risks being kicked out of the meth program altogether, which might prove lethal for her.

The door bursts open and she rushes in without her winter coat. She's freezing. Shivering badly.

"Fuck, it's cold!" she yells. Panting. Out of breath. Cheeks blood red. Breathing into her hands. "I need a hot shower right away!" Angrily kicks off her winter boots. Races towards the washroom while peeling off her clothes.

"Baby, where's your coat?" I yell, totally confused at what's going on. Following her trail to the shower.

"I gave it to a woman in the park…then had to run home…it's so fucking freezing!" She throws her stuff on the floor and jumps into a spray of steaming hot water.

"You what?"

"I met this woman in the park on the way home. She didn't have a coat…and she was *mean!* She told me I should give her my coat! She demanded it! At first I told her to fuck off."

"So where is the coat? Did she steal it?" I ask, still not understanding what's happened.

"No. I got to the other side of the park and then ... I don't know why ... I decided to go back and give it to her ... I told her she needed it more than me."

"You just gave this woman your winter jacket?"

She turns off the water. Steps out of the shower. Takes the towel I hand her. Looks at me like she's done nothing extraordinary.

"Yeah ... I think God wanted me to give it to her ... she might die out there in this weather without it." Walks away from me to the bedroom and curls up in a bathrobe under the blankets. Nothing more to discuss. Conversation over.

Charity. Compassion. Christian generosity. Traits I believe are important and that I'm trying to cultivate in myself—or so I want to believe. But I am false. I'm like the rich man in the Bible who makes a show of his generosity for all to see when all he really donates is a miniscule amount of his fortune to the struggling poor. Jesus compares that rich man to the destitute woman who has next to nothing, yet always donates what little money she does have to the church. It's a humbling lesson I've learned today, and the respect I gain for my struggling girlfriend soars into the heavens. For it's she and not me that's demonstrating the Christ-like qualities of charity and compassion.

Forest-Dwelling

"The most common ego identifications have to do with possessions, the work you do, social status and recognition, knowledge and education, physical appearance, special abilities, relationships, person and family history, belief systems, and often also political, nationalistic, racial, religious, and other collective identifications. None of these is you."
—Eckhart Tolle, *The Power of Now*

The Golden Temple, Kyoto, Japan - 2008

Kyoto in autumn. Zen Buddhist temples. Ancient moss-covered gardens. Sculptured trees standing like ageless guardians. Draped in leaves of brilliant orange, red, and gold. Sacred ponds of raked white pebbles flowing around islands of gray and black stones purposefully placed to inspire contemplation. Morning mists hover in tranquil silence above timeless landscapes. Dissolve into wisps of nothingness at the end of morning meditation.

The allure of spending a few weeks in Kyoto—the heart of Japan's spiritual body and home of ancient emperors—is tugging at my soul. Having retired in April after 30 years of corporate life, it's too late to schedule a trip to see the spring cherry blossoms, so I register to join an informal tour group for an excursion at the height of the fall foliage season in November, 2008. Visits to select Zen temples and Shinto shrines will be led by Robert Ketchell, an English gardener who has studied in Kyoto and has the contacts to get us into secret gardens not normally open to the public.

My daily meditation sessions grow in duration and intensity during the months following retirement, a natural result of divorcing from the distractions and stress of managing a full-time career, raising three sons, and pursuing sensual pleasures with a raging, and at times destructive, social life. On the day of my retirement, I receive a call from a company interested in publishing my first novel, *The Ivory Monkeys*, set in historical Japan and modern-day Toronto. The trip to Kyoto will be my first time back to Japan in 15 years and seems an ideal way to spend idle time while waiting for the final book edits.

Huston Smith, my old philosophy professor from MIT and the Castalia seminar in Switzerland, states that the religious traditions of ancient India, which spring from the largely untranslated Vedic texts, help individuals like me answer that most annoying question that arises from time to time for every seeker on the Xiu Lian Purification Journey: *What's Next?*

People like me pursuing carnal delights in our 20's revel in the immediate gratification derived from activities like: *Eating,*

Drinking, Drugs, and Sex. Anything to stimulate the senses and satisfy our primal desires. But at some point, one despairingly comes to the realization that drinking more expensive wine, having sex with more kinky partners, and ingesting more drugs just isn't enough. There's no long-term satisfaction to be gained from the pursuit of temporal pleasures. As Ram Dass put it after he and Timothy Leary tripped through years of psychedelically-fueled days and nights: *"After the party, you always come down."*

And when that happens, you ask yourself: *What's next?*

Well, to some degree, most people seem to move on when they reach this stage of life. After the partying, they begin to pursue *Wealth, Fame and Power*, thinking that's where it's at. Marriage commitments are made in optimistic good faith. Jobs and careers are launched. At the insistence of the alarm clock ringing Monday - Friday at 5:30 a.m., the scruffiness born of morning hangovers gets replaced with the donning of suits, ties, and expensive polished black shoes. In our 30s and 40s, money is made, homes are purchased, golf and tennis clubs are joined. Vacations with time to relax and contemplate become scheduled in advance for 2 weeks a year, no longer spontaneous excursions decided on a whim. Quality time with the kids is limited to when it's our turn to chauffer them to school and sports practices. If we are dedicated, ambitious, and good at what we do, we get promoted and are rewarded with increased responsibility and power. We purchase bigger homes that come with more expenses to be managed with our bigger paychecks. We dabble in the equity markets choosing investments carefully considered for "long-term financial gain". And when this new kind of success comes through for us, our egos relish in the glorious status we've achieved, labeled on business cards proclaiming our "Senior Vice President" title for all to marvel at. But in the back of our mind, we continue to scratch at those almost imperceptibly nagging questions that just won't go away: *Is this enough? What's next?*

Hindu philosophy tells us the next stage of life is one of *Duty* where we try living with more compassion for others, exhibit more concern for the environment, and do what we can to help the less fortunate. We become active in political causes we believe in and support the churches and sanghas we belong to. If we've had success in our prior stages of life, we may feel pangs of guilt over our wealth, our material possessions, the value of our retirement accounts, and decide to become more charitable. We begin to volunteer our time. We mentor those coming along behind us at work. And our egos take great satisfaction in proclaiming how "humble and generous" we have become. To celebrate our humility, we proclaim the saga of our divine metamorphosis to any and all who will listen. Surely this state of being will result in a fast-track ride to ultimate satisfaction and happiness. And when it doesn't, we once again find ourselves asking: *What's Next?*

As Huston Smith says: *"This is the moment India has been waiting for."*

When we've exhausted ourselves in our seemingly endless pursuit of sensory pleasures, material desires, wealth, fame, power, and duty, we at last find ourselves ready to enter the stage of the *Forest-Dweller.* Having fortified our ego with a lifetime of accomplishments in the material world, and having spent years in meditation practice sitting on our cushions fighting the daily spiritual battle of Kurekshetra so splendidly described in the *Bhagavad Gita*, we are finally ready to try letting it all go.

In ancient times, an individual finding himself awakening to this stage of life walked away from family, home, possessions and literally went into the forest in an attempt to attune directly with God in a landscape of solitude and deafening quiet. Religious scriptures are filled with stories of saints and yogis finding rapture with the Divine on lonely mountains and in stark landscapes. Milarepa, St John of the Cross, Siddhartha, Jesus Christ, and Lao Tzu all had moments of divine revelation in solitude away from the world. Modern-day Forest-Dwelling takes on a different shape for seekers in the 21st century. Today, Forest-Dwelling is more about getting "off the grid." About becoming an anonymous swimmer in a technological sea of cell phones, emails, Internet cafes, and social networking that works globally and ceaselessly to keep us connected to our community. Today's Forest-Dwellers find they can live in the middle of a bustling metropolis or retire to a country cottage or Caribbean island. The location seems less important than creating the opportunity to unplug and withdraw.

For me, retirement is the first step on the path to the forest. The journey to Kyoto will kick off the process by forcing me to unplug my cell phone. I modify my voicemail greeting to let everyone know I will be "unreachable" for two weeks. *It's a good start*, I tell myself. In Kyoto, I'll have a chance to get outside. Be still. Connect with my Guru, Paramahansa Yogananda, beyond the quiet of my meditation room in the center of downtown Toronto.

To prep myself spiritually for Kyoto, I attend a 4-day silent retreat in September at a Carmelite monastery overlooking Niagara Falls led by two monastics of the Self-Realization Fellowship. Meditation in a group setting usually leads to stronger, deeper sessions. In group meditation, no one sitting in zazen posture ever wants to be the first one to move, cough, or get up to relieve a cramp in their leg. The vibes of one's fellow seekers support and reinforce the desire and ability to sit absolutely still for extended periods of time. But in the total quiet of the retreat, I begin to experience a growing sense of loneliness and abandonment tinged with despondency and despair. No longer tied to the demands of a hectic work schedule, having cleaned up my home projects list, and with no reason to set the alarm clock, the virtual walls supporting my daily structure of activities are starting to weaken and crumble. I am becoming transparent, unnoticeable, in the world beyond my meditation seat. The realization of how insignificant "I" am in God's manifested creation is a humbling lesson to learn as St. John taught the Carmelites in the mountains of Andalusia in the 1600s. The specter of my death, much closer now that I am no longer "young," begins to hang around the neighborhood of my thoughts increasing my fear and anxiety about *What's Next?*

Driving home past the shores of Lake Ontario, I feel my persona melting away into the nothingness intimated by a Zen Enso circle painting. *Okay, this is perfect,* I try to reassure myself. *I'm scared and my faith is being tested. I guess that means I'm ready to go…*

On the evening before my departure, my middle son Ryan, 23 years old, and his friend Matt decide it will be fun to join me in Japan. Incredibly, it takes only a few hours for the two to get flights, book a shared hotel room, and pack their suitcases. Their youth-based spontaneity is a not so subtle reminder to me that my time spent in meticulous pre-planning and research for the trip was probably excessive, the result of years of being *careful and prudent* in business. There is great appeal in being able to pick up and go at a moment's notice with little regard to the practical demands of our daily lives and I'm excited to have these two young guys join me as travel partners.

17 hours later, we land at Osaka Airport and catch a bus to Kyoto, a truly unique city on Mother Earth. Home to over 1.5 million people, it's a Mecca the Japanese pilgrimage to in order to learn what it is to be Japanese in the historical and cultural sense. Ordinances restrict the height of buildings and forbid the garish display of Times Square-like advertising on large neon signs. The old-world feel of the place is preserved. In the Gion district around the Kamo River, one can wander down side alleys on a moonlit evening and, if lucky, catch a glimpse of one of the few remaining geishas in the world hastening to an appointment. With virtually no homeless, no graffiti, and no illegal drugs, Kyoto is pretty much crime free. It's amazing to me to see hundreds of commuters leave their bicycles unattended and unlocked outside shops and restaurants with no concern for theft. If I tried that in Toronto—the bike-stealing capital of the world—my wheels wouldn't last 15 minutes.

Sprinkled throughout the city are hundreds of temples, shrines, and gardens. The temples are primarily Zen and the shrines Shinto, Japan's pre-Buddhist indigenous religion. Nearly all of the temples and shrines are active monasteries today, home to abbots, monks, and priests who remain largely invisible to tourists like me descending in droves to those sites willing to open their gates to the public for a few days in the spring and fall. The temples are usually hidden away behind high walls running alongside city streets filled with cars, busses, cyclists, and pedestrians. But it is truly magical how quiet the world becomes the instant one passes through a highly ornamental gate at a Shinto shrine or the vermilion Torii gate at a complex of Zen temples. It's as if there exists some mystical force field protecting the tranquility of the holy places. Ideal for Forest-Dwellers or those like me who need some inspiration and encouragement to find a quiet place to work on killing the ego a little more each day.

In my view, temple monastics have made the leap of faith, have renounced their possessions and identities in the world beyond the temple, and have walked willingly into the forest. To reside in a Zen Buddhist temple is to forsake one's focus on the indulgences and attractions of the five senses. Zen Buddhists view that world as maya, illusion, nothing more than a dream that if pursued can never bring the devotee to enlightenment. The temple monastics turn instead to the inner world, practicing sitting meditation in serene open halls overlooking gardens of simple design and stark contrasts. We Westerners pursuing enlightenment have a tendency to view the monks as "further ahead" or "closer to the end game." following a path from *Here* to *There*. We assure ourselves that we too will be ready to renounce the world *later*, once we've cleaned up our current obligations with family, career, saving the planet, etc. The problem is that *later* never comes, it's always *now*. The path is circular with no past or future, only the present. Saints, yogis, and the monastics of the temples seem to grasp this wisdom that eventually crystallizes for all of us if we persist long enough in our spiritual practice.

In the first days exploring Kyoto, Robert, our guide, leads our group of 10 people from different countries and diverse backgrounds through a series of gardens, many of which contain Japanese teahouses hundreds of years old. Despite the grandeur and elegance of the large temple halls and the pristine beauty of the Zen gardens surrounding them, it's the teahouses that I find most enticing and mysterious, an unexpected surprise of the trip. The teahouse ceremony itself is a cultural activity originating in the 15th century. The intricate ceremony is designed to teach Japanese how to be virtuous in life, humility being the most important virtue to a Zen Buddhist. Vaguely familiar with the formal practice of tea-drinking as a part of Japanese historical and modern day culture, I'm anxious to learn more about the protocol surrounding getting to the garden and entering the teahouse itself via the "dewy path" designed to induce humility in the arriving guests.

We find ourselves at Koto-in, a Zen temple established in 1601 by Hosokawa Tadaoki, a great military warrior who fought with Ieyasu Tokugawa in the period I used for the historical setting of my novel, *The Ivory Monkeys*. Tadaoki's military feats caused him great renown but he is also remembered for being the husband of his famous wife Gratia, a devout Catholic and daughter of the traitor Akechi Mitsuhide, leader of an unsuccessful revolt against the government. Tadaoki and Gratia had the Shoko-ken teahouse constructed in a garden adjacent to the temple near a famous stone lantern that marks the graves of the couple.

It is here that our guide Robert educates us in the basics of teahouse protocol. We begin with a slow, measured walk down a long, straight pathway of paved stone designed to keep our backs turned to the outside world and our minds focused on the unseen mysteries lying around a curve in the distance. We then wind our way to a small bench under a thatched-roof shelter that reminds me functionally of the covered benches deployed at bus stops in Toronto providing weather-protected resting spots for passengers. In the Japanese ceremony, it's here that one sits, meditates, and clears the mind for what is to come while waiting to be called to the teahouse proper. Once summoned, we then proceed to the inner gardens, walking single file along a series of asymmetrically placed and uniquely shaped flat stones to a water basin in which rests a bamboo ladle. To stay on the path, one must traverse it with head down, a further step in enhancing our humility. At the water basin, we splash our hands and faces to symbolically purify ourselves in readiness for entering the teahouse itself. The last act of humility we face is to crawl through a small square entryway onto the tatami mats of the interior waiting room. A difficult task for a Westerner six feet tall! But, since providing a full-height doorway to walk through would tend to encourage our glorious egos and counter our desire to be humble, crawling into the teahouse is the best way and, indeed, the only way to go.

Throughout the days of exploration, we find contact with the temple monastics to be as frustrating and elusive as trying to use one's hands to grab a Japanese koi fish swimming in the garden ponds. The monks, seen few and far between during the 9–5 tourist hours, tend to walk and work in areas of the temple grounds that are inaccessible or off-limits to tourists like us. On the rare occasions when I do find myself approaching monks on the same path, they invariably turn away at the first fork in the road, leaving me with the impression they are intentionally avoiding me, not eager to have their silent time interrupted with idle and unnecessary conversation.

While planning the trip in my Toronto condo, I harbored ego-fueled expectations of joining these monastics for early morning sessions at the temples. Surely a novitiate Forest-Dweller like me would be encouraged by friendly monks to sit lotus-style on traditional green zazen cushions for 1–2 hours of meditation in the picturesque setting of an ancient temple. Our minds would be inspired by the simplicity of the raked gravel gardens before us. I was eager to experience such a tantalizing taste of a day in the life of a Buddhist priest.

Well, the invitation was there and not there at the same time, floating before me like a Zen koan whose meaning might or might not ever be realized. Anyone can sit and meditate on the wooden floorboards bordering the gardens, by themselves or in small groups. Indeed, many Japanese do partake of this opportunity. The formal meditation rooms, however, are off-limits and always empty during the periods of the day when the temple halls are open to the public. One needs a special invitation to sit at the rear of a chamber filled with monks in active practice and there doesn't appear to be any way for people like me, newbie Forest-Dwellers, to receive such consideration. And why should there be? I am insignificant and could only be a distraction to other practitioners despite having trained myself to sit motionless for a full hour in half-lotus position. And so, my morning meditation sessions in Japan are confined to the floor of my small hotel room in the center of downtown Kyoto.

Preparing to depart Japan at the end of the journey, I continue to be overcome with the beauty and vibration of this special place. The opportunity to connect with my middle son Ryan for a few weeks and see first-hand his appreciation and wonder at the majesty of the temples and gardens fills me with a warmth further reinforced by comments from the other tour participants both directly and via email after the trip stating "what a wonderful young man" he is and how much they enjoyed his company and his humor.

⚜ ⚜ ⚜

Had the circumstances been different, I might have stayed on in Kyoto a bit longer, or perhaps for a very long time. One could easily become a full-time Forest-Dweller in Kyoto. Indeed, the timeless city is filled with men and women pursuing their individual paths to enlightenment in the quiet setting of the temple gardens, physically close to, but spiritually eons away from the hustle and bustle of modern urban life.

Back home in Toronto, a Japanese bronze-cast temple bell I brought back from the trip rests on a small altar in my meditation room. Not every day, but occasionally, I ring the bell and let my thoughts melt into the tones arising from the resonating gong. My soul is instantly transported back to Kyoto, home of Zen Buddhism. It's a good way for an aspiring Forest-Dweller to start morning meditation. But alas, little do I realize that my Xiu Lian path is about to change direction again, and not in the direction of Zen Buddhism. I will soon be accepted as a Disciple of my Guru, Paramahansa Yogananda. And shortly thereafter, I'll be directed to meet a new spiritual father, Master Sha, who will resolutely inform me and his other students that now is not the time for Forest-Dwelling...

The Laughing Monk

I received some unexpected guidance in Kyoto from *Soen Ozeki*, a "famous" Zen Buddhist priest and spiritual Dragon. My son Ryan and I meet Ozeki outside the rock garden at Daisen-in, a sub-temple of the Daitoku-ji Temple of the Rinzai sect of Zen. In keeping with the Rinzai teaching of *kensho*—seeing one's true nature through the work of daily activity—Ozeki is engaging visitors by selling books at a table next to the entrance booth. He has written a few spiritual guides—unfortunately for me they are all in Japanese—spread out on a table fronted by tourists eager to purchase a signed copy. His personal magnetism is quite strong and my son Ryan and I find ourselves drawn to him as he performs his work. Catching my eye, he holds up a copy of a book sporting a colorful caricature of his face on the cover. Laughing loudly, he proclaims in reasonable English that: *"I am this man. I am very handsome, yes?"* He then advises us that:

> *"We know each day what we have to do and what we have to avoid. And when we try to do what we must, we might fail. We do fail. Again and again we fail. But that is alright. By failing we gain insight. It is better to try and fail than to get everything right the first time. Ha Ha Ha Ha Ha!"*

Ozeki then pulls out a piece of notebook paper scribbled with Japanese characters and numbers. Ceremoniously and lovingly places it onto the table. Motions me and Ryan to come over. Points to each line and starts reading the text. "Oklahoma, 7. California, 55. Ohio, 29."

I'm thinking he's showing me some sort of census, perhaps where he's logged the number of visitors to his temple from each state. Ryan asks him what's the number for Massachusetts, as we are both from Boston. "Massachusetts? Massachusetts? Ah, 12." Then, pointing his finger to a blue mark next to Massachusetts his voice loudly rings out "Obama!" Roaring with laughter, he continues to read from his list of what is in actuality the 2008 US presidential electoral vote count for each of the 50 states. For each state won by the new president, he repeats the "Obama!" mantra for all to hear. The group of Japanese standing before the priest start shouting "Obama!" also while laughing aloud with Ryan and me.

Perhaps there's some spiritual insight to be gained from this meeting, some deep message from the Divine to consider. Perhaps not. St. John of the Cross warns us against praying for "visions, revelations, locutions, and other miraculous communications from God." If God does choose to speak to us, the manner in which he does so should not be the object of discriminative analysis. Rather, the message itself, as felt intuitively by our soul, is where we need to focus. Even more unseemly is the desire to perform miracles in God's name, a sure way to fire up the ego and promote our "holiness" in ways that will lead to a painful humbling process down the road. St. John teaches that miracles and visions do occur, but are enacted in people "unknowing," spiritual people who, through faith, have become empty vessels devoid of ego and are therefore able to be filled fully with God's infinite light.

Soen Ozeki is such a soul as described by St. John. Filled with light, filled with love, and filled with infectious laughter. When we leave his temple, Ryan and I are smiling widely, and I feel just like a little boy.

DISCIPLE

"A guru is a God-knowing person who has been divinely appointed by Him to take the seeker as a disciple and lead him from the darkness of ignorance to the light of wisdom."
—Paramahansa Yogananda

Gurus of the Self-Realization Fellowship

Cancer. Such a frightening word. Terrible connotations. Harbinger of death. Incurable. Radiation. Chemotherapy. Pain. My sister Marilyn is diagnosed with breast cancer at the age of 39. Married with two children on the verge of High School. A born-again Christian who practices her faith studiously, Marilyn seems an unlikely target of such a cruel disease.

A little conservative in her views. When my girlfriend shoots her debut music video with her rock and roll band, I send DVD copies to all my relatives. The video is a bit steamy. Hot and sexy, just this side of pornographic. Marilyn and her husband Bill watch the video once. Bill tells me later that when he went to view it a second time, the file had been "mysteriously" and "accidentally" deleted. Hmm...

The family gets together to offer love and support to Marilyn while she goes through a lengthy and extended series of medical consultations. Cheerful optimism abounds that they've caught the disease early enough to keep it from spreading. Chances for a full recovery are quite good. Everyone puts on a brave face to confront the enemy. Prayers get offered to the Divine each and every day hoping God in his mercy will show a little of that mercy to Marilyn.

Cancer treatments begin in earnest. Work schedules adjusted to accommodate driving my sister to recurring medical appointments. Hair loss as predicted. Marilyn, my other sisters, and female cousins all joke about picking out the wig. The kids trying to cope, not really understanding what or why this is happening to their Mom. The women in the family all socially networking with each other on a daily basis. Sharing and maintaining currency of information and ensuring the doctor-prescribed regimen of pills, diet, rest, radiation and chemo aren't overtaxing Marilyn's ability to cope. The men of the family less vocal. Roosters worrying silently in the background while the hen's bustle about.

Of all the members of my family, Marilyn always laughs hardest at my jokes and lame attempts at humor. She "gets" me. Doesn't necessarily agree with my lifestyle or the choices I make, but all our conversations seem to end up with a chuckle about what life's throwing our way and how we should deal with our shit.

Remission! A wonderful word to hear from doctors. The bad stuff is going away! Shrinking. Another great word. The bad stuff is getting smaller. Prayers have been answered. God is great! We are blessed! The wig is put in the closet when Marilyn's once long brown hair begins to grow out again. Family celebration at an oceanside restaurant. Lobsters, clams, tartar sauce, french fries, and summer drinks consumed with reckless abandon. The jokes seemingly funnier. The laughter louder. A bullet dodged, the family is able to resume "normal" living.

⚜   ⚜   ⚜

In the fall of 2009 in Toronto, my meditation practice is evolving nicely. Kriya Yoga now the fundamental daily technique I use based on instruction from Self-Realization Fellowship (SRF), Paramahansa Yogananda's North American-based organization. Morning practice followed by 1–2 hours study of my Guru's timeless, priceless writings. His treatises on *The Bhagavad Gita* and *The Second Coming of Christ* are the best religious doctrines I've ever read. Endless tears get shed in joy and gratitude while I drink in and absorb the words and wisdom of the Guru.

Deciding to get more active in local SRF activities, I become a regular attendee at the Sunday morning group meeting in Toronto. Here, a quiet energy flows through the room at all times, lovingly confirming the Guru's presence. In all seasons but winter, windows are left open. We accept the tradeoff of occasional sounds from light Sunday morning traffic for a cool breeze that rustles the white linen curtains shifting gracefully beside us in a slow dance. Silent meditation for twenty minutes. The power of the group setting is intense. Much stronger than when I'm practicing by myself in my condo. Readings from the Guru's teachings inspire us to strive for God with all our heart, with all our soul.

Songs sung by the congregation lift us to heaven, connecting and attuning us directly with God. We are willingly swept up in the current of heaven's love connecting and flowing through all of us like a divine river of light.

At long last, I have morphed into at least a *part-time* Forest-Dweller. No daily corporate job to get up for. After moving to a brand-new luxury condo in downtown Toronto, I convert the second bedroom to an Asian-style meditation room to encourage and promote my daily Kriya Yoga practice. 12 feet by 12 feet, the space is perfect for 4 and 1/2 tatami mats. Traditional Japanese homes have rooms measured in 4-foot increments. Full-size tatami mats are 8-feet by 4-feet in length and can be placed in patterns that totally cover the floor. I find a local Japanese guy whose family ships "real" tatami mats to Canada from Nagasaki, Japan. My mats pass successfully through Canadian Customs as "food" items since technically they are made from rice straw.

I maintain a simple altar with two candles on either side of my Japanese temple gong from Kyoto. Walls adorned sparsely, a photo of Guruji surrounded by smaller pictures of the spiritual Dragons of the SRF path:

Sri Krishna: the Hindu deity who became the Guru of Arjuna and guided him to ultimate victory and enlightenment in *The Bhagavad Gita,* a Hindu allegory of the Xiu Lian Purification Journey.

Jesus Christ: the enlightened Son of God who sacrificed his mortal body on behalf of all humanity.

Mahavatar Babaji: an Immortal light being alive today in a human body. Serving humanity from a non-accessible, secret location in the Himalayan Mountains. Babaji is the Guru of Lahiri Mahasaya.

Lahiri Mahasaya: Disciple of Mahavatar Babaji who revived the practice of Kriya Yoga as a means of attaining union with God. Lahiri Mahasaya is the Guru of Swami Sri Yukteswar.

Swami Sri Yukteswar: Disciple of Lahiri Mahasaya and Guru of Paramahansa Yogananda. Author of *The Holy Science* in which he explains the recurring 24,000-year cycles of the Yugas during which the collective state of human consciousness rises and falls in its awareness of God.

Here, in my private temple, I meditate in sacred space. My spiritual sanctuary exists in the middle of one of the liveliest, active, and most diverse metropolises in North America. But, like the Zen temples of Kyoto, there is a perpetual, quiet tranquility in this room due to the aura of my Guru and the other light beings with whom I connect daily. When sitting silently, the metropolitan sounds of the city are an eternity away.

Having practiced Kriya Yoga now for many years, I complete the SRF training courses and apply to become a Disciple of my loving Guru. My heart thirsts for God more and more each day. My soul longs for release from the struggles I've brought on myself with the choices I've made in this life and all my past lifetimes. The process of purification on the Xiu Lian path is endless, and when not practicing meditation, I have to be wary that my social life with my girlfriend does not derail my progress. As the Guru teaches: "*Keep trying. When you fail, try again.*"

Paramahansa Yogananda describes the battle of Kurekshetra as told in the Bhagavad Gita as a metaphor for the spiritual journey. I find my personal battle of Kurekshetra repeating daily, over and over again. *Am I truly ready to become a Disciple of my Guru? Am I really ready to dedicate my life to God? Should I wait another year or two? I've already sent in the paperwork, when will SRF answer me?*

I receive the letter from Self-Realization Fellowship and open it with shaking hands. Acceptance. What a joy! I will become a Disciple of Paramahansa Yogananda! My soul will be wed eternally to the soul of the Guru. I am elated!

The Christian mystic Saint John of the Cross called the moment one's soul unites with the Divine *The Dark Night of the Soul*. Saint John describes his spiritual union with Jesus Christ so beautifully in a lyrical poem that can be read on so many levels: a lover meeting a lover, a soul meeting the soul of a loved one, a soul uniting in ecstasy with the Divine, the Tao, the Source.

For Saint John, I believe his spiritual union with Jesus was a culmination of many lifetimes of endless purification, testing, and offering unconditional universal service to all souls in all universes. When I first read St. John's lengthy discourse titled *The Dark Night of the Soul*—the same title as his poem—I didn't get what he was trying to say at all. The text consisted of hundreds of pages of intricate, complex Christian mysticism I wasn't ready for. Saint John's philosophical constructs were way over my head. Finally, I put the larger text aside and read the verses of *The Dark Night of the Soul* as just a love poem and found it really touched my heart. All of a sudden, I didn't need to comprehend the textbook discussion about ascending Mt. Carmel, Saint John's literary analogy of the Xiu Lian path home to God. The essence of the teachings had been distilled for me in the poem.

The mind reads books, but the heart reads poetry. Years later I heard *Dark Night of the Soul* set to music by Loreena McKennitt, the Canadian singer/artist and I cried. When such poetry is put to music, the words come alive and our hearts can be awakened and opened wide.

Dark Night of the Soul

Upon a darkened night
The flame of love was burning in my breast
And by a lantern bright
I fled my house while all in quiet rest

Shrouded by the night
And by the secret stair I quickly fled
The veil concealed my eyes

While all within lay quiet as the dead

Oh night thou was my guide
Oh night more loving than the rising sun
Oh night that joined the lover
To the beloved one
Transforming each of them into the other

Upon that misty night
In secrecy, beyond such mortal sight
Without a guide or light
Than that which burned so deeply in my heart
That fire t'was led me on
And shone more bright than of the midday sun
To where he waited still
It was a place where no one else could come

Within my pounding heart
Which kept itself entirely for him
He fell into his sleep
Beneath the cedars all my love I gave
From o'er the fortress walls
The wind would his hair against his brow
And with its smoothest hand
Caressed my every sense it would allow

I lost myself to him
And laid my face upon my lover's breast
And care and grief grew dim
As in the morning's mist became the light
There they dimmed amongst the lilies fair
There they dimmed amongst the lilies fair
There they dimmed amongst the lilies fair
—Loreena McKennitt

The sacred ceremony to become a Disciple of Paramahansa Yogananda gets scheduled for November in New York City. I'll be joined by approximately 20 other North American students. Plane and hotel reservations made. My biggest concern becomes what and how to bring an appropriate offering to the Guru for such a priceless event. Life cannot be better. Tears of gratitude flow daily during my practice. I am extremely blessed!

❈　❈　❈

Setback. Recurrence. My sister Marilyn has her monthly follow-up appointment with the Doctor and he suspects her cancer has returned. Thought to have been stopped, the cancer cells are growing again. Spreading. The disease now infecting Marilyn's liver. More chemo treatments and operations to cut out the offend-ing out-of-control cells. The brown wig hibernating in the closet pulled out for a second round of usage. Outward discussion of a positive outcome amongst family and friends. Demons of suspi-cion and reluctant acceptance of what is inevitable lurking under the surface.

Final planning. Consultation with the specialists who indicate it's time to consider moving Marilyn from the ICU ward to a hos-pice setting. A facility is chosen close to Marilyn's home. Beautiful grounds. Beautiful large, expansive rooms. Beautiful compassion-ate human beings in 24-hour attendance to any of my sister's wants or needs in her final days.

Marilyn sits up in bed. Smiles. Surrounded by family and fre-quent visitors from her church. Laughing at stories of the "old days" with high-school friends arriving for a final visit. Lots of sleep, during which family members patrol the halls like senti-nels on watch for the spectre of Death. We wander along outdoor garden paths alone or in pairs. Questioning God, demanding answers. *Why? Why Now? Why Marilyn? Why not me?*

Practical discussions with brother-in-law Bill about money, insurance, my sister's will, her intentions for the kids, location of a burial plot. Conversations necessary to divert attention from Death's impending arrival. Conversations necessary to divert our focus away from my sister's soul readying itself to leave.

Mom and Dad live in Florida, both in their early eighties. Mom determined to make the flight north for a final goodbye. Dad too frail physically and emotionally to handle a personal visit. I meet Mom at the airport and am so incredibly impressed with her strength to make this journey.

Endless tears when cousin Terry whispers to Marilyn that it's okay to let go—and she does. I make the phone call to my father waiting in Florida. We get through the short conversation as best as two men can. Not the right time for extended conversation; simply an acknowledgement that the pain and suffering has passed for his daughter, my sister.

⚜   ⚜   ⚜

The formal SRF ceremony of the union of guru and disciple is scheduled for the same day as Marilyn's funeral. A bit of a dilemma for me, unable to be in two places at the same time. Best to check with one's soul when these occasions arise. I do, and it's a no-brainer. Marilyn's soul is perfectly fine with me attending the SRF ceremony in New York City and not attending her funeral in Boston.

Funeral services are for the living and provide a setting for final closure for those left behind. The actual burial or cremation process is structured to take care of a discarded body, an empty husk that temporarily housed an eternal soul. I'm okay with missing my sister's funeral service and burial, as I know Marilyn is in a good place now and, if she could tell me in person, she wouldn't hesitate to advise me not to miss the SRF ceremony.

In the coming years as my Xiu Lian Journey continues, I often call Marilyn's soul to "come visit" if I find I'm in a spiritual place like a temple or cathedral that I know my sister would like. We are still able to laugh together at the soul level and I don't foresee us ever losing our mutual, weird sense of humor with each other on our overlapping journeys through *No Time, No Space*.

I manage to get a reservation on short notice at a hotel near the SRF meeting hall in New York where the guru/disciple wedding ceremony will take place on Friday evening. I'm extremely fortunate to find a perfectly round, perfectly unblemished orange at a local food mart in downtown Manhattan in the middle of November. This orange will be my offering to the Guru. The fruit will be the "wedding ring" of our spiritual marriage.

The hall is packed with people. About 20 of us are here today to become Disciples. Some students have invited friends and relatives to witness the ceremony and share in the joy of our Divine Wedding. I sit in the front row with the other novitiates and absorb the vibrations of love and sacredness all around us. Wedding nuptials tie the souls of two humans together for life in the eyes of God. The guru/disciple "wedding" ties the soul of the devout spiritual seeker to their spiritual Master for the remainder of their spiritual journey. On our *Dark Night of the Soul*, we will join with our beloved guru for all eternity. My eternally grateful soul has waited for this union for a very long time...

⚜ ⚜ ⚜

I like the spiritual metaphor of *Ice to Ocean* to describe the Xiu Lian Purification Journey home to the Divine, the Tao, the Source. A human soul wrapped up in a cocoon of karmic debt is like a fragment of ice clinging stubbornly high up on a mountaintop glacier. The glacier represents the Buddhist concept of *maya*: an illusory perception of the world, of reality, that's constructed and fed by our egos and desires. How strongly we cling to maya—Master Sha calls it the "bitter sea"—is based on our past negative karma. The more negative karma we have to work out—caused by our own past mistakes or those we "inherited" from our ancestors—the tighter we are bound to the world of maya. Our souls get frustrated since we have to serve and forgive others unconditionally lifetime after lifetime in order to pay off our karmic debt, all the while being careful to minimize the creation of any new negative karma. When all of our karmic debt is at long last cleared, we free ourselves from the endless cycle of rebirth.

Another way we can accelerate our Xiu Lian Purification Journey to Tao is to find a guru, or spiritual Master. The guru is like a pure mountain stream flowing below the glacier, ever ready to catch us if we would just let go of our egos and let ourselves fall willingly into the current of our guru's love. The stream flows unceasingly, and ultimately unites with the Ocean, which represents the Divine, the Tao, the Source. When we unite with our guru, our egos slowly dissolve as we become one with our teacher, like a chunk of cold ice melting in a warm stream.

For most of us, our soul—the chunk of ice—is going to find it difficult to transform, to let go of the glacier—the illusory world—without a little assistance. Help comes in the form of God's love when we devoutly ask the Divine for a guru to help release us from our karmic bonds and guide us home. When we are ready and when we are sincere in our supplications, God sends his love to us in the form of a spiritual blessing. The blessing acts like the Sun rising on a cold winter morning, warming and loosening the molecules of ice keeping us attached to the glacier of maya.

If we meditate long enough and with enough devotion, when our intentions with God are pure, when we open our hearts and souls fully to him, our connections to the world start to melt away. It's scary because we are high up on the glacier built by our karma and our egos are afraid of letting go. We have to demonstrate *total faith* in the Divine to deliver us safely. God protects us from smashing on the rocks below by guiding our fall into the stream of the guru's love. There we bounce along, a piece of ice floating on top of the water, flowing in one direction only, towards the Divine, the Tao, the Source.

The guru's love is eternal, relentless, and boundless. And over time, like warm water continuously surging over jagged ice, all our rough edges get smoothed. The process might take a while—but each moment we connect with our guru, we become less a separate piece of ice riding the current of the stream and more a part of the stream itself. And when we have fully "warmed up" to and fully accepted the guru's love, the last molecules of ice dissolve and we become truly one with and truly indistinguishable from our Master.

Our soul instinctively knows the path of glacier ice to stream to ocean is a return journey to the infinite Source from which we originated. As the stream nears its final destination, there is no way to slow us down or prevent our homecoming. Our return to Tao is inevitable. And when we at long last arrive at the delta where the stream pours into the ocean, where Guru and Divine meld together, our egos fully dissolved, our karma cleared through self-less acts of service to all souls in all universes, this stage of our Xiu Lian Purification Journey will be complete and the endless cycle of reincarnation will cease.

Sitting in Paramahansa Yogananda's Self-Realization Fellowship Temple in New York City on the evening of my initiation as a Disciple, I'm reflecting on just how far I've traveled on my Xiu Lian Purification Journey. After years of searching, my Guru found me and showed me my path. Yogananda's teachings and my Kriya Yoga meditation practice over the last 25 years have greatly accelerated my spiritual journey and prepared me lovingly for this day. My love of God increases with each period of medita-tion. On a daily basis, my ego detaches more and more from the glacier of illusory existence. I'm letting go and free-falling towards the receptive stream of the Guru's love, which is already embrac-ing me. And although my purification process is not complete— my ego is not fully dissolved—there's still an "I" that's separate and distinct from the Guru—I know I will eventually melt. It's inevitable. I will become the Guru and the Guru will become me. Together we will flow as one back into the ocean of the Divine, the Tao, the Source.

Initiation vows. Divine Marriage. Disciple. The SRF ceremony in New York City is miraculous. The spiritual presence of my Guru Paramahansa Yogananda fills the space in the meeting hall with a loving frequency and vibration that—for the duration of the ceremony and a few days afterwards—lifts the souls of all present to the realm of Heaven. Tears stream endlessly. Hearts open to an expansiveness never before experienced. Bliss is boundless. Happiness is endless. Today is the most significant day of my life so far in this incarnation on Mother Earth. I am home. I am ready to serve others in the tradition of my loving Guru. I will meditate, perform Kriya Yoga daily, and serve all sentient beings to the best of my ability.

Jai Guru, Jai Guru, Jai Guru Jai
Jai Guru, Jai Guru, Jai Guru Jai
Jai Guru, Jai Guru, Jai Guru Jai

Practice to Build the Jin Dan

A Jin Dan is a sacred, divine treasure that can heal all sicknesses in your physical, emotional, mental, and spiritual bodies. The Jin Dan is a golden light ball that sits in your lower abdomen. Master Sha teaches: "In history, this treasure has been delivered only to a very limited number of lineage holders."

No one is born with a Jin Dan. But anyone can start to build a Jin Dan by chanting this special mantra:

Tian Di Ren He Yi

which means "Heaven, Mother Earth, and human being join as one." After your Jin Dan starts to form, energy may start to flow freely in all parts of your body removing soul, mind, and body blockages and allowing you to heal, prevent sickness, rejuvenate, prolong your life, and transform every aspect of your life including relationships and finances.

Building a Jin Dan to the size of your fist can take many years of dedicated practice. If you are able to build your Jin Dan to the size of your whole body, you have reached the immortality state which is a key area of focus for Taoist practitioners.

Master Sha once visited a very spiritually advanced Taoist priest living in the Wudang Mountains of China. After spiritually assessing Master Sha's Jin Dan, the priest commented that Master Sha's Jin Dan was so advanced that he could offer Master Sha no new teaching or advice.

Build your Jin Dan by focusing on the lower abdomen, visualizing light, and chanting *"Tian Di Ren He Yi"* repeatedly for at least 10 minutes per day. The longer you chant, the quicker you can build your Jin Dan and start receiving the benefits of this priceless treasure.

Strategic Planning

"Everything else can wait. But your search for God cannot wait."
—Paramahansa Yogananda

Swami Sri Yukteswar and Guru Paramahansa Yogananda

In the weeks following my initiation as a Disciple of Paramahansa Yogananda, my body is saturated with incredible calmness. After lifetimes of searching, I have at long last found my Master. All my questions have been answered. I understand fully the purpose of my spiritual journey. I'm floating downstream in the arms of my Guru on the river of my soul's emancipation. The roadmap to the ultimate treasure has been revealed to me: the Guru teaches that if one practices Kriya Yoga diligently, enlightenment and freedom from reincarnation is possible in one lifetime.

I'm proud of myself for fulfilling all the pre-requisites for spiritual success. My ego whispers:

You're all set now! Everything's under control. You have everything you want, including your Guru. You've reached a key milestone on the journey. Just stay true to the Guru, true to the teachings, do your daily practices, and you can decide what you want to do next.

Yeah, right. What I don't grasp is that I've fallen into a spiritual trap. I've made the age-old mistake of thinking *I* am the one guiding my Xiu Lian Purification Journey and that *I* know as much as the Guru or the Divine about what should happen next. My stubborn ego won't completely let go and surrender to God. The truth is I'm nowhere close to being an *unconditional* servant of the Divine. The battle of Kurekshetra continues to rage within me daily. My ego admonishes me: *It's time to get practical, to get busy. No rest for the weary. Time to plot out the next phase of your Xiu Lian Purification Journey.*

Strategic Planning. A concept from the business world I'm intimately familiar with having worked as Vice President of New Business Development for multiple businesses in a highly profitable global corporation. Successful enterprises create Strategic Plans annually with the direct involvement and participation of the senior business team. Strategic Plans are kind of fun to work on. They are not as long or complex as the Business and Financial

Plans that get created later in the process to describe in detail the what, when, and how the company's objectives will be accomplished. When you're appointed to the Strategic Planning Committee, you get to define key business objectives for the coming year at a high level. These goals and objectives are written up in what's called an "Executive Summary" document. Generally speaking, successful achievement of the business's high-level objectives will lead to the firm's growth by increasing profits and market share while managing investments and expenses better than the competition.

By taking the time to create well thought out Strategic Plans, you put a stake in the ground for all your employees and business partners to rally around. You create a common set of high-level goals and objectives that everyone can buy into and focus their energy and resources towards accomplishing as a united team. And when the team works together in harmony with each other at all levels of the organization, success inevitably follows.

As a new Disciple of Paramahansa Yogananda practicing Kriya Yoga daily in my Toronto condo, my ego prompts the question: *What are we going to do now? What's next on our spiritual journey?* As the 2009 Christmas holidays approach, I take the time to do a little strategic planning of my own life for the upcoming year.

My soul keeps nudging me to seriously consider becoming a full-time Forest-Dweller. To cut all ties with family, friends, lovers, and society in general. To "go to the mountain" like Lao Tzu, Milarepa, Jesus, and so many other spiritual Dragons did when they needed to purify themselves further on their own Xiu Lian Purification Journeys. Self-Realization Fellowship has a formal monastic program that's part of the Swami Order of India. For Disciples like me, ready to exit society and commit totally to a spiritual lifestyle of renunciation and service, this option is highly appealing.

My life up to now has been blessed in so many ways. In this incarnation, I was lucky enough to be born in the United States and grow up in prosperous economic times. I've been relatively healthy in this life, experienced exceptional business and financial success, and am debt-free. I've experienced many loving relationships with women, my family, and my children. I've even won multiple golf tournaments—including two club championships—that boosted my male ego tremendously for years when hanging out with the guys. I have no desire or need to accomplish *more* in the material world. I don't need *more* money. I don't need *more* victories in business or sports, and—although I love dating—I'm not looking to find a permanent partner and get married again.

I decide to take a few months—there's no rush on the Xiu Lian Purification Journey—and give serious thought to becoming an ordained monk in Paramahansa Yogananda's two global organizations: the Self-Realization Fellowship in North America and the Fellowship/Yogoda Satsanga Society in India and Nepal. Deciding it will be cool to spend six months of each year in the US and six months in India, I envision myself wearing the orange robes of a monastic. Confident I'll be viewed by others as a humble servant. Not seeking recognition or spiritual power, I'll be content to step back from the limelight and remain silent for the majority of time. In my *What's Next* fantasy, I become a handyman maintaining the ashrams, meditation gardens, and temples wherever I'm needed for the remainder of my lifetime of spiritual practice behind the walls of a monastery. Practicing celibacy might be a tall order in the beginning but I'm certainly not the first monk who has struggled with that challenge and am pretty sure I can make that vow.

The first step is to do some basic research on the SRF website about monastic life. If I'm going to become a monk living in ashrams around the world, I better have some idea of just what I'm getting myself into. The SRF website (www.selfrealizationfellowship.org) offers very clear guidance and descriptions of the Monastic Order:

"Yogananda's Self-Realization Fellowship's Monastic Order embraces a fourfold vow of renunciation: Simplicity, Celibacy,

Obedience, and Loyalty. Monastics take vows of poverty (nonattachment to possessions), chastity, and obedience to the head or spiritual authority. There are four stages of monastic life in the Self-Realization Fellowship monastic order, representing a gradual deepening of one's commitment to the renunciant life and the monastic vows. These stages are not of any fixed length. Rather the spiritual growth of each monk or nun, and the readiness of that renunciant to dedicate himself or herself more fully to this life, are always considered on an individual basis."

Okay—I think I can handle the vows. And I like the idea that the four stages of SRF monastic life don't have set timeframes in which you have to pass some sort of test to be deemed ready to go to the next level or be forced to reset the clock and start all over. My biggest challenge will be figuring out how to tell my long-term girlfriend that my love for God is deeper than my love for her and that I'm considering leaving her to become a celibate monk. Hmm...

I read further about the four stages to become an SRF Monastic:

1. *Postulancy*
   "The first stage, or postulancy, usually lasts for two years. Postulants follow a monastic routine that includes group and individual meditation, spiritual study and instruction, and service in whatever areas are assigned to them. The postulant program is designed to give the renunciant a fuller understanding of the monastic ideals and way of life. Its emphasis is on helping the postulant to develop the attitudes and habits that will assist that renunciant in deepening his or her spiritual life and attunement with God and the Guru. This first stage of monastic life helps the renunciant to gauge the depth of his or her desire to embrace the path of renunciation, and at the same time allows those responsible for the renunciant's spiritual welfare to guide him or her to an ever deepening understanding of the monastic life.

2. *Novitiate*

   At the end of the postulant stage, if both the postulant and counselors remain convinced that he or she is well suited to ashram life, the postulant will be invited to take the Novitiate Vow. With this vow, renunciants pledge in a more formal way to live by the fourfold monastic vow of the Self-Realization Monastic Order. During the novitiate period, the novice is expected to demonstrate a growing understanding of monastic discipleship by his or her application of the principles learned at the postulant stage.

3. *Brahmacharya*

   If after several years the novice has demonstrated an increasing desire and ability to dedicate his life wholly to seeking and serving God as a monastic of the Order, he or she is invited to take the vow of brahmacharya. (Brahmacharya is a Sanskrit word referring to the discipline and self-control of one's thoughts and actions for the purpose of achieving union of the self with Spirit.) This vow signifies the disciple's deepening intention to remain a monastic in the Order, living by the vows of simplicity, celibacy, obedience, and loyalty to the end of life.

   After taking this vow, monks are referred to as a brahmachari and nuns as a brahmacharini. Use of the family name is dropped and within the ashram the monastic is addressed by title and first name—for example, "Brahmachari John" or "Brahmacharini Mary." A brahmachari or brahmacharini understands that he or she may be asked to assume greater responsibility in the ashram—perhaps training as a temple service leader, taking on special assignments, or serving in other capacities as directed by those responsible for guiding the monastic spiritually.

4. *Sannyas*

   The final vow of sannyas represents the renunciant's total, lifetime commitment to God, Guru, the Paramgurus, and Self-Realization Fellowship; and to the SRF monastic vows and ideals, which he or she pledges to observe faithfully as a monk or nun of the

Self-Realization Monastic Order. It signifies the monastic's inner determination of soul to set aside all lesser desires in order to live for God alone, and with unconditional dedication and loyalty to serve Him through the path of Self-Realization Fellowship. The sannyas vow is taken only after many years of living the monastic life, and after the brahmacharis or brahmacharinis have proved to themselves and their superiors in the Order that they are ready to make this final commitment. The vow corresponds to that taken by members of the ancient Swami Order in India. When the monk or nun becomes a sannyasi or sannyasini, he or she is given a monastic name of Sanskrit origin, signifying a particular spiritual ideal or quality to exemplify or attain. Monks who have taken this vow are addressed as "Brother" (or, in India, "Swami"). Nuns are addressed as "Sister" (or in India, "Mai").

With the complete dedication of one's life and being to the Divine, the sannyasi strives ever more diligently for perfection of character, of service, and, above all, of love for God. He or she assumes a sacred responsibility to exemplify the high ideals of Paramahansa Yogananda's teachings and society; and, through that example, to inspire and encourage others in their divine quest.

I love the roadmap of the SRF path from:

Disciple > Postulant > Novitiate > Brahmacharya > Sannyas

My soul resonates completely with the objectives of SRF monastic life. I must have been a monk or nun before in many past lifetimes. So eager to return to that lifestyle, I'm smart enough to know that submitting my application to become a full-time monastic is not a decision to be made lightly. The implications of such a choice will have to simmer in my head for at least a few months. Just because I'm so excited about this opportunity today doesn't mean I'll feel the same level of enthusiasm tomorrow or next week. Continuing to practice Kriya Yoga daily, I consciously and subconsciously align my thinking with the goal of becoming an SRF monk. Everything feels right. I'm all set...or so I think. I print out the application and formally apply to become a monk in the SRF Monastic Order. I've done my strategic planning and have laid out my course of action.

But sometimes God has to not-so-gently remind us that *we* are not the ones in charge of *What's Next*. My strategic plan is about to get blown up and I'm about to get physically assaulted...

Practice for Developing Mind Power

An often-debated premise of modern Western science is that we human beings use only a small percentage of our brain cells during normal daily life. The human brain is divided into two hemispheres. Our left hemisphere is associated primarily with logic and reason. The right hemisphere is the creative, artistic side of the brain. Both hemispheres of our brain are connected by a bundle of neural fibers called the corpus callosum. The primary purpose of the corpus callosum is to transfer messages between our brain's right and left hemispheres.

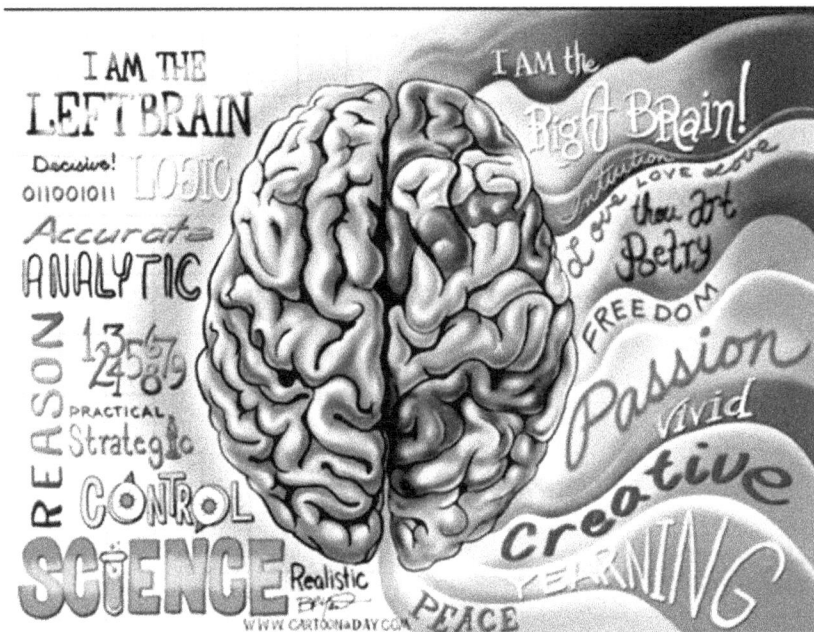

Dr. Zhi Chen Guo, Master Sha's spiritual father from China, discovered three sacred codes that, when chanted in sequence, vibrate the cells in the left-brain, right-brain, and corpus callosum. Stimulation of these cells can lead to the opening of your Third Eye spiritual channel as well as developing the potential power of the mind and increasing your intelligence.

Here's a practice from Master Sha's *Soul Mind Body Medicine* book to develop the power of your brain:

"Start in a sitting position, in a chair or on the floor. Form a little 'O' with your hands and fingers, with the tips of your thumbs almost touching and with the fingers of your right hand resting on the fingers of your left hand. Chant the first code, the number sequence 01777, ling yao chi chi chi in Chinese (pronounced "ling yow chee chee chee"). 01777 is the secret code to stimulate the cells in the corpus callosum, the tissues between the left and right brain that transport messages between the two.

Then chant the second code, the number sequence 908, jiu ling ba (pronounced "joe ling bah"), which stimulates the cells in the left brain.

Now chant the third code, 92244, jiu ar ar si si (pronounced "joe ar ar sih sih"), which stimulates cells in the right brain.

I recommend that you stimulate all the cells in your brain, left, right, and corpus callosum, by chanting all three codes in the following sequence: 01777-908, 01777-92244, 01777-908, 01777-9244. Chant as fast as you can, as much as you can. It will sound like this:

Ling yow chee chee chee – joe ling bah

Ling yow chee chee chee – joe ar ar sih sih

Ling yow chee chee chee – joe ling bah

Ling yow chee chee chee – joe ar ar sih sih."

This is a fun practice to do alone or in a group setting. Once you get the sequence of codes down, remember to chant as fast as you can. You'll be able to feel the energy flowing back and forth between the two hemispheres of your brain!

A PUNCH TO THE BELLY

"When the student is ready, the teacher appears."
                                        —Ancient Chinese proverb

February, 2010. My meditation room in Toronto, Canada. Readying myself for morning Kriya Yoga practice. I've been a Disciple of my Guru, Paramahansa Yogananda, for three months now. Still affected by and in daily soul contact with my late sister Marilyn. Deep into writing my second novel, *Kissing Carmen*, a trashy romance about a single night I spent with a woman in Madrid, Spain back in my corporate working days. Thinking maybe I'll make more money from this steamy tale of lust than my first action/adventure novel, *The Ivory Monkeys,* because the "romance" novel genre is pretty popular right now.

Canadian winters seem more bearable when it's snowing. The snow helps us forget just how cold it is outside. In downtown Toronto, we never seem to get a lot of accumulation. For some meteorologically ordained reason, moisture flowing east across Canada always races over the city in a great hurry to get to Lake Ontario where a disproportionate share of the white stuff gets unfairly dumped on Buffalo, NY. Today, Torontonians are unexpectedly graced with snow. Large delicate flakes drift slowly down from heaven. Cover the dirt and grime of the inner city. Cleanse the air of impurities. Begin to pile up on balcony railings. Gather in swirling drifts around the base of my sliding-glass doors. The cars in the parking lot below sit in imminent danger of being buried alive under white crystals if not swept clean soon by their owners. I turn the heat up a little in the condo, not because it's cold but because it seems the prudent thing to do during a winter storm. Survival instincts kick in, brought on by the weather: *Is there enough food in the fridge? What if the storm gets really bad and I can't get to a store? Is there gas in the truck? The phone charged? What if we lose power?*

Ok, forget the storm. Time to sit. I begin my Kriya practice. The only mind-generated distraction to meditation that arises is the occasional desire to open my eyes and visually enjoy the rare blessing of falling city-snow. *It's all just an illusion,* I silently remind myself. *Part of the world of maya. It's going to snow all day. You can check it all out after you've finished your Kriya practice.*

Suddenly and without warning, I'm struck by what feels like a punch to my belly. Someone or something has assaulted me in the lower abdomen, right below my navel. I open my eyes expecting to see my girlfriend in front of me. Maybe she's angry at some offense

I've committed and decided to attack. But there's no one around. The punch feels just like a physical blow. I haven't imagined this. And, after I've been hit, I can feel something has been left behind in my gut. My Third Eye shows me it's round…a sphere of some type. About the size of a tennis ball. Yellow-gold in color. Just sitting and rotating around in my belly. *What happened? What is this?* I look down to validate the assault, to find tangible evidence of what's just happened. The ball seems to have mass, but no weight. It's moving around slightly as if trying to find exactly the right spot to settle in my abdomen.

Alone in my sacred space, the snow continues to fall outside. I shift my shoulders back and forth. Place my hand on my mid-section to feel whatever has come inside me, to touch it. I look to the wall-mounted photograph of my Guru. Yogananda is smiling knowingly at me, but if the Guru knows anything, he's not about to give up any information or reveal any spiritual secrets this morning.

Now, more curious than shocked, I lift my shirt and visually examine my stomach. Half-expecting to see a red mark or bruise where the punch occurred. But there's nothing there. Very strange. *Okay, let's get back to meditating. I'll think about this ball thing later.*

I finish my session, do some SRF energization exercises, then slide out to the kitchen to put on the coffee. The snowfall is heavier now. Ten stories below my condo, the streets have emptied of vehicles with the exception of Toronto's streetcars which aren't going to let what will amount to "only" a foot of snow slow them down. I forget all about the yellow ball and for the rest of the morning, I enjoy the snow swirling outside from the cozy confines of my living room couch.

Early afternoon. Checking the Internet to see if I still have connectivity at the height of the blizzard. An email from Robert Liu, an ex-employee from my corporate days, catches my attention.

⚜   ⚜   ⚜

I made a special business trip to Toronto in 2002 to interview Robert and three other IT guys who had a lot of expertise writing software to operate really fast printers used in large corporations. My boss at Fidelity Investments wanted to develop code that would maximize our company's flexibility to print high volumes of documents—like the millions of monthly customer statements we produced each month—using any printer vendor's hardware. We formed a company—OPServer, Inc.—under the corporate umbrella of Fidelity, then hired Robert and the three other engineers to supplement a team of 14 software developers that worked for me in Dallas, Texas. I acquired some space near the Eaton Centre in downtown Toronto for the guys to work in, and set up an office for me to use when visiting my Canadian team for one or two weeks each month.

When we decided to sell OPServer a few years later, Robert figured out it would be an auspicious time for him to retire and focus on other pursuits. On his last day of work, Robert came to my office for his "exit interview". I asked him how he intended to spend his "golden" years. How surprised I was when Robert told me he was "spiritual". As far as I could remember, the topic of God had never come up before in the three years of our working relationship. He told me he intended to become a full-time student of someone called Master Sha, a Chinese spiritual Master and Soul Healer he'd been studying with for a few years while still making an income in the corporate world. I replied to Robert that I was "spiritual" as well and was studying to become a monastic in Paramahansa Yogananda's SRF organization. He was as surprised at my declaration of spirituality as I was of his.

"Have you heard of Master Sha?" he asked me.

"No."

"Don't worry. You will!" Robert said those words so emphatically that they stuck with me, and I would not soon forget them.

When I asked Robert to elaborate, he explained that Master Sha is a medical doctor trained in Western medicine in China as well as a doctor of Traditional Chinese Medicine (TCM) and Acupuncture. Master Sha came to Canada from the Philippines around 1990. Robert told me this Chinese doctor is also a world-renowned Master in many Asian disciplines such as Tai Chi, Qi Gong, Kung Fu, Feng Shui, and the I Ching. All of this info seemed interesting enough, but I wasn't sure why Robert was telling me about Master Sha. What was his point?

Robert further explained that a number of years ago, the Divine spoke to Master Sha and that soon after his conversation with God, Master Sha started writing books and teaching people how to heal themselves and others using the power of soul. The underlying premise of Master Sha's Soul Power teachings is:

"Heal the soul first, then healing of the mind and body will follow."

At the same time I was practicing Kriya Yoga to advance my soul journey, Robert was teaching soul healing to spiritual seekers and people looking for new and alternative ways to heal themselves of physical, emotional, financial, and relationship challenges brought on as a result of negative karma.

The concept of being able to self-heal our negative karma was very appealing to me. The premise of soul healing made sense. Paramahansa Yogananda talked about the effects of hauling around our bad karma as a key component of the SRF teachings:

"Your failure or sickness or other troubles started with unwise actions in past lives, and the effects of those causes have been brewing within, waiting for the right time to bubble over. Disease, health; failure, success; inequalities, equality; early death, long life—all these are outgrowths of the seeds of actions we have sown in the past. They cause us to come into this world with varying degrees of goodness or evil within us. So even though God made us in His image, no two people are alike; each has used his God-given free choice to make something different of himself. This is why some people suffer for the slightest reason. Others become angry at the

least provocation. And there are those who eat endlessly without any self-control. Did God make them that way? No. Each person has made himself the way he is. There would be no justice in this world if God had arbitrarily made us the way we are. I sometimes think God must be watching in amazement this big zoo of human beings here, blaming Him because they have a headache or a stomachache, or are always getting into trouble. Don't blame God or anyone else if you are suffering from disease, financial problems, emotional upsets. You created the cause of the problem in the past and must make a greater determination to uproot it now."

I knew next to nothing about Chinese herbal remedies, acupuncture, or the concepts of Traditional Chinese Medicine that Robert explained are all foundational healing modalities, which Master Sha has expanded upon in developing his approach to self-healing. Robert, who is himself Chinese, knew all about these kinds of healing modalities, having dabbled as an amateur Chinese herbalist able to procure rare imported herbs in the apothecaries of Toronto's Chinatown neighborhood, only blocks from my condo. He had witnessed firsthand Master Sha's miraculous healing of people with all types of frustrating medical conditions for which Western medicine and traditional healing methods had no cure. Robert's soul was ready to pursue his own Xiu Lian Purification Journey full-time with Master Sha. He was anxious to leave the business world as soon as possible and focus his time and energy on serving others exclusively. But as much of what Robert shared at his exit interview was intriguing to me, I felt I knew all about karma from Paramahansa Yogananda and I just wasn't interested in becoming any kind of "New Age Healer."

❧   ❧   ❧

After Robert's retirement, we stay in touch only sporadically as he lives in Canada and I'm still traveling the world for Fidelity

Investments building new businesses. But when I move to Toronto in 2008 just after my own retirement from the corporate world to become a Disciple of Paramahansa Yogananda and pursue full-time Forest-Dwelling, Robert picks up the pace of our emails. Since I am now "local" to him and living "in the neighborhood." he starts sending me a stream of email invitations at least once a month.

"Steve, come meet Master Sha. He's in town teaching next month."

My response to my ex-employee becomes a variation of the same polite refusal, repeated over and over. "No thanks, Robert. I'm happy you've found a spiritual Master to follow, but I have my own Guru, Paramahansa Yogananda, and I'm devoted and committed to following his path."

Next month: "Steve, come to our Tuesday night *Power of Soul* group. It's only a few subway stops from where you live. It can't hurt."

"No thanks, Robert. I'm totally focused on my daily Kriya Yoga practice. I'm glad the path you've found is working out for you and happy you met Master Sha. My path with Yogananda is working out great for me!"

And on the afternoon of the February, 2010 snowstorm in Toronto, I receive Robert's latest:

"Steve, we are having an introductory meeting about Master Sha for new students tomorrow night. You should come."

Okay, enough! I tell myself. I devise an ingenious plan to end Robert's relentless pursuit and interest in the well-being of my soul. I email back that I'll go to his meeting the following evening. Not because of any particular interest on my part to learn about Master Sha, but to finally and mercifully put an end to Robert's persistent requests. My brilliant, crackerjack plan is to show up at the meeting at a place called the Estonia House, listen politely to what they have to say, and figure out a way to tell Robert face-to-face about my Guru, and my need to stay focused on the

Kriya Yoga path of Paramahansa Yogananda. That switching the direction of my spiritual practice—and switching Masters—is just not an option for me right now, especially since my Xiu Lian Purification Journey seems to be in such good order and I'm planning to become a monk in Yogananda's Swami Order of India. I'm thinking: *Surely, Robert will understand and accept my apologies. Then, we can both pursue God by climbing valid, but different, paths up the mountain. We can meet each other at the summit after we've both become enlightened. Share a beer or a glass of "heaven's nectar" or whatever it is you get to drink at the bar in Heaven in celebration of the end of your Xiu Lian Purification Journey.*

The next night, I arrive at the Estonia House promptly at 7 p.m. I'm met at the door and introduced to Sher and Lynda, two lovely students who will later become Divine Channels and Worldwide Representatives of Master Sha. Robert looks surprised I actually showed up. Laughs when he sees me sitting in the midst of the other brand new attendees whose souls somehow got them here to learn about Master Sha. During the meeting, Robert, Sher, and Lynda explain soul healing conceptually to the group of about 10 newcomers. Most of us newbies seem to accept the premises of the teachings but we're also anxious to see a demonstration of the *Power of Soul*. We want to witness the teachers practice what they're preaching.

Robert gives us an easy practice to start. One he assures us will be felt physically by everyone in the room. He demonstrates the ancient *Weng Ar Hong* technique that Master Sha references in his book *Soul Mind Body Medicine*. Robert has us stand up and guides us through the series of three chants, each lasting about 20 seconds while we focus our attention on our vibrating Upper, Lower, and Middle Jiao as taught in Traditional Chinese Medicine. Once we've seemingly got the hang of it, we chant *Weng Ar Hong* for about 15 minutes straight. As the chanting continues, the three types of vibrations get stronger and deeper. I'm feeling energized and more aware, more alert.

Sher tells us she can see with her Third Eye, and that light beings entered the room once the chanting commenced. "Not unusual or unexpected." she calmly informs us. "This ancient mantra connects with all the souls who have ever chanted it once anyone starts to recite the mantra at anytime in any place.

After the chanting, the group of newcomers all sit down. The energy in the room has shifted. The hall has heated up. People's faces are brighter, filled with more light. Robert asks a few volunteers to share their experiences and it becomes clear that everyone in the room felt *something* happened, even if we have difficulty expressing our experience in words.

After the *Weng Ar Heng* practice, Sher makes her way to the front of the room to teach us about something she calls *Sha's Golden Healing Ball.* Sher describes Sha's Golden Healing Ball as a round yellow sphere that we can summon to our abdomen. Once the ball arrives, we can call upon it to help us heal areas of the body that are sick or diseased. This light ball is a healing treasure given to Master Sha by the Divine on December 7, 1995, while he was in Vancouver, BC. Sher tells the students that Sha's Golden Healing Ball works because it radiates the "frequency and vibration" of the Divine when called upon to heal illness. And she tells us the ball can subdivide as needed when serving multiple souls who invoke its healing blessing capabilities simultaneously! Sher is going to lead us in a practice to call on Sha's Golden Healing Ball. She tells us we'll be able to ask the treasure, which is a gift to humanity from the Divine through Master Sha, to bless us in any specific area of our body we could use some healing.

Aha! I'm jolted back to the prior morning's meditation session and everything starts to come together for me. *Is this what I received when I felt my belly get punched? A healing light ball from Master Sha? But other than that conversation a few years ago with Robert, I don't even know who Master Sha is. How could he have given me this ball? How is this possible? How did this happen? Why did this happen?*

Sher and Lynda explain that Master Sha teaches "everyone and everything has a soul." Now I'm used to the idea of having a body soul which has reincarnated in this lifetime and many lifetimes before. But it's a bit of a challenge for me to accept Sher's declaration that "every system, every organ, every RNA, every DNA, every cell, and all the spaces between the cells in my body also have a soul." Still, since I'm an open-minded guy, I decide I can play along with and accept the premise of souls as Master Sha teaches—at least for the duration of the exercise.

Sher proceeds to show the group how to use Sha's Golden Healing Ball to heal ourselves. She introduces us to Master Sha's *Four-Power Techniques*:

1. **Body Power:**
   We will place our hands in specific positions in the area of the body that need healing.
2. **Soul Power:**
   We will use the power of soul to heal ourselves. We will *"Say Hello."* that is, we will connect with the souls needing to be healed and request healing for the specific illness or condition from which we are suffering. *(Sher tells us she'll teach us to say an invocation to invoke Sha's Golden Healing Ball for our healing request.)*
3. **Mind Power:**
   We will use creative visualization to picture Sha's Golden Healing Ball—a brilliant golden light ball—shining in the area of the body for which we've requested healing.
4. **Sound Power:**
   We will chant mantras and vibrational sounds to facilitate the healing.

Okay. Let's give this a try and see what happens! All the students stand up and are excited to give self-healing and the Four-Power Techniques a test run. I decide to focus on my Type II diabetes as a chronic condition in need of soul healing. It might be a bit of a stretch to ask for such a major healing my first time at a Master Sha class, but I figure why not put the teachings to the test?

There is no cure for diabetes in Western medicine at this time. I suffer the effects of the disease during periods of stress or when I don't watch my diet closely. My Dad's diabetes progressed to Type I when he reached his sixties and he now has to take daily insulin shots. I would like to avoid Type I diabetes if I can and am open and willing to try Sha's Golden Healing Ball and see if I get good results. But, truth be told, I'm not expecting much. I figure I'll just play along to keep Sher, Robert and the other students happy.

Before we can start using Sha's Golden Healing Ball, Sher does a special calling to bring the treasure to each person's abdomen. She then begins the invocation. We all repeat her words after her and add our specific requests. For me, the invocation is very simple:

"Dear Sha's Golden Healing Ball,
I love you, honor you, and appreciate you.
Could you please give me a healing for my Type II diabetes?
Please do a good job.
I am very thankful."

I visualize the golden healing ball I received the prior morning spinning around the area of my pancreas, the organ in our body responsible for creating insulin. Diabetes ensues if we have excessively high levels of glucose in our digestive system and our pancreas doesn't produce enough insulin to properly regulate those glucose levels. For me, when this situation occurs, I get dizzy, and start to talk non-sensical gibberish. Kind of like drinking 4 beers in half an hour and then trying to deliver a lecture on physics.

For Sound Power, we chant *"Sha's Golden Healing Ball"* as a mantra to a lyrical tune that Sher teaches us. We sing for almost 10 minutes. It's pleasant. I'm a little self-conscious at first about singing to a "healing ball" hovering over my pancreas but I get over it in a hurry since everyone else seems to be concentrating on what they're doing and no one is concerned about me. And keeping my eyes closed helps me focus on the healing process like I'm supposed to be doing.

Sher closes the practice by thanking Sha's Golden Healing Ball, then asks for volunteers to come up to the front of the room so they can tell everyone what they felt during the practice. After sitting back and listening to what the others have to say, I feel safe enough to share my own experience. I tell the group that I requested a healing for diabetes. Explain to them I felt the healing ball physically near my pancreas and that I could visualize golden light in that area of my body. That's it. I've no idea if anything related to my diabetes was actually healed and certainly harbor no expectation that I've been "cured". Sher classifies my experience as "okay, normal, perfect." Reminds me and the rest of the class that chronic conditions like diabetes, cancer, and other diseases almost always take time to fully heal. That some relief may be gained immediately after a practice with Sha's Golden Healing Ball, but that it's not unusual for benefits not to occur until a few hours after the healing, or even the next day. Reminds us of Master Sha's one-sentence secret:

"Karma is the root cause of success and failure in every aspect of life."

If I'm understanding the teachings correctly, what Sher wants us to know is that if *heavy* karma is the cause of our sickness, it may take much longer to self-heal than a few daily practice sessions using Sha's Golden Healing Ball and Master Sha's Four-Power Techniques. The good news is we *can* heal ourselves, and Master Sha is here at this time in history to teach us to do just that!

We are at an introductory lecture covering the basics, so there isn't a whole lot of time available to explain all the details and potential uses of the Four-Power Techniques for self-healing, Sha's

Golden Healing Ball, or the *Weng Ar Hong* mantra and practice. For me, my questions on these topics will have to be answered later. The key now is for me to consider the fact that such tools and treasures actually exist and that it might be worth my while to learn a little bit more about Master Sha.

After the practice, the three teachers close the session by singing a Soul Song blessing to the group. The song is lilting, harmonic, and full of love. Springs from the souls of the teachers, not their human voices. Spontaneous. Not something prepared in advance. Unique. Never possible to be sung again in exactly the same way. Customized for this group, in this place, at this time only.

After the blessing, I'm standing around idly waiting to talk to Robert and Sher. Chatting with a few of the other new students. I'm very uncomfortable. My limited intellect has a big problem understanding Master Sha. In light of the prior day's event—my "punch to the belly"—and the delivery of the golden ball to my abdomen, I'm extremely confused. I've no doubt that the treasure I received yesterday morning was in fact Sha's Golden Healing Ball, but that's all I know at this point. The timing of the delivery of the gift, followed by my "coincidental" attendance at the introductory meeting about Master Sha—after years of avoidance— seems somehow predetermined. *But by who? My Guru? Master Sha? Are two enlightened beings working in concert in the soul world figuring out What's Next for my Xiu Lian Purification Journey?* The most difficult question for me now is *why* I received Sha's Golden Healing Ball. I think back to when I was sitting in my meditation room after receiving the punch to my belly and being the recipient of my Guru's knowing smile. Hmm...

In retrospect, the answer seems obvious. My soul, in loving synchronization with my Guru, Paramahansa Yogananda, needed to learn about soul healing from Master Sha at this point in my Xiu Lian Purification Journey. I was being "prepared" for my introduction to Master Sha by receiving the gift of the treasure. But the exact purpose and all the specifics of what I'm supposed to do now have not yet been revealed to me.

If I hadn't experienced Sha's Golden Healing Ball arriving in my abdomen when sitting in my meditation room with my Guru, I might not have paid anywhere near as much attention to what Sher, Lynda, and Robert were talking about. And since my "invitation" occurred while practicing Kriya Yoga under the guidance of my Guru, I must push aside any troubling thoughts about *why* I have to learn about soul healing, and *why* the teachings must come from Master Sha. I recognize this series of events represents a good spiritual test of my unconditional faith and trust in my Guru.

Paramahansa Yogananda teaches that a true guru always has the best interests of his students at heart. That if there is nothing more a specific teacher can provide the student—or if the student can best learn a particular lesson from another Master—the guru will release, or "transfer." that student to a higher-level spiritual Master who can deliver the lessons the student needs to learn in order to advance on their soul journey. *But is that what is happening to me? Is my Guru releasing me? I've only been a disciple for three months and I'm planning to apply to join Yogananda's Monastic Order and become a fulltime Forest Dweller! Is something else happening? Does Master Sha have something to teach me that Yogananda doesn't and, once I learn it, will I come back to my Guru and then become a monk?*

Spiritual confusion. I don't have the Help Desk phone number. No way to dial up Heaven's Customer Support team, ask my questions, and wait for easily understandable answers.

Spiritual worry. Causing me to bite my nails and suffer confusion about what's happening.

Spiritual conflict. *Is it possible to have two Masters in charge of my Xiu Lian Purification Journey? Does Heaven even allow that?*

I push these agitating, disagreeable concerns to the back of my mind for the time being. Re-focus on the present. Hope my anxiety will chill. Robert frees up first and comes over to ask me what I think. Sher and Lynda say goodbye to the folks they know, then also come over to listen to what I have to say to Robert. I tell them I enjoyed the evening.

"Will you come back?" Sher asks.

"Yes, why not?" I laugh and give them an abbreviated version about my punch to the belly and the arrival of the golden ball. Everyone is impressed by my story but don't consider what's happened to me to be that unusual.

Sher tells me "On the spiritual journey, guidance is delivered at just the right time." The teachers seem quite sure that my experience is simply part of a divinely-guided plan for my Xiu Lian Purification Journey which must now include Master Sha.

Sher pulls me aside and asks me a few questions that probe a little deeper into the current status of my spiritual journey. I open up to her. Tell her about my Guru and other spiritual teachers and Masters I've followed up to this point. She nods at the right time, smiles at the right time. Encourages me when I get snagged trying to explain things in less than adequate words. I voice my budding concern about dealing with "multiple Masters" and she knows exactly what I mean. Tells me most of Master Sha's students have also studied with and have followed other teachers. "This is not a problem. It's a blessing. Master Sha honors all religions, all teachers," she tells me.

Comforting to hear. Sher and I have a prior life soul connection, I can feel it. She reminds me of my Aunt Mary, a devout Catholic and big fan of St. Theresa of Avila, one of my spiritual Mothers.

As I ride the subway home, my ego puts up some resistance about Master Sha. *"Don't make more of these two days then what it is. You've had some interesting experiences, but it probably doesn't mean much of anything. Remember, you're a Disciple of Yogananda now and are about to apply to join the SRF Monastic Order. Master Sha is nothing but a distraction..."*

But my soul doesn't agree with my ego. And as the subway races along below the snow-covered streets of downtown Toronto, all I know for sure is that I want to know more about Master Sha.

Practice For the 1st Soul House

Many Eastern spiritual traditions have teachings referencing the 7 chakras. Chakras are spiritual energy centers located in different parts of the body. The 7 chakras start at the base of our torso and run vertically to the crown of our skull. Each chakra is associated with different aspects of our personalities, and by extension, our soul journey.

You can picture each of the 7 chakras as a vortex of spinning energy. This spiritual, or cosmic, energy is stored in each chakra like energy in a battery. When the batteries are fully charged, there's a lot of power available to fuel your spiritual journey. If you have karmic blockages in any of your chakras and the energy is low or depleted, then physical illness, mental, or emotional imbalances can occur in your body.

Master Sha refers to the 7 energy chakras as Soul Houses because our soul can reside in any of them. Master Sha offers practices to heal ourselves by developing and purifying each Soul House. These practices recharge the battery and replenish the power of each chakra.

Here's a practice for healing the 1st Soul House, or Root Chakra, a fist-sized energy center located at the center of the bottom of your torso, between the genitals and the anus. The 1st Soul House is described in Master Sha's book *Tao Song and Tao Dance*[5]:

"The 1st Soul House is the foundation energy center for all 7 Soul Houses. It is also the key energy center for healing the whole body, especially the reproductive system and immune system, as well as for the anus, rectum, and sexual organs. It is the key for increasing sexual power. It is the key Soul House for enhancing relationships. It is the key powerhouse for developing your confidence and stability. The 1st Soul House connects with Mother Earth and gathers the soul, mind, and body of yin from the whole body."

Do the following practice 10–15 minutes at a time using Master Sha's Four-Power Techniques:

1. **Body Power:**
   Sit up straight. Put the tip of your tongue as close as you can to the roof of your mouth without touching. Put both palms on your lower abdomen below your navel or one palm over the other below your navel.

2. **Soul Power:**
   Dear soul, mind, and body of my 1st Soul House,
   I love you, honor you, and appreciate you.
   You have the power to boost the energy, stamina, vitality, and immunity of my 1st Soul House.
   Please do a good job!

---

5   *Tao Song and Tao Dance: Sacred Sound, Movement, and Power from the Source for Healing, Rejuvenation, Longevity, and Transformation of All Life,* New York/Toronto: Atria Books/ Heaven's Library Publication Corporation, 2011.

Thank you. Thank you. Thank you.
Dear souls of all my spiritual fathers and mothers,
I love you, honor you, and appreciate you.
Please give me a 1st Soul House blessing as appropriate to build my
spiritual foundation.
I am so very honored and grateful.
Thank you. Thank you. Thank you."

3. **Mind Power:**

Focus on your 1st Soul House. Visualize a golden light ball or a
rainbow light ball rotating counterclockwise in that area. If your
Third Eye is open, observe whatever images you receive.

4. **Sound Power:**

Chant or sing silently or aloud:
Hei Ya You Zhong (pronounced hay yah yoe jawng) repeatedly. Hei
Ya You Zhong is a Tao mantra to vibrate and develop the first Soul
House.

After the practice, say:

"Hao. Hao. Hao.
Thank you. Thank you. Thank you."

MASTER SHA

"When the teacher appears, grab the teacher!"
                                        —Master Sha

Master Sha

"**M**aster Sha is coming to Toronto next month!" Sher announces at the Tuesday night *Power of Soul* group meeting. I've been attending the meetings regularly since the introductory evening a few weeks ago. The three-day *Soul Healing and Enlightenment Retreat* will take place at a Holiday Inn in downtown Toronto. Sher goes on to explain to the group of eager students the types of really cool things that are likely to happen at the workshop. Demonstrations of *Power of Soul* healing. Akashic Record readings. Karma cleansings performed by Master Sha with audience volunteers. Soul Song singing and chanting. It's an event not to be missed. Enthusiasm bubbles over amongst the students. Everyone plans to attend. I register for the free healing evening on Friday night, not quite sure if I am ready to commit to the full weekend session as well. I caution myself, *Let's see how Friday night goes before spending the time and money for the weekend sessions.* Truth be told, I'm still not totally ready to go to the next step with Master Sha—or maybe I'm just scared because I can't handle the implications of what becoming a student of Master Sha might mean for my soul journey with my Guru Paramahansa Yogananda.

⚜ ⚜ ⚜

It seems to me that about one-third of the people who follow Master Sha and consider themselves students do so for *spiritual* reasons. They become regular participants in *Power of Soul* groups and attend Master Sha retreats in order to receive powerful blessings for their Xiu Lian Purification Journeys. Many of Master Sha's students have been searching all their lives for a spiritual Father and teacher to guide them to enlightenment, to salvation. Most have studied with other teachers and have practiced some form of meditation based on Eastern philosophies such as Buddhism, Hinduism, or Taoism.

Master Sha is an enlightened Master serving *all* souls with unconditional love, compassion, kindness, and wisdom. Almost all the people I know in the Toronto Power of Soul group who have actually met Master Sha in person became avid followers of his teachings after spending time in his physical presence. Robert, Sher, and Lynda, who run our Tuesday night sessions, are advanced students that have been studying with Master Sha for many years.

But the majority of people who come to learn Master Sha's techniques and practices are primarily seeking *healing*. These people are not necessarily interested or focused on spirituality at all. Many have their own religious belief systems which they are quite comfortable with. They come to Master Sha and use his methods to cure illnesses and diseases, or to get help with severe emotional problems including fear, worry, and anxiety. Many people have strained relationships with their spouses, children, parents, and friends. Others suffer financial hardships including an inability to find a steady job or make enough money to pay their bills. They attend classes to practice Master Sha's *Power of Soul* techniques and study at home reading Master Sha's Soul Power Series books to improve or resolve their relationship and financial issues.

The people who come to Master Sha for healing are often depressed because they've found no cure for their illnesses, or they're frustrated with getting only limited relief from remedies and treatments prescribed by their medical doctors. *They want to suffer less!* They'll pursue alternative therapies, even if their medical insurance plans won't cover all their expenses, in hopes of finding anything to relieve their pain. These people are often at their wit's end, desperate, and are open to exploring New Age, Asian, and Alternative healing options. Somehow, their souls "find" Master Sha, often in unique ways.

One student in our Tuesday night group likes to recount the story of her being in the "spirituality and religion" section of a mall bookstore. One of Master Sha's books, *Soul Mind Body Medicine*, "called" to her by falling off a shelf just as she was walking by. Other students might talk to a friend or relative who's been to a

Master Sha retreat or *Power of Soul* group healing session and find that something resonates within them that urges them to explore the power of soul teachings.

As a medical doctor himself, Master Sha honors all healing modalities, including Western Medicine and Traditional Chinese Medicine. But Master Sha's primary focus is to heal the soul, or souls, of our afflictions first, with the knowledge and expectation that healing of the body and mind will follow. Master Sha teaches that negative karma is the root cause of all our illnesses, hardships, and suffering. He offers ancient wisdom and techniques to his students so we can self-clear our own karma.

I'm learning all about soul healing on Tuesday nights, and getting to practice in a group setting with all kinds of fascinating, intriguing people. I'm seeing for myself that the practices work. And when any of the other students or I have demonstrable success and are able to transform some aspect of our lives, we all share our experiences with each other.

I'm at the point in my Xiu Lian Purification Journey where my mind is actively entertaining "Soul Healer" as a possible future job title for me. This is something I would never have considered prior to taking up my friend Robert's invitation to learn who Master Sha is. My Kriya Yoga practice is flourishing, but for now I hold off submitting my application to become an SRF monk. Something is percolating under the surface of my consciousness. My soul wants to learn much more about Master Sha's teachings. I still harbor a hidden reservoir of doubt about going too far down the Xiu Lian path with two teachers: my Guru Paramahansa Yogananda and Master Sha, but I'm not trying to pick one over the other, or compare the two teachers.

⚜   ⚜   ⚜

Friday evening in early April, 2010. I arrive at the Holiday Inn, site of Master Sha's Soul Healing and Enlightenment Retreat. Check in at one of the tables set up outside the meeting hall. Sift through the name badges lined up for the 100 or so pre-registered guests. Sign application forms and waivers for permission to be filmed as an attendee if I get called to the stage. Find a seat towards the center of the room, maybe 3 or 4 rows back from the front. Listen to welcome and introductory remarks from Shunya, Master Sha's events manager who lives in Hawaii but travels around North America with Master Sha coordinating and emceeing these types of workshops and retreats. Contribute my share to the nervous anticipation building in the audience. Shifting about in our chairs, we await the arrival of Master Sha to the stage.

Master Sha is beaming! Shining! All love and light! Master Sha is so happy to be here! Welcomes everyone and begins his teachings immediately. Draws pictures and diagrams, splashes Chinese characters and English words all over the flipchart beside his chair. Master Sha's frequency and vibration dominate the room. I become aware of how much ... *lower and slower* ... my frequency and vibration is while in the presence of this enlightened being emanating such high energy. Master Sha is feeding us his vibration—his love—while he speaks, and we are all *so* ready to absorb him like dry sponges dropped into a bucket of water. I start to recognize what Robert, Sher, and Lynda have been saying every week in our Tuesday night classes. Master Sha really is like no other human being on the planet.

Healing demonstrations. Volunteers called up to the stage, a few in need of assistance climbing the stairs. Their physical illnesses seem debilitating. Most guests not experienced with public speaking. Unaware of how to use the hand-held microphone, they are gently guided and encouraged by Sande, Master Sha's AV Team manager. The volunteers share vivid, heart-wrenching descriptions of illnesses wreaking havoc in their lives. Receive compassion from the audience. Occasional tears shed by all when the volunteer breaks down, becoming emotionally naked in the spotlight. I'm reminded of The Buddha's First Noble Truth:

"Life is Suffering."

It takes supreme courage to speak in public about our short-comings, our failures, our illnesses, our karma. The volunteers are about to receive a huge blessing for showing the determination to come to the stage. Master Sha is here. Master Sha is the servant. Master Sha can help. Master Sha does help.

Readings from the Akashic Records are helpful to determine the root karmic causes of our illnesses. The Akashic Records are managed by light beings in heaven led by their leader *Yan Wang Ye.* These written records contain the sum total of all our actions, thoughts, and deeds from all of our lifetimes. Nothing omitted here. Nothing skipped, forgotten, or glossed over. Our karmic destinies determined by the "weight" of our good service vs. our deeds which harmed others in the past. High levels of good karma can mean this life and future lives are blessed with exceptional health, plenty of money, beautiful relationships, and business success. Mistakes made in this life or prior lives can mean endless future reincarnations in challenging conditions of bad health, poor relationships, financial and business failures, and more.

Actions have consequences. As the Christian Bible states in Galatians:

"Be not deceived; God is not mocked:
for whatsoever a man soweth, that shall he also reap."

Master Sha asks for and receives permission to access the Akashic Records from those individuals who are up on stage with him in need of healing. With the assent of each person, Master Sha "connects" with Heaven and the Akashic Records and then reveals the specific karmic causes for the physical conditions that have manifested and are the cause of their suffering in this lifetime. Some volunteers look devastated when the mistakes they made in past lifetimes are revealed. Some are overwhelmed with sorrow for their past harmful actions and struggle to hold back tears of anguish. Master Sha comforts them all, tells them it's okay and—when they are ready—asks the Divine to clear the karma for each person's condition. When Master Sha shouts "Transmission!," the flash of light and energy in the room is palpable, especially to those with open "Third Eyes (the spiritual eye that allows you to see spiritual images).

Master Sha teaches that we can self-clear our own karma by doing lots and lots of Forgiveness Practice and by serving others unconditionally to make them happier and healthier. If we sincerely practice and serve unconditionally, we gain virtue in Heaven that's recorded in our Akashic Record book. Little by little, this good virtue (good karma) "pays off" our spiritual debt – our bad karma, also recorded in our Akashic Record book. And when our debt is paid, we no longer suffer the negative effect of that karma. Our health, our relationships, our finances can heal and we can flourish in all aspects of our lives. Depending on the severity of our mistakes and the weight of our negative karma, our karmic debt may take hundreds or even thousands of lifetimes to pay off!

So what actually happens when Master Sha clears our karma? Well, for one thing, the karma clearing is instantaneous. When he gives the "order" for our karma to be cleared, Heaven responds immediately! The Divine offers *Divine Forgiveness* by paying our spiritual debt! The Divine opens Heaven's virtue bank—not ours—and give's Heaven's virtue to the souls we harmed. This virtue blesses their future lives. Areas of darkness in our body are transformed. Our Akashic Record book is updated, with this negative karma removed from the record. Our "account" gets balanced. This priceless service offered by Master Sha is incomprehensible to most people, including myself.

Master Sha teaches that we could have cleared the same karma ourselves by building up credit in our own virtue bank with lifetimes and lifetimes of service. "What's wrong with that?" as Master Sha would say. But when an enlightened being like Master Sha is available to clear our karma instantly, in this Divine way, why wouldn't we take advantage of the opportunity? As Master Sha often reminds us:

"When the student is ready, the teacher appears.
When the teacher appears, grab the teacher!"

Watching multiple volunteers get their bad karma cleared, I'm overwhelmed at what seems totally miraculous to me. Of course, not all the healings occur instantaneously. Some people do receive immediate benefit of having their negative karma cleared—there are countless video and audio testimonials to Master Sha's healing abilities on his website (www.DrSha.com) and in his Soul Power Series books. For others, the healing results might be delayed a few hours or days. Sitting in the meeting room at the Holiday Inn and witnessing people receiving positive results from Master Sha's blessings, I'm anxious to learn more about what's going on. A kind of spiritual hunger is growing within me. *I want to serve humanity as a Soul Healer!*

There's a woman in the audience who "does it for me"—who seals the deal to my becoming a student of Master Sha. She's sitting directly in front of me. Sheila suffers from psoriasis, a painful skin condition for which there is no cure in Western medicine. I can see a patch of the scaly plaque across the back of her neck, just below the hairline. A horizontal Band-Aid sized reddish-white infection. Sheila raises her hand when Master Sha asks for the next volunteer to come up on stage. She is selected and moves, not without effort, up to the spotlight. I don't remember the details of her Akashic Record reading or the history of her disease, only that it is spreading all over her body and that her physical discomfort has become nearly unbearable. Sheila receives a karma clearing and a healing blessing from Master Sha. Bows down in thanks. Sobs to Master Sha who reminds her that "he" has done nothing, that Master Sha is only "the Servant." That it is the Divine that is doing all the work.

When Sheila gets back to her seat, those of us around her smile in support. She is still crying. Weak in the knees after such a powerful healing. The evening continues with more demonstrations interspersed with more teachings. Master Sha continues to radiate love and compassion to all the attendees. But the strangest thing happens as I watch Sheila's neck over the remaining few hours from my vantage point sitting directly behind her. *Sheila's psoriasis is receding! Visibly disappearing before my eyes!* It's another *Aha!* moment for me on my Xiu Lian Purification Journey. And the second *Aha!* moment related to Master Sha, the first occurrence coming when I received the gift of Sha's Golden Healing Ball. I can hardly keep still. At the end of the evening, when we rise from our chairs, I tap Sheila on the shoulder and tell her what I've seen. She of course can't see the fading psoriasis on the back of her own neck, but the woman whom she came with looks and giggles in amazement, corroborating what I've told her.

Sheila's healing confirms for me that Master Sha possesses unique and very powerful healing powers. That soul healing—performed without physically touching the person being healed—actually works. At the end of the evening, I rush outside the meeting room and immediately sign up to attend the Saturday and Sunday full-day sessions at the hotel.

It's been a great night and I'm quite excited about learning more from Master Sha over the next two days. But on the way home, I get attacked by demons of doubt about what I've witnessed. This kind of attack is not unusual on the Xiu Lian journey, especially after significant and life-transforming experiences occur and jolt our mindsets. The demons pepper me with questions:

"Are you sure what you saw is real? Plenty of so-called spiritual healers are charlatans, clever con men taking advantage of innocent people and stealing their money—maybe Master Sha is one of them. Are you sure some of the so-called "volunteers" that went up to the stage aren't "plants" that are working behind the scenes with Master Sha to dupe the audience into thinking they're actually getting healed? There's no scientific evidence that soul healing works!

None of this is logical. Sure, the "show" was entertaining, but that's all it was, a staged event. You should walk away from this now. You don't want to look like a fool, do you?"

I also question my own soul a bit about witnessing Sheila's cure. Would I have decided to become a Master Sha student if I hadn't seen her healing for myself? I hope so. I don't want to be like the unbelievers in the Bible:

"Unless you people see miraculous signs and wonders," Jesus told him, *"you will never believe."*

I don't consider myself one of those individuals who needs direct and personal experience of "miracles" supported by verifiable scientific facts in order to believe what a spiritual Master is teaching. But I do recognize that for many Westerners, brought up in an overly analytical culture, some type of proof or direct experience is necessary before their rational mind "accepts" what they've witnessed as real. Spiritual faith, trust in the Divine, is often just not enough to convince some people that they are not being tricked by what they see happening in front of them.

I lie in bed awake for most of Friday night. My body still buzzing, alive with an electric-like current coursing through me. It's the first time since my summer at Karmê Chöling in Vermont with Chögyam Trungpa Rinpoche almost 40 years ago that I'm going through a withdrawal, a "come down," after spending time in the physical presence of a true Master. My body is adjusting to the difference in the spiritual energy levels of Master Sha in the Holiday Inn meeting room in contrast with the far less intense frequency of the energy in my condo. I have only a few hours to catch some sleep before I have to wake and return to the hotel for the full day of teachings beginning on Saturday morning. When I do finally crash, my sleep is dreamless and amazingly restful. No tossing, no turning. A *Return to Forever.*

Puma In The Snow

There are three basic rules to observe when you're hiking alone in the wilderness:

Rule #1: Don't Leave The Path! Gandalf the Wizard offered this sage advice—which was promptly ignored—to Bilbo and his dwarf friends in J.R.R. Tolkien's *The Hobbit.* Inexperienced hikers often convince themselves they can reach their destination quicker by taking "shortcuts" off marked trails. As Bilbo and the dwarves found out, disasters can occur on your journey if you leave your path to save a little time.

Rule #2: Tell Someone Where You Are Going! It's a good idea to let someone back home know you are out hiking by yourself, where you are headed, and when they can expect you back. That way, if you don't show up for dinner, your friends can start worrying and go look for you.

Rule #3: Everything Is Farther Away Than It Looks. In the wilderness, it's easy to change your plans and divert from the marked trail, especially if there's an attractive landmark or scenic view that appears to be within easy walking distance. In the wilderness, it can be fatal to undertake these "quick" side trips if your destination is in reality a lot further away than it looks, and you are running out of energy and daylight.

In many ways, these "Rules for Hiking Solo" apply to the Xiu Lian Purification Journey as well. When traveling on the spiritual journey, it's a good idea to stick to one's path. Avoid distractions, side trips, and detours. Find a few supportive friends who know what you're up to. Remember the journey is longer than it looks and might take a few thousand lifetimes or more before you reach your goal at "the top of the mountain."

On a cool October afternoon, I find myself violating all of these rules while hiking in the mountains of Nevada by myself. I've got no particular goal or destination I want to reach, I'm just exploring. But no one knows I'm out here. The trek is enjoyable and I'm feeling optimistic about life just the way you're supposed to in the great outdoors. I'm chanting Master Sha mantras and singing Divine Soul Songs to my heart's content. With no one else in sight, I can sing aloud in the province of nature for the benefit of the birds and animals that might care to listen. The trail basks in the glow of afternoon sunlight. The few inches of melting snow from the prior evening mix with the loose soil and muddy the way. In the shady parts of the trail, the accumulation of snow is 3–4 inches deep. It's going to have to get a lot warmer before any of this snow melts.

In the distance, I spy a rock shelf a couple of hundred feet high calling me to come and climb it. I decide it's probably okay to exit the trail, navigate my way through the stands of Mojave yucca, creosote, blackbrush, and spiny agave plants, and scale the rock face in order to reach the top where I'll be able to sit down, meditate, chant, and sing in the late afternoon sunshine.

I'm faced with difficulties from the moment I make my decision to stray from the path. Since there's no trail enabling me to reach the rock face quickly, I've got to scramble through patches of briars and climb up, over, and around large sedimentary sandstone and limestone boulders. I'm wearing hiking shorts and suffer cuts on my legs in spots where the underbrush gets too thick. And I find the snow is much deeper off the trail than I'd expected. My ankle-high hiking shoes sink into the soft snow that flows over the tops of the boots and gets absorbed by my socks, freezing my ankles and feet.

When I realize the sun is about to set behind the jagged skyline of the Sierra Nevada Mountains, I'm forced to admit defeat and failure of my spontaneous expedition. I'll have to retrace my footsteps in the snow as best I can and find my back to the marked trail before dark.

Jumping from boulder to boulder as much as possible to minimize clawing through the underbrush, I'm taken aback when I come across a fresh set of animal tracks in the snow. Some sort of large predator—most likely a puma—has recently passed this way.

Pumas are quite common in the wilds of Nevada and I'm hoping this nearby resident hasn't smelled the blood on my legs from the cuts I sustained in the bushes. Pumas have four toes on each paw. The toe tracks are facing north so I decide it's a good idea to head south. Generally speaking, pumas don't attack humans. But since I'm wandering in the puma's neighborhood, I'm not so sure I won't be considered an appetizing dinner if the mountain lion hasn't eaten in a while or is a female with hungry cubs to feed. If that happens, no one is going to find what's left of my body out in this wilderness.

Panic rises in me. Seizes my stomach. Adrenaline rushes. I hasten my pace in the opposite direction of the paw prints, each one a little larger than the size of my outstretched palm. Just when I think I'm beyond the territory of the puma, the paw prints show up in the snow again. *Have I been traveling in circles? Is this mountain lion tracking me? Waiting for the perfect time to attack?* The hairs on the back of my neck stand on end. I can feel the nearby presence of the predator. I know the puma is near, safely camouflaged in some rock crevice or hiding behind a clump of creosote bushes. Watching me. Sizing me up. Maybe even licking its chops.

Time to settle down. Get grounded. A perfect opportunity to ask for forgiveness from the soul of the mountain lion who's space I've invaded. I speak my Forgiveness Practice aloud:

"Dear soul, mind, and body of the puma who lives in these mountains,

I love you, honor you, and appreciate you.

Please forgive me for entering your territory.

I have no intention of disturbing you or causing you any kind of undue stress.

I honor your space and have no business being here.

Please don't eat me! I just want to leave quietly and you'll never see me again.

Please forgive me. Please forgive me. Please forgive me.

Hao/ Hao. Hao.
Thank you. Thank you. Thank you."

After the Forgiveness Practice, I swear I hear a sound like a sigh. A long exhalation of breath. Maybe it's the wind. Maybe not. I picture the puma closing his eyes. Losing interest in tracking me. Releasing me as an object of prey.

Master Sha teaches that all animals have souls. And even though the soul standing of animals is, generally speaking, lower than that of human beings, all animals are worthy of our love and respect. Be aware of the wild animals around you. Respect their spaces! Respect their souls!

CHANGE OF PLANS

"The purpose of life is to serve."

—Master Sha

Lao Tzu on a water buffalo carrying the *Tao De Jing*

During the Saturday session of the Soul Healing and Enlightenment Retreat in Toronto, Master Sha announces that he will host his first ever Tao Retreat in Ramsau, Austria in early May. The next book in the Soul Power Series, *Tao I, The Way of All Life*, is about to be published and will be taught to students from all over the world who attend the 10-day session in the Austrian Alps. Now this is exciting! It's pretty easy to convince myself that an unexpected and unplanned week in the Austrian Alps with Master Sha will be a nice change of pace for me. *I could use a springtime vacation in Europe. And what better excuse do I need than an opportunity to study the Tao with Master Sha?*

The last time I was in Austria was nearly forty years ago when I spent a weekend in Salzburg while attending the Castalia seminar in Switzerland. But I have to think about this a little bit. *Am I truly ready to become a soul healer with Master Sha and study Tao with him? Is there some further confirmation I need to alter the course of my Xiu Lian Purification Journey in this way? Is Master Sha just a distraction sent by Heaven to prevent me from "going to the mountain" and becoming an SRF monk?*

Returning from the lunch break, we take our seats. The attendees are still buzzing about the upcoming Tao Retreat. The students all of a shared opinion that this event will be of historic significance. That Master Sha will reveal for the first time secrets of how to heal our souls, minds, and bodies with ancient Tao practices and Tao wisdom.

Shunya, the event manager and meeting organizer, takes the stage to make announcements about Master Sha's Mission, the local events schedule, and, of course, the upcoming European retreat. While Shunya is speaking, I notice Master Sha quietly entering the room through a side door. Not wanting to interrupt Shunya's announcements, Master Sha takes a seat on a folding chair off towards the back of the room. I need to use the washroom after lunch, and get up to leave so I can be back before the afternoon teaching and healing sessions begin after the announcements. I realize I'm going to have walk by Master Sha when I leave the hall. I'm not nervous, but more in awe of being in such close physical proximity to such a powerful spiritual Master. Keeping my head bowed in respect, I'm passing by about 15 feet away from where Master Sha is sitting. My head automatically rises—and I find myself gazing into the eyes of Master Sha. Those loving eyes seem familiar to me and hold my attention. I don't know what to do. *Should I stop walking? Should I look away? Do I say hello? Do I just keep going? Just what is the protocol for spiritual courtesy around a fully enlightened being?* Master Sha simply nods his head at me. It's an unforgettable greeting. Without speaking a word aloud, his soul is speaking to me: *"Hello. Welcome. Welcome back."*

I don't get washed over by a flood of past life memories, but my soul suddenly "recognizes" who Master Sha is. He is my spiritual Father. I have known him before. Master Sha has been my Master in *many* lifetimes. I nod back to my teacher in acknowledgement of our spiritual reconnection taking place in real time. If I had any lingering doubts about who Master Sha is before this moment, they've fallen away like dead leaves being blown off an oak tree by a late autumn breeze.

For the remainder of the Saturday session, I feel calm, balanced, and alert. This is my first retreat with Master Sha in person, but it feels like my spiritual Father has never been very far from my soul.

⚜   ⚜   ⚜

On Sunday afternoon as the Soul Healing and Enlightenment Retreat begins to wind down, Master Sha talks more about the upcoming Tao I Retreat. Explaining that he is not going to teach traditional Taoism based on Lao Tzu's *Tao Te Ching*, Master Sha tells us he will instead focus on Taoist concepts of longevity and immortality using *The Power of Soul* practices and techniques. Master Sha stresses the importance for each of us in the room to receive these teachings in Austria next month. He reminds everyone in the room that it is no coincidence we've found our way to this retreat. Whether we are existing students who've followed Master Sha for years, or new students like me, Master Sha tells us we are "chosen." *Well, what exactly does that mean?* I wonder. *Chosen for what?* Master Sha is about to tell us. The room gets so silent you could hear a pin drop, all the students on the edge of their seats. I can only paraphrase Master Sha's message as best as I remember it:

> *"Mother Earth is in transition. Humanity's karma is heavy. Wars, pollution, economic struggles, the spread of communicable diseases, and misuse of technology for greed, power, and wealth are causing lots of people to suffer now and will be the cause of further suffering if we don't address the karma of humanity now."*

Master Sha's words make me uneasy. *Okay, I get it. Everybody knows the planet isn't in good shape right now. So what am I supposed to do about it? I'm nobody. I try to help when I can in my own small way...* Master Sha continues:

> *"I am the servant. I am here to help Mother Earth and all humanity get through the coming transition. You are also servants chosen by Heaven to help humanity also. It is no coincidence you have found me; that you have come to this retreat. The purpose of life is to serve. We all have to serve humanity during Mother Earth's transition."*

Many of the other retreat attendees and I get more anxious and uncomfortable as Master Sha speaks. The room is hotter. I feel like a grade-school student who's misbehaved in class with his friends and is getting admonished by the teacher. Master Sha tells us:

> *"In your past lives, if you wanted to advance on your Xiu Lian spiritual journey, you would go to the mountain and meditate*

for twenty, thirty, even fifty years! In this life, we cannot go to the mountain. Humanity needs us. Mother Earth needs us. There is work to do. We need to become teachers and healers. I am teaching you, I am giving you the tools to serve humanity."

Master Sha is not asking politely if we want to help out humanity in our spare time, on weekends, or whenever it's convenient for us to serve. He's rather firmly telling everyone in the room we have a job to do. That Heaven is preparing tasks specifically for us.

Well, this is not what I'm expecting to hear at this point in my personal Xiu Lian Purification Journey. My ego is not happy and gets obstinate with me: *Tell me again why you can't become a monk and meditate? Who's in charge here? You've been doing great on your spiritual journey up to now! You've earned the right to meditate and practice your Guru's Kriya Yoga techniques in solitude. You deserve it! Who is Master Sha to tell you it's not time to go to the mountain?*

My soul tenders a different response and helps me get over the uncomfortableness of being told by a spiritual Master I've just met that he has work for me to do. My soul pushes the fear, doubts, and concerns of my ego to the back of my mind. *"You are here for a reason. You were supposed to meet Master Sha in this time and place. You know this now. You've witnessed a miraculous healing on Sheila and you've seen other people getting healed by Master Sha all weekend. It's time to become a full-time student of Master Sha and learn soul healing."* I make the decision to put aside my application to become a monastic in Yogananda's Self-Realization Fellowship and learn to become a Master Sha Soul Healer.

⚜ ⚜ ⚜

Master Sha announces that he will close the Soul Healing and Enlightenment Retreat with a *Tao Energy Circle* blessing. Before we begin, he asks for a show of hands to see who plans to come to Austria with him in May. Maybe a third of people raise their hands. The rest of the students want to go, but are wrestling with the practical considerations of how to get the time off work and manifest the needed travel funds quickly since the event is less than a month away.

Sande, Master Sha's AV Team coordinator, wants to film this special blessing which is being performed by Master Sha for the first time in a group of this size. We clear the room of chairs and our personal items, leaving a big open space in which to form the circle. Master Sha sits on the floor in half-lotus position in the center of the room. The rest of us all line up one behind the other in rows moving away from the center like the spokes of a big wagon wheel. It takes a bit of time for everyone to get settled. Sande wants to get the lighting just right and is facing some challenges. Master Allan, a Divine Channel and Worldwide Representative of Master Sha, sits adjacent to Master Sha at the head of one of the wheel's "spokes." There's an excessive amount of light shining off Master Allan's shaved head and Sande is having difficulty deciding whether or not to adjust the lights and leave Master Allan in place, or move Master Allan to a less desirable spot in the energy circle away from Master Sha. The students joke aloud to the AV team that the light shining off Master Allan's head is "spiritual radiance," and that no matter where Sande places him in the circle, she'll have the same problem.

The delay in getting started finds me crouched on my heels in cramped quarters, unable to move or stretch out my legs. But I'm in a spot right behind Master Sha's left shoulder, and being this close to the teacher convinces me to endure the kind of physical pain I haven't experienced since my Kundalini Yoga classes in college so many years ago where the students were required to sit on our heels for extended periods of time.

After a seemingly interminable delay, Sande announces the lights are good and the cameras ready to record the Tao Energy Circle event. Master Sha begins. I don't remember the specifics of the invocation he used to start the blessing, but I do recall the massive waves of energy pouring out from Master Sha over each of us once the blessing started. Energy so strong I believe it would have knocked me down if I were standing at the perimeter of the circle or anywhere else in the meeting hall. And like ripples generated in the center of a pond into which a huge boulder has been tossed, the waves flow out equidistantly from Master Sha in a 360-degree pattern. This energy sweeps through us, passes between the cells holding our physical bodies together in time and space. Uplifts us, carries us along beyond the meeting room, beyond the Holiday Inn, beyond downtown Toronto and out into the universe. Light beings, angels, Buddhas and Bodhisattvas arrive and join us, their golden souls melding into the circle. Indescribable power flows instantaneously throughout the hall, blasting out from Master Sha. There's no duality here! We've reached a state of *Wan Ling Rong He* – all souls joined together as one—all the oneness origi-nating from Master Sha's Jin Dan, the energy core in his abdomen.

When the Tao Energy Circle practice ceases, we shake, we cry, we laugh, we are all overwhelmed. Master Sha laughs with us also and asks a few people to share their experience. Impossible to explain adequately in words. A few students do their best.

Master Sha then turns to look at me over his left shoulder. "What are you going to do?" he asks. His smile is such pure love. But my soul knows Master Sha is asking me a different question than what he asked the others. Master Sha isn't asking about my experience of the energy circle blessing, he's asking something much deeper. He's asking if I'm going to become his student.

My soul answers right away. "I'm going to the Tao Retreat in Austria with you Master Sha. Thank you!" Everyone laughs, includ-ing Master Sha. I'm in deep now! I've committed to Master Sha that I'm going to continue my Xiu Lian journey as a student of the Tao. My intent to "go to the mountain" and meditate in silence has taken an unexpected turn. The mountains I'll be going to are the Austrian Alps. And instead of meditating alone, I'll be studying with hundreds of Master Sha students from all around the globe.

❧   ❧   ❧

When I return home Sunday evening after the retreat, I'm excited about everything I've witnessed, everything I've experienced, and everything I've learned from Master Sha about soul healing over the past three days. But I'm most excited about going to Europe to study the Tao with Master Sha. To have an unprecedented opportunity to learn from an enlightened Master with a bunch of my new friends from Toronto seems too good to be true.

When I hang up my winter coat in the hall closet, I notice my old woodblock print of Lao Tzu that I acquired 38 years ago while an undergrad at the University of Massachusetts. Lao Tzu is looking at me with big black eyes from the back of the water buffalo he's riding. The *Tao De Jing* scroll is securely tucked under his arm. And if I'm not mistaken, the old Tao Master is speaking, telling me: "I want to go to the Tao Retreat."

What?

"I want to go to the Tao Retreat." That's all. *Hmm… this is strange. Am I really hearing voices from a woodblock print in my condo. Is this another "Aha" moment or am I just going totally crazy?*

After three days of intense spiritual experiences at the workshop, I'm too tired to question why Lao Tzu's image is communicating to me. So I simply respond, "Okay. I will take you."

The black eyes of Lao Tzu sparkle mischievously. Somehow the old Master is staring into my soul to acknowledge my commitment to the journey ahead, to Master Sha, to the Tao.

On the Xiu Lian Purification Journey, our spiritual fathers and mothers sometimes arrange for a change of plans. Prior to attending my first Soul Healing and Enlightenment Workshop, I had no plans to go Austria and study the Tao with Master Sha. Master Sha teaches us the importance of *Divine Flexibility* and this quality is advantageous to have on the spiritual journey when plans change unexpectedly. Like Lao Tzu says in the *Tao Te Jing:*

"A good traveler has no fixed plans, and is not intent on arriving."

Ten Da's

The Ten Da are qualities which any traveler on the Xiu Lian Purification Journey should aspire to nurture and develop in themselves. They are the nature of Tao. Master Sha considers the Ten Da so important that he's painted a sacred calligraphy for each Da and hangs them on the center stage at his retreats.

Each Da can be chanted as a mantra. You can also chant all Ten Da's together. For example, if you'd like to increase your compassion, chant "Da Ci Bei" (greatest compassion) silently or aloud for as long as you'd like. Developing the Ten Da qualities advances you on your soul journey in countless ways!

1. *Da Ai* — *Greatest Love* (pronounced *dah eye*)
2. *Da Kuan Shu* — *Greatest Forgiveness* (pronounced *dah kwan shu*)
3. *Da Ci Bei* — *Greatest Compassion* (pronounced *dah sz bay*)
4. *Da Guang Ming* — *Greatest Light* (pronounced *dah gwahng ming*)
5. *Da Qian Bei* — *Greatest Humility* (pronounced *dah chyen bay*)
6. *Da He Xie* — *Greatest Harmony* (pronounced *dah huh shyeh*)
7. *Da Chang Sheng* — *Greatest Flourishing* (pronounced *dah chahng shung*)
8. *Da Gan En* — *Greatest Gratitude* (pronounced *dah gahn en*)
9. *Da Fu Wu* — *Greatest Service* (pronounced *dah foo woo*)
10. *Da Yuan Man* — *Greatest Enlightenment* (pronounced *dah ywen mahn*)

TAO JING

Tao Ke Tao
Fei Chang Tao.
—Master Sha, *Tao I: The Way of All Life*

Tao I Retreat
Ramsau, Austria, May 2010
Robert Liu introduced me to Master Sha

Springtime in Ramsau, Austria. Site of Master Sha's first *Tao I Retreat*. Situated high in the Austrian Alps, Ramsau is a quaint European mountain village that depends on tourists for its economic well-being. A destination for serious downhill and cross-country skiers in winter, mountain hikers and campers in summer. It's May, 2010 and the retreat is scheduled to occur between the two busy seasons for visitors to Ramsau. At this time of the Alpine spring, Master Sha's Tao students are the only group in town. There are about 300 of us crammed into every available hotel, motel, and bed and breakfast inn we can find in the small Austrian village. A large Community Center and Meeting Hall is located at the base of the mountain adjacent to currently idle ski lifts. Big enough to hold the sessions with Master Sha, and also the site of the only operating restaurant in town.

Master Sha's students have arrived from all over the world. Every continent represented. Tao I is a homecoming of old souls all intent on furthering our soul journeys by learning to serve others unconditionally under the guidance and direction of our teacher. I meet so many people in this spiritual family that I feel I've known across multiple lifetimes and this experience is shared pretty much across the board by everyone else. We're a bunch of ancient beings on the Xiu Lian Purification Journey. Still navigating time and space in human bodies. Trying to clear our karma. Trying to reach enlightenment. Trying to raise our soul standing in this life so that we don't have to reincarnate and come back again in the next. Brimming with confidence that Master Sha is the answer to all of our questions. Against the backdrop of the beautiful snow-capped peaks surrounding the valley, we students are primed to hear both ancient and new wisdom from our humble and loving teacher.

On the morning of the first day of the retreat, Master Sha welcomes the students in a formal opening ceremony. To celebrate our arrival from points all over the globe, Master Sha decides to transmit what he calls a *Feng Shui Golden Light Ball* to bless the valley, the local inhabitants, and the retreat attendees.

A Feng Shui Golden Light Ball is a divine treasure, which Master Sha can manifest in any location in which he is serving. A Feng Shui Golden Light Ball radiates pure divine love, forgiveness, compassion, and light at a very high frequency invisible to the naked eye. I never even knew this type of spiritual treasure or blessing existed! My Third Eye is only just starting to open, but I sense the arrival of the Feng Shui Golden Light Ball as soon as Master Sha completes his invocation to transmit the treasure. The huge ball hangs in the sky above the retreat building and below the peaks of the surrounding mountains. I "see" it as yellow/orange like the sun. Spinning slowly. Radiating the energy of Divine Love, Divine Light, Divine Forgiveness and Divine Compassion to everyone and everything in the valley. And this Feng Shui Golden Light Ball is massive! At least 10 times the size of the Ramsau Conference building.

Divine and Tao treasures are sometimes the catalyst for "unusual" things to occur in the vicinity where they show up. About fifteen minutes after Master Sha's blessing, we are enjoying a short break before the formal teachings begin. A number of students, including the few smokers in attendance, gather outside around the front of the building to engage in small talk and reconnect with each other at the soul level. Everyone has unique and fascinating stories to tell about how their soul overcame immense challenges in order to make it to Austria and the Tao I Retreat.

A few car alarms have started blaring inexplicably in the parking lot. While the students mill around outside in the spring sunshine, Ramsau's two on-duty two police cars come rushing over the hill from the village and race down towards the convention center. The police cars enter the parking lot with red lights flashing and tires squealing. The police drive around the perimeter of the buildings, like hounds trying to flush out an elusive fox in the bushes. But there are no car thieves or suspicious persons to be found, only students of Master Sha.

Kitchen staff wearing stained white aprons run out to question the officers. No one in charge. No one sure of anything. No one knowing what to do next. Looking like Keystone Cops, the police have been outwitted by an invisible foe.

We learn that the building's security alarms had gone off at the same time Master Sha was transmitting the Feng Shui Golden Light Ball. The police responded as they had a valid reason to suspect "something unusual" was going on at the retreat.

Over lunch later that day, there are lots of chuckles amongst the spiritually aware with open Third Eyes. Because at Master Sha's Tao I Retreat, "something unusual" is most certainly going on. The students smile at each other knowingly, sure the unseen culprit causing electrical malfunctions in the building and setting off car alarms in the parking lot was Master Sha's Feng Shui Golden Light Ball.

⚜   ⚜   ⚜

Master Sha is teaching us the major concepts from the sixth book of his Soul Power Series: *Tao I: The Way of All Life*. Today, we are learning about *Tao Normal Creation* and *Tao Reverse Creation* as applied to our soul's Xiu Lian Purification Journey.

The Tao Normal and Reverse Creation Cycle represents how all things are created from Tao (the Source) and how all things eventually return to Tao. The Great Cycle simplified by Master Sha so new students like me can easily understand how it works. It's simplest to think about the cycle in two parts: the Tao Normal Creation Cycle and the Tao Reverse Creation Cycle, each of which have four steps. In the Tao Normal Creation Cycle, all things are created by the Source, by Tao. Master Sha teaches:

Tao Normal Creation Cycle

1. **Tao Sheng Yi (Tao creates One)**
   "Tao is the Creator and The Source. "One" is the Hun Dun or "blurred" condition in which there is no time or space. The blurred Hun Dun Oneness condition is timeless, spaceless, formless, shapeless. The laws of Yin and Yang aren't applicable in the Hun Dun condition."
2. **Yi Sheng Er (One creates Two)**
   "The blurred Hun Dun Oneness condition creates Two. Two is Heaven and Mother Earth."
3. **Er Sheng San (Two creates Three)**
   "This three is one plus two. One is the blurred Hun Dun Oneness condition. Two is Heaven and Mother Earth. Heaven belongs to yang. Mother Earth belongs to yin."
4. **San Sheng Wan Wu (Three creates All Things)**
   "Three creates all things in countless planets, stars, galaxies, and universes, including humanity."

In the Tao Reverse Creation Cycle, all things return to the Source, to Tao.

Tao Reverse Creation Cycle

1. **Wang Wu Gui San (All things return to Three)**
   "All things in all universes return to Three, which is Heaven, Mother Earth, and the blurred Hun Dun Oneness condition."
2. **San Gui Er (Three returns to Two)**
   "Two is Heaven and Mother Earth."
3. **Er Gui Yi (Two returns to One)**
   "Heaven and Mother Earth return to the blurred Hun Dun Oneness condition."
4. **San Sheng Wan Wu (One returns to Tao)**
   "The blurred Hun Dun Oneness condition returns to Tao."

Tao Normal and Reverse Creation Diagram

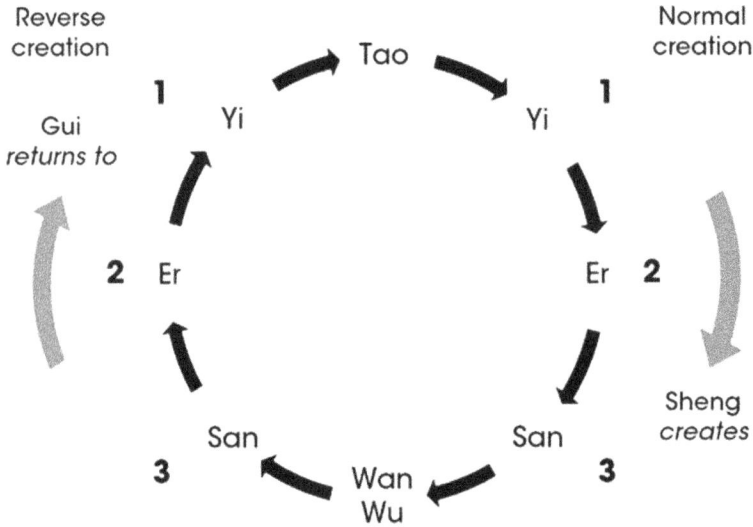

Reverse creation

Normal creation

Gui returns to

Tao

Yi **1**   Yi **1**

2 Er   Er **2**

Sheng creates

San **3**   San **3**

Wan Wu

Most of the world's major spiritual traditions preach that the soul's desire is to *Return to Forever.* Organized religions are all like ice cream to me, the particular flavor you choose from the menu is up to you and your soul:

Buddhist souls seek enlightenment through meditation.

Muslim, Jewish, and Christian souls expect to rise to heaven and reside with their one God after a lifetime of virtuous living.

Hindus aspire to union with Brahma. They seek infinite joy, infinite knowledge, and infinite bliss by practicing all kinds of traditional and highly advanced types of yoga and meditation.

Taoists seek to meld with The Source using ancient practices to gain longevity and immortality.

Here in Ramsau, high in the Austrian mountains, Master Sha is teaching his students Tao practices and techniques to facilitate the Tao Normal Creation and Tao Reverse Creation cycle in this lifetime. Regardless of which religion you practice, your soul most likely has some work to do before it can be uplifted and *Return to Forever*. If you carry heavy karma because you've made mistakes in this life or prior lives, you can think about knocking on heaven's door when your body dies, but you're not likely to enter Eternal Paradise without doing some clean-up work first.

Huston Smith likens the purification process to polishing a lamp that's covered over with dust, dirt, and grime. The muck on our souls obscures the light within us trying to shine through. The lamp may be on but we can't see the light and others also have difficulty seeing the light within us. We are blind to the fact that we are one with God. To become enlightened, we have to clean off the dirt of all our bad karma created from past lifetimes and this lifetime, and purify our thoughts, words, and actions in order to let our inner light shine forth so the doorman at heaven's gate can give us the nod to enter through the pearly gates.

It isn't easy to talk about, let alone comprehend this stuff. The more words, analogies, and metaphors we use to depict the Tao, the less we are successful in describing the indescribable. Master Sha's *Tao I* book contains a 75-line sacred text called the *Tao Jing*, which Master Sha received from the Divine directly. The first two lines of Master Sha's *Tao Jing* and the first two lines of Lao Tzu's *Tao De Jing* are basically identical.

"Tao Ke Tao
Fei Chang Tao."
The Tao that can be explained by words or comprehended by thoughts
is not the eternal Tao or True Tao.

High in the Austrian Alps, Master Sha teaches us that the Tao is beyond description. Beyond human comprehension. Lao Tzu says the same thing in the *Tao De Jing*:

"Look, it cannot be seen — it is beyond form.
Listen, it cannot be heard — it is beyond sound.
Grasp, it cannot be held — it is intangible.
It is called indefinable and beyond imagination."

Master Sha teaches the Hun Dun "blurred" condition is created by Tao. The Hun Dun "blurred" condition then creates Heaven and Mother Earth. Duality gets established. Yin and yang, us and them, male and female, light and dark. From Heaven and Mother Earth, the 10,000 things—all things—are formed.

Tricky to talk about which is why Lao Tzu suggests that it may be best to simply keep silent and not try to wax poetic on this and other aspects of the Tao:

"Therefore the wise go about doing nothing, teaching no-talking."

My limited intellectual understanding is that the first lines of Master Sha's *Tao Jing* and Lao Tzu's *Tao De Jing* are both a rather short, concise variant of the story of Genesis shared by Islam, Judaism, and Christianity in the Old Testament scriptures. God, The Divine, The Tao, The Source—call it what you like—exists as One and from the One springs all of creation. Once Heaven and Earth are formed, everything else in the physical universe follows, including human beings. Buddhists talk about life as illusion once duality appears in creation. Spiritual "duality" means we believe we are different, separate, and distinct from our Creator. That our true divine nature has been hidden or lost, and is in need of rediscovery, of enlightenment, to dissolve the *illusion* of separateness so that we can return to the Source. Just like the final step in Master Sha's explanation of Tao Reverse Creation: *Yi Gui Tao (One returns to Tao).*

Lao Tzu says the way to *Return to Forever*—to "go home."—is to follow The Way. The *Tao Te Ching* talks about the subtle attributes of the "superior man" who follows nature's way, lives in harmony with all the rest of creation, and is therefore able to avoid suffering and sickness.

In the Tao I Retreat, Master Sha is teaching us *The Way of All Life* in order to achieve healing, rejuvenation, longevity and immortality. We learn and practice variations of the Four- Power Techniques for soul healing and many of the participating students benefit from good results, including relief from chronic illnesses they've suffered for many years.

In this out of the way meeting hall, in this out of the way mountain village, in this group of about 300 trekkers on the Xiu Lian path, I know I'm in the right place. My soul is ecstatic to be here with Master Sha and his students who are my soul brothers and sisters. I am one of them. I fit in with this group of ethnically diverse spiritual seekers. We all stand at different points on the circle of Tao Normal and Reverse Creation, and we are all at different stages of our Xiu Lian Purification Journey. But at least for the duration of the retreat, our souls are all joined as one ... which also happens to be the mission of Master Sha:

Wan Ling Rong He (All Souls Join As One)

When all souls join as one, all souls will have transformed and returned to Tao, the final step in the grand Tao cycle. In order for *Wan Ling Rong He* to manifest, we all need to purify our own souls, hearts, minds, and bodies, transform our collective karma, and forgive and serve others unconditionally.

Master Sha stresses to his students that *now* is the time to serve others who are suffering due to karmic burdens. He teaches us that Mother Earth is "the bitter sea," a place to clear our karma and advance on our soul journey by uplifting our soul standing. Mother Earth is in transition and this transition could last many years. Many people could lose their lives. Pollution of the planet, global economic woes, potent communicable diseases, war, famine, and drought may be coming upon us in greater force in the years ahead. The tough times have already begun. "Just look around you," Master Sha advises. "See what is happening on Mother Earth. We *will* get through this transition period, but not without casualties and loss."

Sitting in the meeting hall, I'm dealing with uncomfortable thoughts: *I'm just a tiny, insignificant player in the unfolding cosmic drama. I don't have any power to change the world. So what am I supposed to do? What does Master Sha expect of me?*

Flowering Plants and Friendly Neighbors

If there is light in the soul,
There is beauty in the person.
If there is beauty in the person,
There will be harmony in the home.
If there is harmony in the home,
There is honor in the nation.
If there is honor in the nation,
There will be peace in the world.

—Feng Shui Chinese Proverb

Feng Shui (pronounced "fung shway") is an ancient Chinese practice for improving the energy flow of spaces. In Traditional Chinese Medicine, when energy in the body, known as *qi*, flows without blockages, one is healthy and free of illness. This concept of *qi* also applies to the spaces around us, our environment. When the *qi* around the spaces of our homes and businesses flows without blockages, those environments will be robust and flourish.

Master Sha offers a special treasure called a *Feng Shui Golden Light Ball*. This treasure, which radiates golden light, can be downloaded to people's homes and businesses. The golden light ball incorporates Feng Shui concepts from ancient China to improve the flow of positive *qi* and create an environment filled with love, peace, and harmony. What's more, it creates a *Divine* feng shui.

In addition to his other credentials as a Master of many Chinese disciplines, including Qi Gong and Tai Chi, Master Sha is also a Chinese Feng Shui Master. I get intrigued when I first hear Master Sha describe the benefits of having a Feng Shui Golden Light Ball to the participants attending the first Tao I Retreat in Ramsau, Austria in May, 2010.

When I learn that we students can receive our own Feng Shui Golden Light Ball for our residences and businesses, I apply for the treasure for my condo. At home, I have a meditation room with an altar on which many of my spiritual items reside. I'm thinking the Feng Shui Golden Light Ball might shake up the *qi* of the space in a positive way. I honor for the treasure and Master Sha gives the order to Heaven to create and download the ball to my condo address in downtown Toronto.

Historically speaking, I've had tremendous difficulty keeping plants alive ever since I started living on my own. Flowers and foliage just don't do well around me wherever I'm residing. Despite my best efforts to water plants properly and place them in an appropriate amount of sunlight, the leaves on my plants seem to always be wrinkly, turned down, and colored a shade of dead brown.

When I return home to my condo from Austria, I'm anxious to check if the Feng Shui Golden Light Ball is really here. My Third Eye shows me an image of the ball near the ceiling of the short hallway between the living room and my bedroom. To me, it looks kind of like a slowly spinning disco ball from the 70s, silver, shiny, and sparkly. Within ten minutes of watering my two plants, the leaves fill with color, rising and expanding like a heavenly angel slowly unfurling her wings. I can feel their happiness in a way that can't be accounted for simply because I fed the plants a little water after returning home.

When you live in a large, hotel-style condominium complex, you get to see and interact with your neighbors only sporadically. You occasionally see each other in the elevator, the parking garage, the mailroom, or if you happen to be coming or going from your respective condos at the same time by coincidence. Although my neighbors that live up and down the hallway aren't unfriendly people, none of us seem to go out of our way to converse much when we do encounter each other in the hallway. Master Sha teaches that having a Feng Shui Golden Light Ball can improve the relationships of people within its sphere of influence. This aspect of a heavenly treasure can be especially helpful if you own a people-oriented business like a restaurant!

To my surprise, I find that after returning from Austria and living with the Feng Shui Golden Light Ball in the condo for a week, my neighbors have become much more friendly to me as well as to each other. We start asking questions about one another's health, families, and jobs. We start commenting on the weather or the local sports team's chances of making the playoffs. It's not a profound in-depth analysis of our respective spiritual journeys, but it's a start at connecting with each other as human beings. I'm witness to the fact that the waves of golden, vibrating, healing energy from the Feng Shui Golden Light Ball aren't confined to my living space alone but extend beyond the walls of my condo into the adjoining units, generating a positive effect on the people who live around me. This newly-created healing frequency of love, peace, and harmony radiates continuously.

To this day, I'm frequently and pleasantly surprised when a guest enters my condo and breaks into a smile while taking off their shoes in the front hallway. "Oh, wow! This place feels amazing! And I haven't even gotten past the front door! What's going here?" If they only knew...

Extraordinary Abilities

The miracles of Earth are the laws of Heaven.
                                        —Jean Paul Richter

Master Sha

My experience at the *Tao I Retreat* is astounding! I never dreamed I'd find a *living* Master to guide me on my Xiu Lian Purification Journey, let alone one with such high spiritual standing as Master Sha. My Guru, Paramahansa Yogananda is pure love, but since I was born a year after he transitioned, I never got to meet him in the flesh. I never had the opportunity to experience the Guru's love face to face. Master Sha's soul frequency and vibration are incredibly high, incredibly fine, and infinitely beyond my ability to understand with my limited intellect. I am so grateful to have been invited to study with such an enlightened being. But I also find that, as a new student with low frequency and low vibration, being in the presence of Master Sha can come with its own set of unique challenges.

At the end of each teaching session at the Tao I Retreat, I find myself totally drained of energy. After the first few days, I realize that I'll have to skip some sessions to sleep, recover, adjust my body, integrate all the blessings, and recalibrate my energy to what I've been witness to in the meeting hall. Many other students experience similar responses and are overcome with spiritual exhaustion from the high-level frequency, and dealing with their karma while purifying their souls, hearts, minds, and bodies.

My Third Eye is not as advanced as other students of Master Sha, but I do occasionally receive images when a person's karma is being cleared on stage at the retreat. Using my Third Eye drains me of so much energy. Weakens my stamina and immunity. After only a day or two at Master Sha's Tao I Retreat, I find myself perpetually tired and rundown, susceptible to communicable diseases, battling the onset of a cold or the flu.

"You're purifying!" one student counsels me.

"Be thankful!" suggests another.

"Master Sha is here to help you if needed!" one of Master Sha's Divine Channels reassures me. "Let's do the practice to build up the energy in your Snow Mountain energy center."

The Snow Mountain practice helps immensely and I soon find myself looking forward to getting up from my seat every few hours, standing in the back of the hall, and repeating this chanting practice to boost my energy, stamina, vitality, and immunity. Incidentally, Master Sha teaches that this important energy center, the Snow Mountain Area, should be well developed before opening the Third Eye. The Snow Mountain Area energy center provides nourishment for the brain and Third Eye, so using the Third Eye to see spiritual images can drain the Snow Mountain Area.

❧ ❧ ❧

Master Sha is providing the retreat participants some basic training in the teachings from *Tao I: The Way of All Life*. Master Sha is a great teacher when it comes to the tricky subject known as Tao. And like all good educators, Master Sha balances his serious teachings with colorful stories and anecdotes from his own life or the lives of other Masters such as Buddha or Jesus. He encourages us to read *The Journey to the West*, a Chinese classic written in the 16th century. The story is a fictional account of a Buddhist monk from China charged by his superiors to travel to India and return with sacred texts to help spread Buddhism throughout China. The monk is accompanied by three companions, including a mischievous character known as the *Monkey King*. These high-level spiritual beings assist the monk along the journey by using their extraordinary abilities against evil demons and forces trying to disrupt their journey. The work is an allegory of the Xiu Lian Purification Journey, which, like the Hindu classic *The Bhagavad Gita*, can be read as an entertaining story or a spiritual text, depending on where you are in your soul journey. Master Sha asks us to read the book to give his students an idea of how beings in the soul world can serve those of us struggling daily in the "bitter sea" of Mother Earth.

❧ ❧ ❧

We students collectively shed a sea of tears in Master Sha's meeting hall over the course of the 10-day retreat. Tears of joy. Tears of love. Tears of purification. What a cleansing and uplifting of souls takes place in the Austrian village of Ramsau!

We deeply understand that we need to serve others humbly. The other students and I feel like chosen ones blessed to be in the Master's presence. We are here to learn what our roles are in supporting Master Sha's task of joining all souls as one (*Wan Ling Rong He).* Finding ourselves with an enlightened Master in this idyllic setting high in the Austrian Alps, our souls remind us we've been prepping for this retreat for many past lives so that we can receive this level of spiritual training with Master Sha now, in this current life, in this current place and time. The wisdom Master Sha is revealing to us is wisdom we've always known deep down in our souls. The teachings are not new. The wisdom has been hidden or forgotten by us as a result of our repeating negative karmic patterns over and over again, lifetime after lifetime. Master Sha is re-educating us, re-awakening us to the truth we always knew. Tao I is not the first time this group of souls has met!

Master Sha calls himself a "servant," chosen by God to teach us, love us, heal us, and empower us so that we in turn will be able to better serve humanity. Master Sha serves all souls in all universes, and we are following gratefully in his footsteps on the journey to reach *Wan Ling Rong He* under his loving guidance and direction.

❧ ❧ ❧

On the last day of the Tao I Retreat, Master Sha distributes a CD to each participant. The CD is a blessed gift on which he's recorded a musical version of the *Tao Jing,* the 75 phrases which have been the focus of the core teachings during the retreat. Master Sha's relative by marriage, Mr. Chiang, an award-winning music composer who lives in Taiwan, has written the music score and Master Sha sang the words.

Seated in the meeting hall and hearing Master Chiang's angelic spiritual melody for the first time, tears of joy flow from me and many of the other students. To this day, the *Tao Jing* is the most beautiful music I've ever heard.

In the months following the retreat, I learn this song by heart, singing along with the CD whenever I'm out doing errands, or driving around Toronto. In the summer months in Canada, my truck windows are usually open. When I'm stopped at red lights, I'm initially a little self-conscious about singing aloud and being heard, judged, or criticized by Toronto's ethnically diverse pedestrians. But most people just smile at me when they hear me singing, and no one ever asks me to roll up my windows or stop.

⚜   ⚜   ⚜

In late April, 2010, Iceland's Eyjafjoell Volcano exploded. Plumes of gray ash spewed eastward, spreading over the European continent. Over 8 million travelers got stranded at every major airport in multiple countries during the natural disaster. As the polluting ash rained down from the darkened heavens, the economic cost to industry escalated into billions of dollars. The Eyjafjoell volcano caused the most massive disruption of travel to and from Europe since World War II.

The explosion of the volcano overlaps with the final days of the Tao I Retreat. Master Sha offers a blessing to calm the volcano and ease the havoc for the airlines personnel assisting travelers, and those of us scheduled to return home on flights out of Salzburg Airport. Most flights heading West are cancelled and the students are scrambling to book any available hotel rooms near any airport they think will open up for outbound flights. After the beauty and tranquility of our time spent with Master Sha, stress levels are rising. Those with limited resources haven't anticipated or budgeted the extra funds needed to stay in Austria beyond the end of the retreat. Master Sha tells us not to worry, that he will give a *Soul Order* to assist everyone trying to get home. All we need to do is chant the healing mantras we've been taught, trust in the Divine, and call on Master Sha's soul to overcome the challenges of traveling during this massive natural disaster.

When I check with British Airlines, I learn my return flight to Toronto via London the following day is cancelled. No surprise there. *Okay, this is a good test!* I tell myself. *Time to see if my faith in Master Sha can be validated outside of the retreat in the real world.* I call British Airlines and politely inquire about alternate booking options. The Customer Service Rep checks for me and just as politely informs me that "At this time, Mr. Colwell, I can get you to London on your original flight but I don't have seats on any transatlantic flights right now. You can contact us again tomorrow evening when you arrive at Heathrow Airport."

"How about Business Class or even First Class?" I ask the gentleman who I'm sure has been overworked and overstressed dealing with this crisis. "If I upgrade, are there any seats available? Can you check again please?"

"Of course, sir. Let me put you on hold."

At this point, I start chanting "Master Sha, Master Sha, Master Sha. Can you please help me to get home on any available flight?" It's not that I'm pessimistic about chanting Master Sha's name, but I'm mentally preparing for a scenario where I'll have to scramble to find accommodations somewhere in the UK for an unknown amount of time until transatlantic flights resume service. Still, my soul tells me to keep chanting Master Sha's name.

When my Customer Service rep returns, he's excited. "Mr. Colwell? I'm not sure what happened but I checked the same schedules I was looking at earlier for you and there is now a flight available tomorrow evening that actually gets you into Toronto 20 minutes earlier than your original flight! I've booked you on that flight…and there is no additional charge for the flight change. I don't know why I didn't see it before."

Wow! I know why he didn't see it before. I hadn't started chanting Master Sha! My faith gets a mega-boost after seeing for myself the power of Master Sha's blessings. I leave Austria a changed man and tell everyone sitting around me on the flight home about my good fortune and the reason for it: Master Sha.

⚜   ⚜   ⚜

When I return home from Austria, my friends can see I've been transformed once again. The path of my Xiu Lian spiritual journey has been adjusted and a new direction has been clearly laid out before me. My Guru Paramahansa Yogananda sent me to learn from Master Sha. I've followed my Guru's guidance and have now become a student of Master Sha. I will study to become a Soul Healer and Teacher. I have no other choice. Master Sha is my path. Master Sha has become my Xiu Lian Purification Journey.

My Guru and Master Sha's love flows through my veins, my entire being, 24 hours a day. My Kriya Yoga sessions, my daily meditations, and my chanting practices do not subside or lessen in intensity once I return home to Toronto. My love for Guru Paramahansa Yogananda actually increases, as does my love for Master Sha. I become a regular participant and student at our Toronto *Power of Soul* group meetings in addition to continuing Kriya practice with my SRF group on Sunday mornings. Over the next 6 months, I attend as many Master Sha events and retreats as I can. *This is what I'm supposed to be doing!* My soul is as happy as it's ever been. What I don't anticipate is that there will be a huge emotional upheaval with this shift in the direction of my path. And though I don't begrudge anything that's happening, the spiritual testing and the emotional pain lying in wait for me will severely test my commitment to the Xiu Lian Purification Journey with Master Sha.

Divine Soul Songs

Divine Soul Songs are songs received by Master Sha directly from the Divine. They are *not* composed by human beings in the human realm. Master Sha's Divine Soul Songs can be chanted or sung in any language. Master Sha teaches that Divine Soul Songs carry *Divine frequency and vibration with Divine love, forgiveness, compassion, and light,* which bless all humanity and all souls in all universes. When you sing or chant Divine Soul Songs, you are serving all souls everywhere! And it feels so good!

Many people are too embarrassed to sing in public. They feel their voice is not suitable for being heard by an audience. Others feel confident only when singing alone in the shower or driving in their car listening to their favorite CD. Singing in church is also "safe" for many people who feel spiritually inspired to praise God in song only in the company of other devotees. Many spiritual traditions include devotional group singing as part of their rituals. Singing to God sincerely touches our hearts and can cause us to cry spontaneously just like people who burst into tears during an Italian opera when the tenor sings, regardless of whether or not they understand the lyrics.

An early memory I have of singing the praises of God comes from the late 1950s. My family regularly attended Catholic Mass at the Blessed Sacrament Church in Wakefield, Massachusetts. I despaired when the Catholic Pope changed the rules and Mass was no longer sung in Latin. Even though I didn't understand the meaning of the Latin words, I loved the music for what it was, joyous praising of the Divine in song. I was only 6 or 7 years old, but recall the angelic voices of the choir echoing throughout the high-ceilinged church and filling my soul with love each Sunday. When listening to the choir singing, the notes touched my heart and pulled at my soul. But I was too young to consider that the angelic music might have been reminding my soul of the Xiu Lian path I'd been traveling for countless lifetimes and that I'd probably heard and sung many of these same songs in prior lifetimes as a Christian.

Master Sha received his first Divine Soul Song: *Love Peace and Harmony*, in California on September 10, 2005, while walking through the Redwood forest with three of his advanced students. One of the students asked Master Sha if he would request a song for the Mission from Heaven. Master Sha obliged the student, Heaven obliged Master Sha, and the Divine delivered *Love Peace and Harmony* to Master Sha in Soul Language, which is the language all of our souls can speak with each other.

Love Peace and Harmony is a Divine gift to humanity and all souls. When you chant *Love Peace and Harmony*, you are serving. You are helping to change the frequency and vibration of all souls in all universes. On Master Sha's website, there are many stories of people who have received miraculous healings by singing *Love Peace and Harmony*.

Master Sha founded the *Love Peace Harmony Movement* in 2010 with a goal of having 1.5 billion people singing the song simultaneously by the year 2020. He did not copyright the *Love Peace and Harmony* song. Anyone can download an mp3 of the song from Master Sha's website for free and share it with others. There are many other Divine Souls Songs available in the CDs that are included with many of Master's Sha's books, and on Master Sha's website (www.DrSha.com). Check them out! Remember when you sing a Divine Soul Song, the divine frequency and vibration of each song is healing, rejuvenating, and transforming you and others around you!

I've included the lyrics for *Love Peace and Harmony* in English, Soul Language, and Mandarin Chinese below.

Love Peace and Harmony

English
I love my heart and soul

I love all humanity
Join hearts and souls together
Love peace and harmony
Love peace and harmony

Soul Language
Lu La Lu La Li
Lu La Lu La La Li
Lu La Lu La Li Lu La
Lu La Li Lu La
Lu La Li Lu La

Mandarin Chinese
Wo ai wo xin he ling
Wo ai quan ren lei
Wan ling rong he mu shi sheng
Xiang ai ping an he xie
Xiang ai ping an he xie

Temple Dogs

Before enlightenment: chop wood, carry water.
After enlightenment: chop wood, carry water.
—Ancient Zen Proverb

Baba's Barn, Boulder, Colorado
Master Sha's First Divine Temple established in 2008

Tracy. My Canadian girlfriend of many years. Previously tolerant—if not oblivious—of my daily meditation practice. Completely intolerant of my studies with Master Sha. Views my new teacher as a rival. An enemy to be dealt with quickly and harshly. A growing cancer needing to be decisively and ruthlessly cut from my body. Initially hopeful Master Sha will turn out to be just a passing fancy for me, now gravely concerned at the focused attention I'm paying to my soul journey.

As the lead singer in a successful band that releases a new hard-rock CD every few years, Tracy's lifestyle becomes the antithesis of mine. When I get serious about pursuing my Xiu Lian Purification Journey on a full-time basis after meeting Master Sha, Tracy gets doubly serious about her music and modeling career as if we're in a competition to see who can fulfill their respective dreams first. I promote her band by financing a few music videos for Canada's Much Music television station. But while I'm busy practicing Kriya Yoga and slowly withdrawing from Tracy's world of sex, drugs, and rock 'n roll, she's active with photo shoots, magazine, and radio interviews. Basically, Tracy's awake during the hours I want to sleep and sleeping during the hours I'm doing my spiritual practices.

Tracy believes in a Christian God, but is not a member of any particular denomination of Christianity that gathers weekly for service. It's hard to get up on Sunday morning and go to church if you don't get home from a Saturday night gig and after-party until 7 a.m. My soul warns me of the fallacy of trying to meddle in another person's spiritual journey, so I don't attempt to "convert" Tracy or steer her to Master Sha. And although she is unable to overtly prevent me from studying with my new teacher, Tracy is clearly worried at the diminishing amount of time and attention I'm focusing on her.

Of course, I'm not the first aspirant on the Xiu Lian path to wrestle with a partner who has little interest in their spiritual journey or is struggling to acknowledge the existence of their soul. I know other students of Master Sha and other teachers that have strained relationships with their partners and families because they've made a personal commitment to direct their time and effort to the Xiu Lian Purification Journey. It makes perfect sense to me why the monastics of many spiritual traditions take a vow of celibacy and choose to live behind the cloistered walls of seminaries and monasteries to minimize distractions from the opposite sex and the outside world. Master Sha doesn't require his Divine Channels or advanced students to take a celibacy vow. I know many married couples who are students of Master Sha, many raising families. But students like me, trying to manage their journey with a partner on different or conflicting spiritual paths, often face serious relationship challenges.

Tracy and I struggle to weather the storm as best we can. I place my trust in the Divine, hoping against hope to find a solution to our dilemma. Some days and some nights are better than others. But the intertwined thread of our life together is unraveling. Our story is drawing to a close. We both know it. It's unavoidable. Our love is withering like a dying limb on the once flowering tree of our affection. Unstoppable. I really don't want to cut off the dying branch or let it fall to the ground on its own. I don't want "us" to die. My heart is desperate to see my lover flourish, rejuvenate, grow new buds, and flower once again. I would love to see her find God in her heart and pursue the Divine with passion and fervor. But it's not right for me, nor my place, to manipulate Tracy's soul like a bonsai specialist wrapping wire around the branches of a tree's limbs to force it to grow in the direction he wants.

We face the crisis together resignedly. Neither of us know what to do. We are lovers who've lost our love. The only solace we share is the belief that our souls are eternal and maybe we will meet again in a future lifetime and be given a chance to work out whatever karma still exists between us. And when we can't bring ourselves to make the necessary and inevitable split, the Divine steps in and makes it for us.

❧ ❧ ❧

This story of *Flying With Dragons* began in December, 2010 in Niagara Falls while I was driving home to Toronto after a Christmas visit to Boston to spend the holiday with my sons and grandkids. It was there on Rainbow Bridge separating Canada and the US that I was detained by Canadian Immigration authorities, deported, and barred from returning to my home and life in Toronto. Why then? It was the only time in years of border crossings that I'd ever been questioned about my legal status in Canada. The Divine most certainly played a role in the events that occurred on that frigid, stark, December evening and I was angry at his intervention. I silently screamed at God like a child whose toy is taken away: *No! What are you doing messing up my life like this? Why do I deserve to suffer like this?*

The Divine was prepping me to move on, to begin a new chapter on my Xiu Lian Purification Journey. I resisted of course, unable to bear the thought of not being in total control of my own spiritual destiny. Still harboring a big ego and attachments. Still wanting to meticulously plan my actions and activities based around what "I' wanted to do and not being open to God's will and plans for me. Heaven was busy preparing a change of scenery for me, giving me an opportunity to start fresh, to do my spiritual practice in new locations with new friends. Giving me a chance to disassociate from an environment and lifestyle not 100% in alignment with Master Sha and my Xiu Lian practice.

My girlfriend and I could have made more of an effort to stay connected during the time I was barred from Canada. We could have leveraged social media outlets to communicate more often than we did. We could have met outside of Canada, taken a vacation to Europe, and survived the year-long ban. But we didn't. We chose not to. Both of us cognizant of what had to happen between us. At the soul level, I believe Tracy slowly changed her perspective regarding Master Sha. She no longer wanted to interfere with or derail my spiritual journey with my teacher like she had in the days immediately after I received the "punch in the belly" from Sha's Golden Healing Ball during that snowy winter morning almost one year earlier.

Everyone suffers. Everyone has pain. It's the human condition. Many people are happy to tell you all about their suffering. They wear their pain like a badge, pinned to their chest like a "scarlet letter" for all to see. Their suffering a built in excuse for why they can't move forward. It's the lucky ones who figure out it's best to accept one's suffering for what it is—the result of past bad karma due to the mistakes we've made—and move on under the guidance of a spiritual teacher or guru who can help.

Driving away from Las Vegas, Nevada, I take the time to reflect on all the myriad chapters of my spiritual journey. Uprooted from a comfortable lifestyle in Toronto and having bounced around between my sister's home in Boston and my brother's condo in Las Vegas for a few months, I'm excited now about moving to the Rocky Mountains, to a climate that's sunny 300 days a year. It's time to meet and play with new Dragons on the Xiu Lian path.

⚜   ⚜   ⚜

Boulder, Colorado. This college town tucked up against the Colorado Front Range foothills is only a geologic step away from the massive Rocky Mountains running 3000 miles from the northernmost part of British Columbia to southern New Mexico. Boulder is also a spiritual community filled with temples, ashrams, yoga studios, health spas, Reiki and massage specialists, Tibetan clothing stores, and health-conscious restaurants scattered about the downtown outdoor mall. Naropa University and the Shambala Institute are headquartered in Boulder, the two Buddhist spiritual organizations founded by Chögyam Trungpa Rinpoche in the 1970s. Boulder is a spiritual seeker's Disneyland. The "New Age" movement probably started here!

My Xiu Lian Purification Journey brings me to Colorado for a couple of reasons. Master Sha held his second Tao Retreat in Estes Park, Colorado in October, 2010. After driving out from Las Vegas to attend the event, I fell in love with the mountains and the climate. In between intense teaching sessions with Master Sha, the students got to experience the tail end of the annual Elk Rut. During the annual rut, massive and majestic big-horned bull elks challenge each other for breeding rights to the female elks. The wailing cries of the males echo across the meadows surrounding the lodge lending a surreal atmosphere to the Tao Retreat. Estes Park is a magical place to be learning Tao from Master Sha.

My brother, Joe, lives in Denver and my youngest son Danny lives in Colorado Springs, about 45 miles south of Denver. Since I no longer have a permanent residence in the US or Canada, I decide Colorado will be an attractive state in which to purchase a property and start my life anew. But the primary reason I pick Boulder as my new residence is because it's the home of Master Sha's first Divine Temple in the United States. I'll be able to do my practices there with no distractions in the form of a non-spiritual partner, or the temptations of the Las Vegas strip available to me while living in Nevada.

Master Amritam, one of Master Sha's Divine Channels and Worldwide Representatives, became a student of Master Sha in 2007 after meeting Master Sha and his spiritual father from China, Master Guo, at an event in San Francisco. Master Amritam is the sole daughter of a stand-up comic. She grew up traveling around the country with her father, hanging onto his coattails and getting to meet many famous entertainers such as Bob Hope, Rosemary Clooney, and Patti Page. In her early twenties, her soul awakened and called her to India where she studied with multiple spiritual Masters before becoming an advanced student of Osho. When she returned to the US after many years, she purchased a six-acre farm in Boulder and converted the barn, formerly home to cows and horses, into a meditation temple. She invited many spiritual Masters to teach at the temple, including Master Sha, who visited Boulder in 2008. Master Sha recounts the formation of the Temple, known as Baba's Barn, in the introduction to his *Power of Soul* book:

> *"On March 9, 2008, at 1:45 p.m. Mountain Daylight Time, while I was teaching an Opening Spiritual Channels Workshop at the Boulder Broker Inn in Colorado, I received divine inspiration to create the first physical Love Peace Harmony Center in Boulder. I asked the Divine to create this center to offer divine healing, prevention of sickness, rejuvenation, and prolongation of life, as well as transformation of consciousness and every aspect of life, including relationships and finances. The Divine responded to my request and transmitted Divine Soul Power to Baba's Barn in Boulder. The Divine guided me to name this place a 'Love Peace Harmony Center.'*
>
> *The Divine told me, 'Dear my servant and servant of humanity, Zhi Gang, I love you. I have created this Love Peace Harmony Center because of your request. I have transmitted my soul healing and blessing power to it. Tell every student in this workshop that they can come to this center with their loved ones. To all who enter, I as your beloved Divine will offer healing, blessing, and life transformation.*
>
> *This is how the first Divine Love Peace Harmony Center was formed.*
>
> *This Love Peace Harmony Center carries divine presence. It is the first of many Love Peace Harmony Centers that will be formed worldwide. I wish you and your loved ones—I wish as many people as possible on Mother Earth—will receive this divine soul healing, blessing, and life transformation."*

After settling into my new condo in downtown Boulder in April, 2011, I started visiting the Temple regularly to chant and meditate. The upper barn loft is covered from floor to ceiling with white cotton draperies. Photos of Master Sha, statues of holy beings including Mother Guan Yin, and other sacred objects decorate the room. But the real power of the Temple lies in the many spiritual beings that Master Sha "downloaded" when he converted Baba's Barn to a sacred space. Like all of Master Sha's Divine Temples around the world, when guests enter the space with pure intention and connect with Heaven, they are instantly transported away from the cares and concerns of daily living to a place where the Divine is present, love flows, and healing of all aspects of life is possible.

It's a great honor and responsibility to run a Divine Temple of Master Sha. Master Amritam has a team of volunteers to assist her and I join the team partly from a willingness to serve but also partly because I'm new in town, don't know anyone, and want to jumpstart my Xiu Lian Purification Journey again by serving in some capacity. Master Amritam passes around a checklist of areas where she needs assistance. The group all laughs when they see I've filled out my form and checked: grass-mowing, leaf-raking, audio-visual support at events, taking trash to the dump, and computer support.

"You want to do *all* these things?" Master Amritam questions me.

"Sure." I reply without hesitation. "I can help in many ways on the farm … and I've got a pick-up truck!"

Chop Wood, Carry Water. The old Zen proverb seems most appropriate for me at this stage of the journey. One way to stay humble and serve the Divine and our fellow aspirants on the path is to take care of the little things. We can't all be leaders, CEOs, and Managers assigning tasks to those who work for us. Someone has to take out the trash, make sure there's toilet paper in the bathrooms, cut the grass, and sweep the floors. At Baba's Barn, there's a never-ending list of farm chores, maintenance, and upkeep projects to keep me and the other volunteers busy. It's a fabulous opportunity to serve the Mission. A lot of the chores take place outdoors. I work with a team to plant, weed, and water the garden.

I get to work up a sweat chopping down the thistle bushes that eternally threaten to overrun the grass. We have a riding mower that works most of the time, and when I'm cutting the six acres of grass around the property, I get chased by the three *Temple Dogs* that live on the farm.

Temple Dogs are special. Temple Dogs are spiritual. Their souls are ecstatic to be resident on a property with Master Sha's frequency and vibration buzzing all around them. Floppy, a Bassett Hound who's been adopted by Master Amritam after displaying anti-social tendencies is the boss of the group and senior supervisor of all dog activities. Floppy occasionally bites people he doesn't like, but seems to be ok with me once he gets to know me. JJ is a frisky Cairn Terrier, and Star is a Maltese mix. JJ and Star are in love and accompany each other around the farm like a married dog couple, sniffing out rabbits and mice while avoiding snakes and coyotes. A coyote once snuck up on JJ and grabbed him by the neck. The coyote was probably envisioning a tasty Terrier dinner, but got rudely interrupted by Floppy who moved faster than anyone thought possible when he saw the coyote's teeth sinking into JJ's neck. Floppy courageously liberated JJ from the clutches of the predator who had to leap over the boundary fence to avoid becoming Floppy's dinner.

My first year on the farm is one of the happiest in my life.

Chop Wood, Carry Water. I'm doing my practices and meditation daily.

Chop Wood, Carry Water. I'm serving at the Temple three or four days a week and meeting other students on the Xiu Lian path.

Chop Wood, Carry Water. I'm getting to practice healing using my Divine Healing Hands and other treasures I've received from Master Sha.

Chop Wood, Carry Water. I'm reading all twenty of Master Sha's books in order, studying the wisdom, and doing the suggested practices to clear my bad karma.

Chop Wood, Carry Water. I'm learning to speak less, listen more.

My Xiu Lian Purification Journey is back on track.

Sarah

I bow to Sarah, the young woman sitting across from me in the Soul Healing and Enlightenment booth I'm working with two of Master Sha's advanced students. We've set up a booth at the Yoga Journal Conference in Estes Park, Colorado a week before Master Sha is coming to the Boulder Temple to teach. Sarah has just received a Divine Healing Hands blessing. She requested the "free blessing" after wandering by our booth, picking up a copy of Master Sha's latest book we are giving away, and asking me a few pointed questions about Master Sha's mission. Divine Healing Hands blessings are a good way for people to directly experience The Power of Soul as described by my spiritual father in his books. I'm happy Sarah stayed and let me serve her with a 5-minute soul blessing and healing.

"You are safe." I tell Sarah.

"Excuse me?" she asks. I'm struck by the depth of her eyes. Dark and shining. No hint of anxiety or fear. I trust the soul behind those eyes completely, and feel like cool water being drawn into the hot springs pool of her spirit.

"You are safe." I repeat. "Someone has given you protection…this is the first time I've seen it." I inform my client. The barest trace of a Mona Lisa smile forms around Sarah's lips and I think to myself: *Have I known you before? What are we supposed to do for each other…here, now…in this moment of time and space?*

Her eyes tell me to go on. "It's like your body is enclosed in a big white cocoon." I tell her, recalling the stark image that came to me through my Third Eye during the Divine Healing Hands blessing. I pause to see if she has any questions. She doesn't speak but strengthens our visual connection so I go on. "It's…permeable, it lets the good light in, but blocks anything bad…are you aware you have it?"

Sarah sits in quiet contemplation for a few moments. Carefully chooses her words. "Well, I know I have something that's helping me…I haven't told anyone about it but I guess *you* see it." I nod, sensing she'll reveal more to me if I'm patient and don't speak. "I've tried to kill myself four times …" she confesses without blinking or turning away. The disclosure hurts me, awakens my sense of compassion, and immediately an arc of spiritual red flowers starts streaming from my heart to hers. "After the last time, I know I received a gift from God … maybe it's this protection-cocoon-thing you see … I'm not sure … but I realized then that I'm not going to try to hurt myself again … that there's something I'm supposed to do in this lifetime to help others."

It's not the time or place to ask Sarah to reveal more of her story, and somehow that's all right. She doesn't need to be intimate with me in that way right now since there's a line of people waiting for their Divine Healing Hands blessing just out of earshot of our conversation but close enough to see something spiritually significant is being discussed. My soul urges me to encourage Sarah to pursue her own Xiu Lian journey. Her "protection package" is a priceless divine treasure and I agree with her there's a reason and a purpose behind it.

"Come to Master Sha's free Soul Healing evening next Friday night in Boulder. You can meet him in person! If anyone can tell you what you're supposed to do, it's Master Sha." *Please come. Don't miss this chance.*

Sarah stands up to leave, still wearing her mysterious smile. I hold out my hand to her, ready to thank her for her time. A handshake is not what she wants. She hugs me for not nearly as long as I would like, then slides her arms down to take both my hands. "Maybe I'll see you there …"

CRISIS OF FAITH

*"Do not worry about pain, and do not be afraid of disasters.
Both are part of the process of purification, life trans-
formation, and soul enlightenment.
Do not let pain and disaster stop your growth.
Be confident and patient as you take your spiritual journey."*
— Master Sha, *Soul Mind Body Medicine*

The Xiu Lian Purification Journey is not linear. There's no straight line from Point A to Point B, from human existence back to Tao. Master Sha describes the path as circular in his Tao Normal and Reverse Creation Cycle teaching. As much as each serious student practicing Xiu Lian would like to move quickly and directly to sainthood, enlightenment, and the Tao with a minimum of pain and effort, most of us are most assuredly going to encounter bumps in the road. Detours that set us back. Roadblocks that have the potential to derail us entirely from our spiritual path. Shit happens. Karma is the root cause of success and failure in every aspect of life including the Xiu Lian Purification journey. And when we are on the spiritual path, sooner or later, karma rears its ugly head. As Master Peter Hudoba, one of Master Sha's Divine Channels, says: "When karma attacks you, you are powerless."

It's not unusual for students on the Xiu Lian Purification Journey to experience a *Crisis of Faith* when their karma activates. Master Sha teaches there are all kinds of karma: personal, ancestral, relationship, and financial karma, to name just a few. Karma can be the source of fear, doubt, and intense uncertainty about whether or not we should continue our journey with our chosen teacher. And just like a married couple that decides to separate when they find the "honeymoon is over" after a few years of blissful and exciting life together, many students can find themselves suddenly and unexpectedly becoming disillusioned with their guru. They may even choose to leave their Master's mission and search for a new guru when they stop resonating with the teachings. Other students leave their chosen path when they face heavy challenges in life and feel they aren't getting the support they need from their spiritual family or their physical family. Severe illness, death of a loved one, loss of a job, failure of a business, and divorce can all take a heavy toll on one's belief in a loving Divine that's supposed to take all our pain away if we just pray to him earnestly.

In many spiritual traditions, becoming an advanced practitioner requires the student to "give up" or renounce the habits, lifestyles, and comforts of the world. Monastics may be required to make vows to Heaven and withdraw from day to day contact with non-spiritual friends and families except when serving their communities. For many students, these requirements become too extreme, and they choose to return to a secular lifestyle.

The Buddhist Master Chögyam Trungpa Rinpoche, founder of Naropa University and the Shambala Institute, lost many students because of his active practice of *Crazy Wisdom*. Rinpoche smoked and drank. He is rumored to also have had extramarital sex with many of his students, all the while teaching advanced aspects of Tibetan Buddhism to his followers. Although many of Rinpoche's students resonated at the soul level with his Buddhist teachings and meditation practices, they couldn't reconcile Rinpoche's outwardly hedonistic lifestyle as consistent with their vision of how a pure Master should behave, and so they left his Mission. Of course, the *Crazy Wisdom* conflict about "passing judgment on a Bodhisattva" was exactly what Rinpoche wanted his students to consider.

There are an infinite number of reasons why a student or disciple of a Master can lose faith in their teacher. When a Crisis of Faith occurs, the student must attempt to reconcile the conflict or they could end up abandoning their teacher to the detriment of their Xiu Lian journey.

I get hit with my first Crisis of Faith in the fall of 2010 at a retreat in Toronto. In a question and answer session with Master Sha in the group meeting hall one evening, a student asks some questions about a former Divine Channel who left the Mission a few years earlier. I never met the person—he left before I became a student of Master Sha—but I've heard rumors that this particular Divine Channel had a difference of opinion with Master Sha about how and where he should serve the Mission. Sitting in the middle of the group of students, I find myself getting extremely angry and upset over this discussion. I squirm in my seat. Am unable to keep still. *Why do they keep talking about this guy? He's gone. Who cares? It's obvious he had a big ego and didn't want to follow Master Sha's guidance. We have more important work to do now. Why does Master Sha keep talking about him?*

This small episode should have been a warning to me that my soul was purifying deeply and that my emotional reaction to Master Sha and the other students was not appropriate. I could have examined my reaction to the discussion once I calmed down, but I chose not to. I could have done Forgiveness Practice with Master Sha and all the souls that had upset me, but I didn't. The incident festered in my mind like an open sore for the next few days. Seeds of spiritual doubt about Master Sha and the Mission started to sprout in my mind: *Am I with the right teacher? Is this the right group of people I should be hanging out with to advance my own spiritual journey? Am I better off going back to Self-Realization Fellowship and becoming a monastic?* The mini-crisis passed in the weeks after the retreat, and I stopped questioning my purpose and role in Master Sha's Mission. But the incident left a bad taste in my mouth that I haven't forgotten to this day and for which I continue to do Forgiveness Practice for being disrespectful to Master Sha with my thoughts.

I experience a more serious Crisis of Faith after attending a special retreat in Orillia, Canada in January, 2012. The retreat is for Master Sha's "advanced" students—you must be personally approved by Master Sha to receive an invitation to come to this very sacred gathering—and I'm thrilled that I'm included in the group that will learn very ancient Tao wisdom and secrets not available to the general public.

Like most organized spiritual groups, Master Sha's Mission is a legally incorporated business with full-time employees and part-time volunteers supporting standard business operations and functions including Sales and Marketing, Finance, Legal, IT, Event Management, and Customer Service. The primary purpose of the business team is to promote and facilitate the expansion of Master Sha's Mission throughout the world. At the advanced retreat, Master Sha asks for students with professional expertise and backgrounds to come forward with creative thoughts, ideas, and their résumés if they feel they can help the Mission move ahead in any of these key business areas.

My 30-year corporate background working in IT and New Business Development for Fidelity Investments, a global financial services company, qualifies me to throw my hat in the ring. My soul wants to serve and help spread the Mission in any way possible. After all, Master Sha teaches us that:

"The purpose of life is to serve."

Excited about the opportunity before me. I polish up my résumé, and submit it to the Mission for consideration.

Things don't move as quickly as I'd like, but if there's one lesson we learn on the spiritual journey, it's that patience is truly a virtue. I counsel myself daily while waiting for a word from the Mission. *Okay, no problem. The business enhancement project has only just been announced. It's a work in progress. Drop this anxiety! Trust that the answers are forthcoming. After all, you know from experience that growing a business globally takes time to manifest. Heaven and Master Sha will bless the coordination of the business initiatives and ensure our success.*

After a few weeks, I'm verbally offered and accept the IT Manager role in the organization. I'm so happy! I'll get to tangibly serve the Mission by leveraging my business experience, and have fun doing it! Over the next six weeks, I undertake a series of exploratory interviews, meetings, and teleconferences with the existing IT and Customer Support personnel scattered all around North America. I'm trying to learn about the skill sets and business backgrounds of my team members, how the current IT operation is structured, what hardware and software systems are used, and what business processes are currently in place. I'm informed I'll have a chance to present my preliminary thoughts and recommendations to Master Sha and the Mission's Board of Directors at the next retreat.

When I meet with Master Sha and the business team to review my initial findings a few months later, I point out areas of risk, where we have single points of failure in either systems or personnel, and what major applications could be enhanced by upgrades or replacement. Stressing the long-term benefits of implementing integrated systems and business processes that can scale to support the objectives of Master Sha's growing worldwide organization, I supplement my findings with real-world examples of successful projects from my 25-year career at Fidelity Investments.

I feel good in the days immediately following the meeting, but although I'm hopeful about my new role and the future of the Mission's business, a little voice in the back of my head starts to nag me over the next few weeks. Reminds me that, although my suggestions about how to build a global systems infrastructure were listened to, my recommendations have not been formally accepted. No one has said "no," but no one has said "yes" either.

It's not atypical in the corporate world for major business initiatives requiring significant investment to get delayed, put on hold, or even cancelled when market conditions change or decisions are made to shift business priorities. While the business leaders take the time to strategize the overall goals and objectives of the Mission over the next few months, I find myself losing enthusiasm, and thinking maybe it was a mistake to accept the IT manager role.

Discouragement. Depression. Despair. Isolation. Impure thoughts and attitudes attack me as the weeks and months go by and I'm not asked to begin the implementation of any of my recommended proposals to upgrade the IT infrastructure of the Mission. The intensity of the negative feelings heightens daily and the Crisis in Faith explodes into full bloom at the beginning of summer. *Is this some sort of spiritual testing about my commitment to Master Sha whom I love so deeply? Am I failing him? Is this business stuff getting intertwined in a negative way with my Xiu Lian practice? Maybe I should back off and just concentrate on my spiritual practices.*

When little children act out, misbehave, or otherwise get themselves in trouble, their parents or teachers have to find a way to deal with the situations. "Time Out" is often an effective method for dealing with an upset child. When a child is put in "Time Out," he or she goes and sits somewhere quiet, away from others. Interaction with classmates or peers is forbidden during "Time Out". The wayward child is given a chance to reflect on what attitude and behavior needs to be modified before they'll be allowed back into the company of others. In late summer of 2012, I reluctantly decide I'm in need of a "Time Out" from Master Sha's Mission.

I desire seclusion, quiet, and rest so I can rethink my commitment to my Xiu Lian Purification Journey as a soul healer and student of Master Sha, and whether or not to continue as a part of the Mission's business team. I'm not in a good place spiritually or emotionally. Although my love and trust in Master Sha as a teacher is unshakeable, I'm angry, upset, and depressed about the lack of activity on the IT side of the Mission.

I publicly announce to friends and family at the Boulder Love Peace Harmony Center that I'm "undergoing renovations" and "leaving the Mission." I draft an email—my letter of resignation as IT Manager—and send it off to the Mission. And, like a convicted felon voluntarily delivering himself to the prison in which he'll serve his sentence, I place myself in "Time Out", cutting my ties with Master Sha's organization. I have no idea what lies ahead for me, I'm just anxious to get away...

Bosphorus Moon

White lilies in a clear vase
Whisper secrets to the red wine sleeping in my glass.
Turkish folk songs stir longing in love-starved souls.
Warm breezes from the Bosphorus smuggle smiles to dining patrons.
An autumn moon hides shyly behind ragged
patches of charcoal clouds.
Chants of the muezzin call the Muslim faithful to evening prayers.
Exotic exhortations at the border of East and West.
Istanbul. When have I known you before?

—Istanbul, Turkey

In November, 2012, I connect with my brother Joe and four of his friends who've invited me to join them on a trip to Istanbul. I've always had a yearning to visit this 7000-year-old city, the historical capital of both Muslim and Christian empires at different points in history. The metropolis, known by many names—Byzantium, Constantinople, Istanbul—is like a bridge straddling the continents of Asia and Europe.

We pay a visit to Topkapi Palace, once home to the Ottoman Empire Sultans, and start our tour at the Imperial harem and courtyard of the eunuchs that guarded them. The palace tour is interesting, but what unexpectedly affects me in the core of my being are the spiritual artifacts we find on display in the Chamber of Sacred Relics.

Muslims revere this chamber because it contains personal possessions of The Prophet Muhammad including one of his cloaks, two of his swords, a bow, one tooth, a hair of his beard, and an autographed letter. There's a preserved footprint of The Prophet here also that draws the attention of many of the tourists.

The Turban of Joseph is one of the antique artifacts housed in the Chamber of Sacred Relics. When I pass by this stained cotton treasure from the Old Testament slave who rose to become the second most powerful man in Egypt—a Vizier serving under the Pharaoh—my skin starts to tingle like I've been connected to a gentle current of electricity. Looking around me, I find no other visitors to the Chamber, including my brother, seem to be sharing my experience so I move on to the next exhibit, a glass case containing the Staff of Moses. This historical wooden stick—shorter than I thought it would be—is said to house miraculous powers as documented in the Old Testament. For believers, the Staff of Moses was able to draw water from a rock and divide the Red Sea into two halves as recounted in the Book of Exodus.

The frequency and vibration of the staff are astounding! Maybe 100 times stronger than what I felt when standing in front of the Turban of Joseph. The vibrations emanating from the staff feel warm. I start to sweat. Some sort of energy is encasing me, nourishing me in what feels like warm honey. My Third Eye starts to open, and although I'm not receiving any distinct visual images, I am enjoying a spiritual connection between my soul and the soul of the spiritual Dragon Moses.

But then, despite the energy I'm feeling, I start to get a little skeptical about the validity of this piece of wood behind the glass, thinking it might be nothing more than a tourist prop enabled by the Topkapi Palace's curators to entertain tourists like me. After all, how could a piece of wood a few thousand years old be preserved like this and not rot away? My brother Joe notices something's up and asks if I'm okay. We move on, but I'm a little disturbed about the doubts I felt in the Chamber of Sacred Relics.

Lying in bed later that night, I can't sleep. Maybe if I'd stayed in the vicinity of Moses's staff for a more extended period of time, I'd have received a message. Maybe if my analytical mind hadn't questioned the authenticity of the relic, Moses would have given me some guidance. The soul world often wishes to communicate with us, but we have to be open, trusting, and ready to receive the messages when they come. I fall asleep thinking I should have remained in the Chamber of Sacred Relics a little longer...

Love, Peace, and Harmony

"You have the power to heal yourself."

—Master Sha

Cahuita, Costa Rica, January 2013

Still in "Time Out" mode after my trip to Istanbul, I decide to forego Master Sha's January 2013 Advanced Retreat in frigid, snowy, ice-bound Ontario, Canada. My ego and vanity surge like a tsunami wave about to break on the shore of an unsuspecting coastal village. I don't want to go back to a retreat and expose myself to the inevitable questions like: "What's going on, Steve? Weren't you going to run the IT projects for the Mission? What happened to all the business plans you talked about last year? Where have you been the last six months?"

My heart whispers: *Let's go someplace warm instead. Look for a tropical beach that isn't too crowded. Go alone where no one can find you. Don't tell anyone you're going! Find a place to meditate and recharge your spiritual batteries.*

Costa Rica. I've never been there. When I check it out on the Internet, I learn I have two choices. I can visit the Pacific side of the country and stay at one of the many oceanfront resorts that offer all-inclusive packages for beach access, food, and drinks. Alternatively, the Caribbean side of the country is less built up and less touristy. Because the Atlantic side of Costa Rica has a lot of government-protected coral reefs, the beach communities are kept small. No major multinational hotel chains are allowed to build on the coast. The Pacific side resorts attract wealthy Americans looking for a tropical beach but within a gated and security guard-patrolled "safe" environment. The Caribbean side attracts a younger, single, more adventurous crowd. Surfers are welcome here, and the nightlife is dominated by open-air bars and restaurants serving $2 Imperial beers to a shorts and flip-flops clientele. If you're in need of creature comforts and a stable Internet connection, the Pacific side of Costa Rica is for you. If you're like me and want to get "off the grid" and away from society, Costa Rica's southern Caribbean coast is a much more attractive option.

I book a cheap 7-day stay at a 14-room beachside "hotel" in Puerto Viejo near Cahuita National Park. The park was established in 1970 to protect a large coral reef off Costa Rica's Caribbean coast.

No phone, no television, no "guaranteed" Internet. Puerto Viejo is a perfect spot for someone in spiritual "Time Out" mode. My tiny 2nd floor room has a small kitchen and a balcony overlooking the beach a few hundred yards from my bed. Behind me is the lush and verdant tropical rainforest filled with thousands of species of exotic birds and wildlife. My half-empty suitcase is home to a half-dozen t-shirts, shorts, a bathing suit, sandals, and my laptop computer on which I plan to do some work in my copious "spare" time.

The hotel staff reverently refer to me as their "author in residence" when they learn I'm writing my second novel. *Kissing Carmen* recounts the story of a one-night stand I had in Madrid, Spain while working in the corporate world a few years back. Since there's a lot of Spanish spoken by the characters, I have a built-in excuse to consult daily with Minerva, the live-in manager/bartender/lifeguard who helps me with proper Spanish grammar, usage, and spelling.

Minerva is happy to help me out. Sets up a small plastic table and chair poolside so that I can work outside of my room. Informs new guests that "Mr. Steve" is a writer and shouldn't be disturbed whenever they see me working. Beside my desk is a hammock I take full advantage of throughout the day when I'm not actively typing. Lucia and Rommel, the two senior staff personnel, get on my case when I take to the hammock to create exciting new twists to the plot of the love story.

"Ah, Mr. Steve is very busy working!" they announce to anyone and everyone around the pool when they spy me gently swaying back and forth in the hammock. Eyes closed. Clutching an Imperial beer in my hand.

Most days I spend writing in the morning, then visiting the beach or rainforest after lunch. An afternoon nap is required after such vigorous activity so I can be well rested for dinner and then a night of bar-hopping along the beach to chat up the locals and tourist girls who've made their way here from all over the globe.

With no technological distractions in the form of cellphones, TV, or the Internet, and with no means of transportation other than a bicycle I can rent from Minerva as needed, I realize I've landed in a Costa Rican version of Heaven. There's no reason to go back home so I extend my stay an additional 5 weeks.

Cahuita

Howler monkeys roar in the jungle, my wake-up call at dawn.
Hummingbird suspends its flight before me to read my thoughts.
Neon-blue butterflies dance through the rainforest.
Ora pendulas warble and gurgle, searching for breakfast bugs.
Teardrop shaped basket nests hang from
branches like Japanese lanterns.
Wild horses ramble in pairs on the beach,
deep hoof prints sunk in sand.
A tired sloth ambles across rafters, rests on
speakers above the dance floor,
Disinterestedly watching the foreplay of dancing drunks below.
Barely bikini-ed tourist girls bronze their skin, ogle local surfer boys.
Endless waves crash the beach, erasing all cares and concerns.
Costa Rican flavor of No Time, No Space.

Costa Rica works for me at this stage of my suspended Xiu Lian Purification Journey. I unwind. De-stress. Swim in the ocean daily. Make frequent treks through the rainforest. Physically, I'm in good shape. My body is toned from all the exercise and tanned from all the sunshine.

Costa Rica is the perfect place to hide from the "civilized" world and all its challenges. I start looking at beachfront properties for sale. Consider a permanent move to this Central American country where I don't even speak the language. Think of starting an oceanfront bed and breakfast for income and amusement. A small business to keep me busy. But, as has happened to me so many times before, the Divine has other plans...

⚜   ⚜   ⚜

I'm pedaling past the Puerto Viejo Christian Congregation Church about a mile down the road from my coastal hotel. A hand-painted sign announces a Sunday gathering of the faithful at which "All Visitors Are Welcome to Come and Worship God!" I've seen this sign at least a hundred times before when bicycling up and down the beach. Why haven't I paid any attention until now? Why am I interested today? All of a sudden? Out of the blue?

Hmm...I know I've been remiss in my spiritual practices since I left the United States, but I'm not sure if the best place for me to re-start my spiritual journey is a Spanish-speaking Protestant Christian gathering. Still, my soul is restless after all the rest and relaxation of the past five weeks, and whispers to me I need to attend Sunday's upcoming service.

My self-imposed "Time Out" is drawing to a close. I can feel it in my bones. Like a little kid whose "time in the corner" has taught him how to behave, I feel I've learned some lessons about having a big ego and about expecting everyone to do things my way. I've had my time to pout during little vacation away from the cares and concerns of the world. My soul tells me it's time to get back to work as a soul healer. I miss the students in Colorado, but I miss Master Sha even more. When I get back home, I'll sign up for the next Master Sha retreat I can find in North America and try and pick up from where I left off on my spiritual journey.

On Sunday morning, I go to church. When I bicycle into the property across the street from the beach, I'm greeted warmly by the Pastor. A fifty-something Spanish man sporting a generous waistline. Welcomes me with a big smile. Speaks passable English. Hands me a Spanish language Bible even though I tell him I can't read it. Waves frantically for everyone to take their seats. The outdoor service is about to commence. Church-going families occupy rows of white plastic lawn chairs under an awning protecting them from the elements of either tropical sun or drenching rain. Curious children stare at me unabashedly. Wonder who the white man is. Some point fingers. Others giggle under their breath.

Pastor Pedro begins the service in Spanish, then calls on one of his bi-lingual female parishioners to come up front and translate what she can into English for my benefit. For the next 45-minutes, no translation is needed as Pastor Pedro leads the Christians in singing a series of psalms. I find myself getting lost in the music—pure heart-felt Christian praising of the Lord. It doesn't really matter that the words are sung in Spanish. I simply hum along with the crowd and get swept up in the intensity of their passion and zeal. When Pastor Pedro really gets loud, the congregation rises from their chairs and everyone, including me, start dancing in the aisles. We gain more room by overflowing into the adjoining pasture occupied by a few grass-eating goats looking slightly annoyed at the intrusion of human interlopers to their feeding grounds. After the singing, the parishioners embrace each other to express their love before returning to their seats to cool down and await the next segment of the Sunday service.

Pastor Pedro, dripping in sweat, hugs me tightly. Summons me forward to the front of the stage. Asks me to introduce myself via the interpreter. Wants me to tell the congregation how I praise Jesus in my church back home.

Hmm... This will be interesting. I'm not sure how to talk to this group about Master Sha.

Pastor Pedro hands me a microphone. Asks me to speak slowly so the interpreter can keep up. Takes a seat. Leaves me facing the congregation on my own.

"Hello everyone. *Buenos días.* I'm Stephen from Boulder, Colorado in the United States." The crowd gives me a small, polite round of applause.

"My church back home is a church of 'Unity'...and we love Jesus!" I proclaim and receive a stronger round of applause. My declaration is technically true. I don't know anyone in Master Sha's Mission who doesn't love Jesus, and Master Sha is all about unity and oneness.

"Tell us how you serve our Lord and Savior Jesus Christ!" Pastor Pedro shouts aloud in encouragement.

I've reached the point I fear the most. My soul tells me I shouldn't start talking about karma, past lives, reincarnation, and spiritual Third Eye images to this particular group of God-fearing, evangelical, Spanish-speaking Christians. I need some help and make a quick request to God. The Divine steps in at this critical juncture and offers me a way through my blockages.

"Well, rather than go into the details of my church, how about I sing you all one of our songs?" I'm pretty sure the group would want to hear me sing rather than listen to me expound upon the details of how my "church" is structured. The assembled group claps wildly at my suggestion and Pastor Pedro nods his head in encouragement.

"I'm going to sing you a song called *Love Peace and Harmony*. And I'll sing each verse in a different language. The first verse I'll sing in English." Spontaneous applause rises from the congregation.

"The second verse I'll sing in something called Soul Language." I get some quizzical looks. The group has never heard of soul language and looks questioningly at the interpreter as if she might not have gotten the translation right. "Think of soul language as 'speaking in tongues' just like in the Bible." I suggest to the puzzled group.

Ok, they like that. Mutter "oohs" and "ahhs" in anticipation of hearing me sing soul language.

"And the third verse, I'll sing in Mandarin Chinese!" Well, the vast majority of the Puerto Viejo Christian Congregation Church aren't visibly thrilled about me singing anything in Mandarin

Chinese. The assembly looks a little disappointed and only a few people clap out of politeness.

Everything seems ok. All I have to do now is perform. I am about to sing in public by myself for the very first time since my sixth grade talent show to this audience of Christians sitting outdoors in a Costa Rican coastal village. Closing my eyes, I ground myself by focusing on my 1st Soul House, the energy center located in my abdomen below the navel. I call on Master Sha to help me, and when I'm ready, I open my eyes and realize I'm still very, very nervous.

There are a few tricks for speaking in public that I mastered when giving presentations to large groups in the corporate world. One involves picturing your audience naked and yourself as the only person clothed. Scanning the crowd of Costa Rican families before me, including the elders, I quickly abandon this approach to calming my nerves. Instead, I use the technique of staring just over the tops of the heads of my audience. The view is magical since what I end up looking at are the incoming waves of the Caribbean Ocean just a few hundred yards beyond me across the street.

I don't remember singing *Love Peace and Harmony* at all, but to my great surprise, when I finish the English, Soul Language, and Mandarin Chinese verses of the song, I receive a standing ovation. And I do believe that if anyone had a bouquet of roses with them, they would have tossed them to me just like patrons at an opera throw flowers to an appreciative diva.

Scanning the audience before me, I notice two of the women seated near the front are wiping their eyes. The song touched their hearts and souls. I know I'm not that good a singer; they aren't crying because my singing voice has moved them to tears. They're crying because they've heard the Divine Soul Song of *Love Peace and Harmony*, which carries divine frequency and vibration, for the very first time. Hearing *Love Peace and Harmony* can have that effect on people.

After the Sunday service wraps up, Pastor Pedro and members of the congregation ask me to come back the following Sunday. I apologetically inform them I'm heading back to the States next weekend or I'd surely join them again.

The Sunday service in Costa Rica has rejuvenated me and I'm anxious to reconnect with Master Sha and his students in person as soon as possible. I have no regrets about taking my "Time Out" when I did. It was necessary for me then, but now it's time to get back on the spiritual path.

Thank you, Master Sha. Countless bow downs, Master Sha.
Thank you, Master Sha. Countless bow downs, Master Sha.
Thank you, Master Sha. Countless bow downs, Master Sha.

Advising Anna

Puerto Viejo, Costa Rica. March, 2013. I've been working for 5 weeks now on my new novel, *Kissing Carmen*, trying to complete the final edits, cover art selection, and contract details with my publisher. Minerva, the manager at the hotel where I'm staying, has gotten a sneak preview. She tells me this is a book women will want to read and share with their friends. We'll see.

Time for a break. I head downtown for a late afternoon lunch on the veranda at a local restaurant. Grab a seat with a view. Stare at the waves of the Caribbean Sea crashing the beach only 100 meters away. Check out the pedestrians dancing in and out of the shops and restaurants on the street below me.

Anna, my waitress, saunters over after a few minutes. Like most service staff working the bars and restaurants in Puerto Viejo, she's in no hurry. "What can I get you?"

"Sangria, please."

Anna smiles.

"What is it?" I ask.

"Nothing…it's good…the Sangria. I just finished making it."

"Cool. That's what I want…and the 3 tacos lunch special."

Anna returns with the Sangria in a tall glass with fresh watermelon and pineapple slices swimming around ice cubes in an ocean of pink liquid. The timeless tropical drink tastes perfect. Anna seems familiar to me. Her accent sounds like home. It's a good excuse to begin small talk with the pretty girl.

"Where are you from?" I ask politely.

"Massachusetts." she answers, looking at me a bit more intently.

"Ah, I thought so. Me too." We laugh together. Turns out Anna lived in Amherst, where I went to college so long ago. I'm too embarrassed to tell her the actual years I attended the University of Massachusetts since she wasn't even born then.

"What brought you here?" I ask. She tells me she went to college for one year, but quit because it wasn't for her. "Jeez! That's what happened to me too when I was at UMass."

Her already wide eyes grow a little wider. "Really? What made you quit?" she wants to know.

"Hmm ... Well, I just wasn't into it anymore ... and decided to go to Switzerland for the summer to figure out my life ... and there was a girl involved."

Anna laughs loudly now. "Me too ... I mean there was a guy ... there is a guy, and I decided to go someplace really far away, so I came to Costa Rica."

I tell her I think it was the right call for me at the time. She says she feels the same way. Just needs time by herself apart from everyone else. Time to forget her boyfriend.

"And your family?" I ask. "Let me guess. They keep sending you emails asking when you're coming back."

"How do you know that?" she questions me, sounding kind of surprised, though it seems obvious to me her family would be worried and wondering when she was returning home.

"I told you. It happened to me too when I was in Switzerland." I take another sip of my Sangria.

Anna slides onto the stool beside me, her interest in the bar's few other customers put temporarily on hold. Glances back at the bar to confirm the other waiter is not too busy. Makes eye contact with her co-worker. Silently sends him a command to "watch the store" for a bit.

"What do you think I should do?" she asks.

Wow. She's asking an important *life decision question* within 5 minutes of meeting me. And she's not asking casually, the way you'd ask what's good on the dinner menu.

I find I get these types of questions more frequently now that I'm on the Xiu Lian path. I'm in my element and totally want to help Anna out. I'm reminded again of Master Sha's teaching:

"The purpose of life is to serve."

Anna is another opportunity to do just that. Offer service. One person on the planet trying to help another.

"Well, if you are trying to figure out if it's time to go back home yet…and I can't tell you that it is or it isn't…you have to ask your heart, your soul." I place my fingers on her heart chakra and tap there a few times. "Your heart will never lie to you. But your mind? Well…your mind can mess you all up."

Anna bursts out in a big belly laugh. "That is so true! Whenever I start thinking I need to figure out what to do next, I mess myself all up in my head."

"All I can tell you is never make big decisions with your head. Talk to your soul…your heart…and you'll always know what to do because the answer you get will *feel* right. You won't have any doubts like you can get when you make decisions with your mind."

We look into each other's eyes. We find comfort in each other. And we arrive in my favorite condition: *No Time, No Space.* After a really nice half a minute or so, Anna puts her hand on my knee.

"Thank you." she whispers. Two small words, but they're all that's needed. I know I've helped Anna. She comes back a few more times with my lunch and more Sangria. We are obliged to carry on social small talk for the remainder of our limited time together but it's apparent something more has happened between us. The undercurrent of our spiritual connection swirls powerfully around the two of us. I get up to pay the bill. Anna and I hug each other briefly. Wish each other well. No need to schedule a follow-up appointment.

Brief encounters like the one I had with Anna are typical of what happens at this stage of my Xiu Lian Purification Journey. Little opportunities to offer service come more frequently. Like the spiritual Dragon Mother Teresa advised:

> *"There are many people who can do big things,*
> *but there are very few people who will do the small things."*

LITTLE DRAGONS

And I thought, I'd seen someone,
Who seemed at last to know the truth.
I was mistaken,
Only a child, laughing in the sun.
                    —*David Crosby*, Laughing

Back in my condo in Colorado, I'm in the kitchen cleaning dirty dishes before heading to the airport. My son Steve is flying in from Boston with my two grandchildren: Matthew, age 5, and Mikayla, age 3. It's the first time the kids have been on a plane. "Papa C," as I'm called, is probably more excited than the kids about our upcoming vacation in Colorado!

Looking out the tiny window above my kitchen sink to the courtyard below, I'm entranced by a little boy who is just learning to walk. Head down. Arms outstretched. Legs wobbly. Navigating his way across a patch of grass striving to reach the fountain artfully splashing water over stones outside our Community Center. There's a woman, probably the child's mother—or maybe an older sister or babysitter—following the boy. Shadowing the child's shaky footsteps. And it occurs to me that this is what our gurus do with their disciples. They silently position their souls behind us, encouraging us to take baby steps as we learn to walk the Xiu Lian path. The guru protects us from spiritual danger, picking us up whenever we stumble on our soul journey. As human beings, we sometimes get caught up in the fulfillment of our own desires—just like the innocent child in the courtyard with a focused desire to reach the water fountain. The guru understands our struggle with desires. And even if the teacher doesn't always condone our actions, the guru's love for us is unshakeable no matter what we do. Our gurus never judge us, always forgive us, and express that unconditional love by guiding our wayward souls through the frequent rough patches of our Xiu Lian Purification Journey.

Although I haven't spent as much time with Matthew and Mikayla as I'd be able to if we lived closer to each other, I've become acutely aware of the spiritual relationship that exists between the souls of my two grandchildren. Matthew is Mikayla's protector. Of course, most older brothers naturally look out for and protect their little sisters, especially when they become teenagers and start becoming the focus of attention from boys in the neighborhood. My own soul tells me Mikayla's soul is ancient. She's been reincarnating for many lifetimes in order to fulfill whatever tasks Heaven has assigned her. Matthew has shared many of those lifetimes with her. In this lifetime, they are tied together karmically once again. My own Xiu Lian journey is somehow linked to theirs, but it has yet to be revealed to me just how and when our family relationship will activate on a spiritual level.

As we drive back to my condo in Boulder, I give Matthew and Mikayla a list of possible activities for the following day and tell them they can decide where they'd like to go and what they want to do. Water World, an amusement park in Denver with dozens of water slides and kid's rides, is the chosen option. When we arrive at the ticket counter the next morning, Mikayla takes my hand and accompanies me to the window to pay our entrance fees. The attendant informs me that since Mikayla is only three years old, her admission to the park is free. My son Steve and Matthew are standing off to the side waiting for us to come back with the tickets.

When we return, Mikayla shouts out, "Daddy, I'm free! I'm free!" We all burst out laughing and Mikayla just smiles at us. I interpret Mikayla's declaration as a spiritual statement rather than an indication of her financial status at Water World. She's filled with innocence. Harbors no hang-ups. Basks in the company of three generations of men who love her.

A prime objective of the Xiu Lian Purification Journey is to learn to be as free as a child, just like little Mikayla. Free of attachments, free of desires, free of karma. Jesus preached:

> *"Truly I tell you, unless you change and become like little children, you will never enter the kingdom of Heaven."*

I resonate with this advice whenever I'm in the presence of Master Sha. His frequency and vibration is so much higher than the students, his soul standing so incomprehensively closer to the Divine and the Tao than our own.

Just like I'm a grandfather with a certain level of wisdom and knowledge to impart to Matthew and Mikayla, Master Sha is a spiritual father sharing wisdom and guidance with his students. I sometimes liken Master Sha to a Harvard Professor of Astrophysics facing a classroom full of naïve, elementary school children. It takes elementary school students years to learn the basics of reading, writing, and counting numbers before they'll be ready to attend any advanced classes in mathematics and science. Master Sha has to temper his teachings and show infinite patience for his students if we are not spiritually ready to receive his advanced wisdom.

We all learn from each other on the spiritual journey. As a little Dragon, Mikayla teaches me an important lesson at the amusement park when she announces she's "free". I also want to be free like Mikayla in the manner Jesus taught so that, one day, I too will be ready to enter the Kingdom of Heaven.

⚜   ⚜   ⚜

My sister Jeanne is babysitting her granddaughter Zoe and speaking to me, computer to computer, on a Skype video call. Zoe scrambles up Grandma's legs to see who's talking on the PC monitor, probably hoping it might be her Mom or Dad. Zoe and I have never met in person. The little girl studies my face. Leans in quizzically for a closer look at this unknown relative from Colorado. Interrupts my sister by shouting a blast of two-year old gobbledygook at my face on the PC screen. I know it's not nonsense she's speaking, and inform Jeanne that Zoe and I want to speak in Soul Language for a few moments. Jeanne asks what Soul Language is and I tell her I'll explain it to her after my chat with Zoe.

Master Sha teaches his students how to speak the natural language of our souls. A special mantra is used to facilitate the speaking of Soul Language, similar in concept to what Christians call "speaking in tongues." Everyone can speak Soul Language to other people, but Soul Language can also be spoken to our spiritual fathers and mothers residing in the higher realms of the soul world. The trick is to repeat the mantra as quickly as possible until your Soul Language comes out. For this to happen, you have to let go of any ego-driven analysis about what is happening by keeping your attention focused on your heart-chakra, the seat of soul communication. "Speak from the heart, not from the head," as the saying goes. And for heaven's sake, don't be self-conscious about the sounds that come out of your mouth or your Soul Language will stop abruptly!

With practice, advanced students of Master Sha are able translate their own or other's Soul Language on the fly. When translating the Soul Language of others, I may receive spiritual images along with the translated English equivalent of the words. The images may come to my Third Eye as colors or pictures, as well as sounds or feelings.

Much like learning a foreign language, the more you practice, the easier it is for your Soul Language to flow, and the easier it becomes to translate messages you are receiving if you've asked a question of your own or another's soul. At this point in time and space, Soul Language remains largely unknown, a mystery to most people, but as we move forward together on our collective spiritual journey, Master Sha teaches that Soul Language will become a primary means of communication between spiritual beings and an integral component of our Xiu Lian practice.

One of Master Sha's Divine Channels and Worldwide Representatives tells a fascinating story about Soul Language that got me interested in learning how to communicate in this manner and hear what my own soul has to tell me.

Two of Master Sha's Divine Channels were traveling together in China after visiting the healing center of Master Zhi Chen Guo, Master Sha's spiritual father. The two Disciples came across a Buddhist priest and a nun in their travels. As one of the Divine Channels is Chinese, he started a conversation with the Buddhist priest in that language. He introduced the other Divine Channel as a woman who only spoke English. The priest in turn introduced the nun as someone who only spoke Chinese. Somehow, the conversation turned to the subject of Soul Language and the Buddhist priest revealed that the woman he was with could speak in Soul Language! The two women began speaking in Soul Language, translated each other's Soul Language, and held a full-fledged conversation!

On our Skype call, Zoe and I blabber back and forth with each other in Soul Language epistles jettisoning from our hearts in 10 – 15 second blasts. It's a bit too fast for me to translate all her words in real time but I find that whatever this little girl is speaking infuses me with happiness and joy that is overwhelming! The part I do hear clearly is that Zoe's soul is happy to meet me at this time, and especially happy that someone understands her! Her soul has a lot to say. She laughs out loud whenever she pauses in her Soul Language, and laughs again after I answer in mine. My sister smiles broadly, just happy to witness what I'm sure she thinks is just silly game-playing.

Master Sha teaches that all human beings are born with the capacity to speak Soul Language. In fact, Soul Language is the universal language – the language of all souls. He also teaches that many young children have open Third Eyes that allow them to receive images from the soul world, including from our spiritual fathers, mothers, and guides. The reality is that these capabilities in young children too often get suppressed as we grow. Most modern societies don't condone "seeing invisible friends, hearing angels, and talking with beings that aren't really there." The unfortunate result of this kind of societal pressure is that, at a young age, our Third Eyes can close and we forget how to speak to our souls in Soul Language. As we grow to become adolescents, if we show unacceptable social behavior regarding our Third Eyes, we can get criticized, ostracized, and shunned by our friends and families. Society often treats adults displaying spiritual capabilities such as "hearing voices" or "hallucinating" as unstable and lock them up in the mental health wards of hospitals that force psychotropic drugs upon the "mentally ill".

Fortunately, Master Sha and other spiritual Masters are with us, guiding and encouraging students to open all of our spiritual channels for the purpose of advancing our respective soul journeys. May you develop your Soul Language soon and start communicating with your own soul as well as the souls of your spiritual fathers and mothers!

Soul Language

Master Sha talks about *Soul Language* in his Soul Power Series book: *Tao Song and Tao Dance*:

> *"Soul Language is the voice and language of the soul. Although everyone's Soul Language sounds different, Soul Language is a universal language. All souls understand Soul Language."*

In 1994, Master Sha was traveling in China to visit the rural clinic of his spiritual father Dr. and Master Zhi Chen Guo. He witnessed nearly 20,000 people gathered in Master Guo's Healing Center speaking Soul Language together. Master Sha relates that "the vibration was beyond comprehension. I could feel heat penetrating my body...I really wanted to bring out my own Soul Language."

Master Guo taught Master Sha the ancient wisdom he'd discovered to elicit one's Soul Language. Master Guo learned Soul Language in 1974. While meditating one morning, the Divine sent Master Guo a code: *San San Jiu Liu Ba You Wu* in Mandarin Chinese. In Chinese, this code corresponds to the numbers 3396815. Master Guo started chanting this sacred code from Heaven and realized each number chanted in Chinese vibrated a different section of the body:

San (3) stimulates the chest.
Jiu (9) stimulates the lower abdomen.
Liu (6) stimulates the ribs.
Ba (8) stimulates the navel.
Yao (1) stimulates the head.
Wu (5) stimulates the stomach

Master Guo started chanting the Chinese mantra *San San Jiu Liu Ba Yao Wu* faster and faster and his Soul Language started to come out.

In *his Tao Song and Tao Dance* book Master Sha teaches:

"When you chant San San Jiu Liu Ba Yao Wu *(3396815), energy flows in the body. Energy starts to vibrate in the chest, and then flows to the lower abdomen. From there it moves to the ribs and then goes to the navel. Next it radiates to the head. Finally, it moves down to the stomach. This movement of energy in the body is a sacred, healthy, pattern. Moving energy in this pattern just by chanting* San San Jiu Liu Ba Yao Wu *is a sacred divine healing and rejuvenation."*

The keys to learning to chant Soul Language are:

1. *Chant* San San Jiu Liu Ba Yao Wu *slowly at first, then go as fast as you can.*
2. *Don't worry when strange sounds start coming out of your mouth.*
3. *Don't "think" about what is happening while you chant.*
4. *Don't "listen" to your Soul Language or try to figure out what it means.*
5. *If your Soul Language stops suddenly, just start over and start chanting again slowly.*

Young children speak Soul Language naturally before they learn the cultural language of the adults around them. When you first start practicing Soul Language, it may take some time before your Soul Language comes out. Once it does start to come out, you won't forget how to speak Soul Language ever again.

So why would we want to learn to speak and translate Soul Language? Since everyone has a soul, and all souls speak Soul Language, you can use Soul Language to communicate with your own soul. Your soul may be quite old. Your soul has experienced many prior lifetimes on Mother Earth. Your soul remembers those lifetimes and the lessons you learned. Your soul has wisdom to share with you that can help you on your Xiu Lian Purification Journey.

Once your soul communication channels open and you're comfortable translating your own Soul Language, you'll find that you can translate the Soul Language of others as well. This translation capability will enable you to learn soul wisdom from others including babies who haven't yet learned to speak in their native language!

I was a little self-conscious when I first started practicing Soul Language so I decided to spend time practicing in my bathroom, where no one could hear me or see me repeating *San San Jiu Liu Ba Yao Wu* faster and faster. How exciting it was when after three or four days of sporadic practicing, my Soul Language emerged!

Give this practice a few tries on your own or in the presence of someone who knows how to speak Soul Language. A whole new world of spiritual wisdom will open up for you!

BACK NINE

"So comes snow after fire, and even dragons have their endings."
—J.R.R Tolkien

Divine Channel Training Retreat
Asilomar, California - September, 2013

After surviving my Crisis of Faith and limping back from an extended stay cruising the tropical beaches of Costa Rica, I return to Colorado and restart my Xiu Lian practices. The summer season at the Love Peace Harmony Center is in full swing. Master Sha is coming to Boulder!

The entire property is in need of a makeover. Lawns to be trimmed. Flower-beds to be manicured. Invading thistle bushes to be contained. Weeds to be pulled up by hand before they overrun the vegetables in the organic garden. The underground sprinkler system in need of repairs. Farm clutter to be taken to the dump or sold off during a yard sale. Baba's Barn to be scrubbed squeaky clean. We have three weeks to prepare for Master Sha.

Master Sha's events planning team has asked the Colorado students if they have any specific subjects they would like to request Master Sha to teach. The weekend schedule coalesces to yield three separate and distinct workshops:

Friday Evening: *Free Soul Healing Evening (open to the public)*
Saturday: *How to Boost Your Finances*
Sunday: *How to Find Your True Love*

I volunteer to "stage manage" all three events. A stage manager at a Master Sha event has several responsibilities including making sure Master Sha has a flipchart, paper, and colored markers with which to write. The stage manager also ensures that when people come up to share their experiences, they have a working microphone and know where they're supposed to stand. But the best part of being stage manager is I get to sit in the front row so very close to Master Sha for the entirety of his teachings!

During the Saturday workshop, Master Sha deviates a little from the formal topic of how to clear financial karma and starts talking about his Divine Channel in Training (DCiT) Program. He wants people who are serious about serving humanity to consider joining his program and offers to "check" with Heaven to see if any student who applies is spiritually "ready" to become a Divine Channel in Training.

But just what are Divine Channels?

Divine Channels are specially chosen advanced students who commit their lives to serving humanity as Worldwide Representatives of Master Sha. In July, 2003, Master Sha himself was chosen by the Divine to be a Divine Channel and Servant of humanity. Being a Divine Channel means one serves humanity unconditionally with *Total GOLD* where "G" stands for Gratitude, "O" stands for Obedience, "L" stands for Loyalty, and "D" stands for Devotion.

For me, the hierarchy of Divine Channels to Master Sha is somewhat akin to the Cardinals of the Catholic Church who report directly to the Pope. Divine Channels must commit their lives entirely to service by offering healing blessings and spiritual teachings to souls in need both before and during Mother Earth's transition. I'll repeat the essence of what Master Sha teaches about the difficult times that lie ahead:

> *"Mother Earth is in transition. Humanity's karma is heavy. Wars, pollution, economic struggles, the spread of communicable diseases, and misuse of technology for greed, power, and the pursuit of wealth are causing lots of people to suffer now and will be the cause of further suffering if we don't address the karma of humanity now."*

Divine Channels are granted many of the same healing and blessing powers that Master Sha offers. Master Sha tells the students in the Love Peace Harmony Center that it is not easy to be accepted as a Divine Channel in Training. If anyone wants to apply today, Master Sha will ask Heaven to assess the readiness and purity of each applicant. If we are accepted into the program, Master Sha will say: *"Congratulations! You are blessed."* If not: *"Don't be disappointed. Purify more. Serve more. Wait for next time."*

Almost everyone takes a deep breath before Master Sha asks: *"So…who in this room is ready to apply to become a Divine Channel? Stand up!"*

It's decision time for me and the other students attending the retreat in Baba's Barn. My mind starts to race. Master Sha scans the audience. My ego silently whispers: *Do you really want to become a Divine Channel and Worldwide Representative of Master Sha? Are you ready to commit your life to serve unconditionally? Is this your true calling? You came close to becoming a monastic with Yogananda, but then it didn't happen. You didn't make the commitment. You'll be giving up lot if you join this program. Your life won't be your own. Maybe you should wait…*

Master Marilyn, one of Master Sha's Divine Channels, who's flown in from California, knows me from many past retreats. She is standing in the front of the class along with Master Sha. Surveying the audience to see who is ready to apply. I sense her gaze moving my way. Terror sets in. Panic seizes my stomach. *And I physically crouch down behind another student so Master Marilyn won't see me!* But it's too late.

"Stephen, you should apply. It's time," Master Marilyn tells me while peering over the shoulder of the person I'm hiding behind. The students around me, most of whom don't know me all that well, turn and size me up. I feel like I'm standing naked on stage in a blinding spotlight.

"I don't think so, Master Marilyn. I'm not ready," I whimper, wishing I could be back on the beach in Costa Rica.

Master Marilyn is a retired elementary school teacher. She's glaring down at me now like I'm one of her students who has fallen out of linc. She responds to my meek protest by scrunching up her face. Purses her lips. Extends her right arm. Points a finger at me like a farmer aiming a loaded shotgun at the boy who's gotten his daughter pregnant outside of marriage, letting him know he's headed to the altar whether he's willing or not.

I don't remember exactly what happened next but do have some partial recollection of lights flashing and thunder rumbling. Something negative exits my body. A big glob of black energy escapes through the barn's window behind Master Sha, and carries with it all my doubts. My resistance has suddenly and miraculously vanished.

Standing up straight, I raise my hand just as Master Sha begins to check the students on my side of the room.

"Stephen ... yes."

I've been accepted into the Divine Channel in Training Program! My heart is pounding. My soul ecstatic. Master Marilyn smiles. I receive heart-felt congratulations from the students around me. My Xiu Lian Purification Journey has taken a giant step forward today. I'm on the road leading me back to Tao. A step I might have missed if I hadn't receive the blessing, assistance, and support of Master Marilyn.

Thank you, Master Marilyn!
Thank you, Master Marilyn!
Thank you, Master Marilyn!

If I've learned anything on this Xiu Lian Purification Journey, it's that we can't complete the journey alone. We all need a little help here and there. A little shove to get us going when we're stuck. A helping hand to hold when crossing a spiritual bridge spanning treacherous water filled with obstacles. It's not easy to ask for directions when we don't even know we're lost. Or accept assistance from others when it's offered without our asking. Our egos are like professional hit men when it comes to getting in the way of our spiritual progress. *I can do this alone. I don't need anyone's help,* we silently assure ourselves. Yeah, right.

On the Xiu Lian path, having humility helps. Learning to let go helps. Trusting in Heaven helps a lot.

⚜   ⚜   ⚜

After my acceptance as a student in Master Sha's Divine Channel in Training Program, I sign up to attend a mandatory training retreat in California being held at the beginning of September, 2013. Master Sha announces he's going to train up to 400 Divine Channels worldwide and most of the North American-based team will gather together at Asilomar, a Pacific seaside community that's part of the beautiful Monterey Peninsula.

In Master Sha's Mission, the timetable for a Divine Channel in Training to become a Divine Channel is not fixed. It's a similar process in Paramahansa Yogananda's Self-Realization Fellowship. SRF Monastics moving through a 4-stage program from Postulant > Novitiate > Brahmacharya > Sannyas have no fixed timeframe in which to complete each stage of their training. In both organizations, one's readiness to move to the next level is determined by the student's purity, openness of their heart, and alignment with their Master.

In Asilomar, I begin the next stage of my Xiu Lian Purification Journey in the company of over 200 students also aspiring to become Divine Channels. It's not uncommon for any of Master Sha's students to share during a retreat about how their karma has adversely hindered their life by causing them to suffer from debilitating illnesses such as cancer, multiple sclerosis, chronic back and neck pain, diabetes and other physical diseases either not easy to heal or for which there is no cure in Western medicine or Traditional Chinese Medicine. I listen to these testimonials with a moderate degree of compassion. But having been blessed with relatively good physical health throughout my life, I just don't have any personal experience of agonizing, life-threatening diseases.

Looking back, I may have gotten just a little too cocky about my "good fortune" at avoiding severe physical challenges in my life. I may have spoken a little too soon in some informal discussions with other students at DC training. Whether I was exceptionally cocky or not, Heaven determined it was time for me to learn a lesson in Asilomar during the DCiT Retreat.

The "Poop Karma" incident began one afternoon while I was in the meeting room. I'd been asked to take photographs of the sessions and so had free license to move about hall freely.

An hour or so after lunch, I start to feel sharp pains in my abdomen. I get up to go the washroom. I feel a bit constipated and as a result, aren't able to "do my business." *Okay.* I tell myself. *No big deal. I'll just try again later.* Well, the pain in my lower body starts ratcheting up, becoming more intense. I've been constipated before, but never like this. I have to leave the hall a few more times to try to go to the bathroom, but nothing is happening. I excuse myself from the hall, and go back to my lodge where I curl up in the fetal position on the bed and just lay there in agony. It feels to me like a big steel pipe is clogging my bowels. This isn't "normal" constipation. I start thinking about those intestinal illnesses where, if the fluid and fecal matter in your bowels backs up into your stomach, you can die quickly. Yuck.

Finally deciding I needed to go to the Emergency Room, I begin to make my way down the walkway outside of my lodge to the reception building a few hundred yards away. I don't make it more than a few feet when the pain became so intense I have to get down on my hands and knees and crawl. All of Master Sha's students are in the Meeting Hall, so there's no one around to witness my struggle.

When I drag myself into the reception area, the woman behind the desk rushes over to ask me what is wrong and immediately calls for an ambulance to take me to the hospital. She finds out that, apparently, there are no ambulances available on Monterey Peninsula to come out to the resort at this time, so she opts to call a local taxi instead.

As a student of Master Sha, we are taught that the root cause of all illnesses is karma and that if we can transform the negative karma attacking us, we can heal our sicknesses and diseases.

We each have the power to heal ourselves! The healing may not be instantaneous, especially for chronic or life-threatening conditions. Therefore, as a medical doctor, Master Sha is very strict about advising everyone to solicit proper and timely medical treatment when we get sick or are in an accident.

While waiting for the taxi to show up and cart me away, I call Kristina Darling, one of my fellow Divine Channels in Training from Colorado who is also attending the retreat, and ask her to let people know I'm heading to the Emergency Room. Kristina gets a little animated, implores me wait, and says she'll be right down. "Okay," I mutter, the pain in my abdomen too intense to stay talking on the phone.

A few minutes later, the taxi still hasn't arrived, but Kristina and two of Master Sha's most senior Divine Channels, Master Francisco and Master Cynthia, come running around the corner of the building. Both of these Divine Channels have very advanced Third Eyes which are scanning me up and down to receive a quick assessment from the soul world about my condition.

"I'm calling Master Sha," Master Cynthia announces. "He may need to do an emergency blessing ... Steve, I see a thick, solid black darkness in your bowels."

What? That's just great, I think to myself.

"Isn't Master Sha down on the beach giving an interview?" Master Francisco asks.

Despite my intense pain, I don't want to interrupt my Master and spiritual father. "If Master Sha is busy, I'll just go to the hospital. I don't want to bother him." I volunteer. I'm not trying to act like a martyr. Not trying to "take one for the team." But I do feel I'm insignificant in the universe relative to Master Sha. That Master Sha's tasks are more important to humanity than my health. And that I truly don't want to disturb Master Sha in whatever it is he's doing.

Master Cynthia ignores me and calls Master Sha who asks her and Master Francisco to check again with their Third Eyes and see if my condition is severe enough for me to get in the taxi which is just pulling into the property. To my surprise, both Master Francisco and Master Cynthia tell Master Sha that my condition doesn't require hospitalization and that it can be healed with a karma clearing.

I'm facing a significant spiritual test now. *Do I have total faith in Master Sha, my spiritual father? Do I have total trust to follow the readings from his two Divine Channels? Is this killer pain going to go away without me going to the Emergency Room and seeing a Doctor? Do I tell the taxi driver to just leave? That I'm going to get my karma cleared and don't need any Western medical Doctors to treat me?*

Master Francisco poses the question. "What do you want to do?"

I turn to face the taxi driver and hotel staff, all waiting anxiously for me to get in the vehicle and go to the hospital. "I'm going to stay. You can go. Thank you for coming." I pay the driver $10 for his troubles.

Master Sha performs the karma clearing over the phone. Everyone looks at me after the blessing to see how I feel. I thank Master Sha and go inside the building to sit down and see if the pain subsides. For the moment, there is no immediate relief from the throbbing ache in my intestines. A few other students show up. Come over to offer sympathy and support. Michael and Sharon Lawrence, and their daughter Lilly, join the "Steve Watch".

I visit the Men's room twice, partly out of the need to poop, and partly because I'm embarrassed and want to get away from everyone rooting for me. I'm having no success at either. After the second try, when I exit the men's room, I find myself standing face to face with 5-year old Lilly who's staring me down and looks like she has something important to say. Master Francisco, Kristina, Sharon, and Michael sit behind her. My "cheerleaders" are pumping their fists in the air and chanting loudly. The resort staff look on with an equal mix of trepidation and amusement. Not at all sure what to make of this group of Master Sha students.

Lilly puts on a serious face and, like Master Marilyn a few months earlier, points her finger at me like a parent to a child.

"You're good!" she exclaims. "Now go do it!"

Okay, Lilly. I turn around. Go back to my stall. And immediately release everything that was backed up in me. When I emerge from the men's room with a big smile, I receive a huge ovation from the cheerleaders. I feel like dancing and give Lilly a big squeeze and hug!

Master Francisco advises me to go back to my room and rest for the remainder of the afternoon. Tells me he's going to have a lot of fun telling the story of my "Poop Karma" to everyone at the retreat.

The next day I get in line to go up on stage with a bunch of other students. When it's my turn to share, I pass Master Sha, turn to him, bow down and thank him for the karma clearing blessing I received. Master Sha smiles. "Tell the story! ... Master Cynthia, Master Francisco, come up!"

We have some fun recounting the Poop Karma story to the great delight and amusement of the audience full of the Divine Channels-in-Training. Master Sha tells the audience: "You know, they told me this was a life-saving blessing for Stephen."

I immediately bow down on the stage in thanks to Master Sha and the Divine.

"They tell me that this very high-level karma has been waiting for many years to activate. It would have killed him yesterday if he wasn't here at this retreat with Master Sha. It was waiting to see if he is *serious* about being a Divine Channel in Training. If he wasn't serious, the karma wouldn't have activated at all."

Master Sha continues on with an expanded teaching about how sometimes our negative karma sits back and doesn't become active as long as we're *not* committed to serving others. It's when we get serious about serving others that the negative karma can activate in hopes we won't endure the suffering, and will back off of our spiritual path and commitment to service. Master Sha uses my experience as a good example of how spiritual testing occurs and gets tougher—not easier—as we move forward on the Xiu Lian Purification Journey. Heaven tests us time and time again *after* we've increased our commitment to serve and demonstrate that commitment by our actions.

Master Sha teaches that these kind of spiritual tests are blessings for our journey. That when we pass our tests that are the cause of so much pain and suffering, we often receive rewards such as good health, good relationships, and financial abundance.

Thank you, Master Sha! Countless bow downs!
Thank you, Master Sha! Countless bow downs!
Thank you, Master Sha! Countless bow downs!

⚜ ⚜ ⚜

I used to compete in a lot of amateur golf tournaments around New England. When you're playing in a competitive match, the format of the event usually calls for a round of 18 holes divided into the "front nine" and "back nine." You can have a lousy front nine and be losing to your opponent badly, but you know you still have time to correct your mistakes, re-focus, and get back on track to winning the game by having a really good back nine. Doing well at the end of the round can more than make up for the errors you make at the beginning.

If the average human being today can live till about 90, and you equate your life to a round of golf, the front nine and back nine will each last for about 45 years. At age 63, I'm well into the "back nine" of my life. I'm well aware of the many mistakes I've made and the negative karma I've created on the "front nine" of my life. Mistakes that have set me back on my Xiu Lian Purification Journey time and time again. But the round isn't over, and there's still a few holes left to play. I'm supremely confidant that having become a Disciple of Paramahansa Yogananda and a Divine

Channel in Training of Master Sha on the back nine of my life, I'm well positioned to finish the round in a positive fashion.

I'm looking forward to the remainder of the journey with hope and optimism knowing the love of all the heavenly Dragons I've met, the love of my Guru Paramahansa Yogananda, and especially the love of my spiritual father, Master Sha, will carry me back to the Divine, The Source, The Tao.

Master Sha teaches that the Tao Normal and Reverse Creation Cycle is a universal principle. Everyone and everything springs from Tao, and eventually, everyone and everything returns to Tao. Whether you're a pragmatist or romantic, a mathematician or a poet, a believer or a skeptic, Tao is Tao. All things return to Tao and "even Dragons have their endings".

Dad

I receive the phone call from the hospital in Boca Raton, Florida on the third day of Master Sha's Advanced Retreat in Ontario, Canada.

"Your father is dying. If you want to say goodbye, you must come to see him now."

"How much time does he have?" I ask the nurse who's calling me before anyone else in the family because I'm first on the family emergency on-call list.

"It's only a matter of days. Hurry."

My 83 year-old Dad is in the Intensive Care Unit suffering from multiple organ failure. The nurse explains his kidneys have all but shut down and, although the Doctors are employing every treatment method available, there are no good options left to explore.

In many ways, I'm ecstatic and amazed that my father has lived into his 80's alongside my Mom, his loving wife for over sixty years. Dad was a multi-pack a day smoker when I was just a boy. Suffered a major heart attack at age 60 and endured triple by-pass surgery. Had a pacemaker installed in his mid-sixties. Had another double-bypass surgery in his late 60's. Developed Type I diabetes that requires him to inject insulin daily. Despite all his health challenges, Dad remains an avid golfer and Scotch-drinker through it all, playing regularly with his other retired Florida-based buddies. He made his last of 16 hole-in-ones when he was 81 years old!

Although the Advanced Retreat is key to my soul journey, there's no question I'm going to leave Ontario, fly to Florida, comfort my Mom, and see my Dad a final time. My brother and sisters coordinate travel arrangements. It won't be possible for all of us to be in Florida at the same time but we ensure at least one of us will always be with Mom and take her to the hospital daily.

I inform the retreat coordinators that I have to leave. They understand the situation completely, but ask me to wait a few hours until Master Sha can be informed. The message that gets relayed back to me from Master Sha is: "Your father isn't ready to transition yet. You don't have to leave the retreat right now."

Okay, my mind is spinning. So the hospital doctors are wrong? I should stay and receive the teachings, healings, and blessings at the Advanced Retreat? What if Dad dies while I'm here and I've missed the chance to say goodbye? Will I ever be able to forgive myself? The medical staff say all Dad's organs are failing and there's nothing they can do. They're recommending hospice. Is this another spiritual test of my faith and unconditional belief in Master Sha? What am I supposed to do?

I make the tough decision to trust in Master Sha and remain at the retreat. Master Sha calls me on stage daily. Asks me to report the status of my Father's condition to the group of students. Offers countless soul healing blessings for Dad's conditions. Everyone chants for my father. Everyone gets involved. For the next 14 days, Dad hangs on. Mom says he seems better. I tell her Master Sha is involved and everything will be fine.

Towards the end of the retreat, Master Cynthia does a private reading of the Akashic Records for my Dad's karma. He has heavy karma in multiple areas. I honor for Master Sha to clear the karma. I can feel my Dad's soul become joyous. He won't have to carry that karmic debt throughout his future lives. Dad's soul is truly grateful to Master Sha.

The retreat ends and I fly directly to Florida. When I arrive at the hospital, Dad is sitting up in his chair next to the bed. A dietician is talking to him about eliminating all salt from his diet when he goes home. *When he goes home! Wow!*

Although Dad's kidneys are still barely functioning, there are multiple long-term care facilities in the area. Mom and I visit several of them and make preliminary arrangements for Dad's transfer once the doctors give him the okay.

My father grew up Catholic, went to Catholic school, and attended Mass every Sunday with my Mom for as long as I can remember. Although he wasn't a Christian fundamentalist or believer in a literal translation of the Bible, he did believe in Jesus Christ as the son of God and wasn't averse to holding a lively discussion about religion if he felt the participants could be respectful of each other's opinions.

When I started talking about Master Sha to my Mom on my annual visits to Florida, Dad would listen as objectively as he could and never tried to dissuade me from my beliefs about the Tao, karma, reincarnation, and the power of soul healing as taught by Master Sha. Nor did he get upset when I took Mom and my sister to see Master Sha at a free soul healing held in Daytona Beach on one of Master Sha's trips to Florida.

The last time I talk to my father is at his bedside the day before he's moved to hospice where he transitioned the following day in the presence of my Mother and me. Dad's systems have taken another turn for the worse. Our premature enthusiasm about his discharge to a long-term care facility is quietly calmed. My Mom bravely resigns herself to the inevitable.

While Mom is down the hall getting a coffee at the hospital cafeteria, Dad sits up in his chair as best he can, furrows his brow and focuses his eyes on me.

"Tell me again about the Tao," he says.

The innocent request takes me by surprise. *Just what do you want to know? Why are you asking me about the Tao now? You're a life-long Catholic. I'm hesitant to even tell you what Master Sha has done to clear your karma. Too afraid you might say you don't believe in any of that stuff.* We'd had some discussions about the Tao in the past, but our talks were purely theoretical, like political science students debating the merits of capitalism vs. communism.

I look questioningly into my Dad's eyes as if to make sure he's grounded and really wants to me to explain the Tao. He does. I don't know how to begin. Because any attempt to explain the Tao is destined to come up short.

Tao Ke Tao
Fei Chang Tao.
The Tao that can be explained by words
or comprehended by thoughts is not the eternal Tao.

"Just think of Tao as The Source," I tell my Dad.

He looks at me for a few moments. Remains silent. Then, his eyes light up. He "gets" it. Understands. Nods his head. Gives me a knowing smile. There's nothing more to be said. My Dad and I are at peace.

ACKNOWLEDGEMENTS

I thank my spiritual Father, Dr. and Master Zhi Gang Sha, from the depths of my heart for all his boundless love, teachings, guidance, and support. I thank Master Sha for inspiring me to complete this book and share my story with others. I cannot thank Master Sha enough.

Countless bow downs. Countless bow downs. Countless bow downs.

I thank my spiritual Guru, Paramahansa Yogananda from the depths of my heart for finding me, loving me, and awakening me to my soul journey.

Jai Guru Dev. Jai Guru Dev. Jai Guru Dev.

I thank Master Avninder Sangha, my partner, and best friend, without whose unconditional love, laughter, and light, this book would not have been possible.

I thank the team at Heaven's Library and the Institute of Soul Healing and Enlightenment. Master Allan Chuck and Master Elaine Ward deserve all credit for keeping the material in alignment with Master Sha's teachings. Any misuse, mischaracterization, or errors in the text and spiritual practices referring to Master Sha is solely my responsibility.

I thank Master Nina Mistry who created the cover art. Artistic creativity is truly a gift from Heaven, and I am so grateful to

Master Nina for her joy and eagerness to contribute her talents to this project in the form of a powerful Tao Dragon!

I thank Christine Falcon, who offered free services to copy edit the manuscript. I am so grateful to Christine for her creative suggestions to correct and improve my grammar and sentence structure to the benefit of the final product.

Lastly, I wish to thank the Heaven's Team in charge of this project and all my spiritual fathers and mothers in all realms for their love, guidance, teachings, and support.

I am extremely honored to be a servant of you and all souls everywhere.

Hao. Hao. Hao.

www.ingramcontent.com/pod-product-compliance
Lightning Source LLC
Chambersburg PA
CBHW081226090426
42738CB00016B/3207